R0006314831

D1531113

Advances in Teacher Education
Volume 5

WHAT COUNTS AS KNOWLEDGE IN TEACHER EDUCATION?

ADVANCES IN TEACHER EDUCATION

James D. Raths, series editor
(formerly edited by Lilian G. Katz and James D. Raths)

Volume 1: 1985
Lilian G. Katz and James D. Raths, editors

Volume 2: 1986
Lilian G. Katz and James D. Raths, editors

Volume 3: 1987
Martin Haberman and Julie Backus, editors

Volume 4: 1991
Lilian G. Katz and James D. Raths, editors

Volume 5: 1999
James D. Raths and Amy C. McAninch, editors

Advances in Teacher Education
Volume 5

WHAT COUNTS AS KNOWLEDGE
IN TEACHER EDUCATION?

edited by
James D. Raths
University of Delaware

and

Amy C. McAninch
University of Missouri, Kansas City

Ablex Publishing Corporation
Stamford, Connecticut

Printed in the United States of America

ISBN: 1-56750-424-8 (cloth)
      1-56750-425-6 (paper)

ISSN: 0748-0067

Ablex Publishing Corporation
100 Prospect Street
North Tower, 3rd Floor
Stamford, CT 06901

Contents

Preface

This thematic volume of *Advances in Teacher Education* was inspired by the growing controversy in our field regarding two of its most fundamental problems: (1) What is the nature of knowledge about teaching? and (2) Who produces it? Throughout most of this century, the epistemological foundations of research on teaching and teacher education have been derived from positivism and its emphasis on measurement and quantitative methods. Researchers on teaching produced the knowledge, which was to inform policy and the practice of teaching.

However, over the last two decades, science, traditional conceptions of knowledge, and the university itself have come under attack. Some scholars claim that the positivistic tradition in educational research is reductionistic and objectifies teachers (for a review of criticism of positivism, see Chapter 3 in this volume) For example, Doyle (1997) assesses the scientific quest for teacher effectiveness in the following way:

> The practical issues of effectiveness require a small set of generic, context-free, and scientifically grounded indicators that can be applied uniformly across a broad range of teaching situations. The search for such indicators inexorably led to a minimizing of information, a condensing and simplifying of knowledge, an economy of expression and deliberation....
>
> Thus, what we came to know about teaching through these methods was not "true" at all, regardless of how carefully investigators attended by their rules to what "actually" happened. The observations may have been conducted "objectively," but they weren't about the phenomenon of teaching. (p. 95)

Instead of the distortion of generalizations, Doyle suggests that narrative offers the only possibility for truth. At the extreme, science is held to be a form of narrative, a story with no special epistemological status (see Carter, 1993).

In a similar vein, Eisner (1995) asserts that no single theory or combination of theories can ever sufficiently deal with the complexity and distinctiveness of the individual classroom. Statistical relationships expounded in scientific theories are "always less complex than the specific contexts and decisions teachers have to make and the particular contexts within which they must work" (p. 101). He claims that stories "get at forms of understanding that cannot be reduced to measurement or to scientific explanation" (p. 102).

In addition to questioning the value of science in research on teaching, Eisner (1988), among others, criticizes what he calls the "hegemony of propositions" in education research. He claims that we, as a research community, seem to believe that what can't be stated in propositional form has no value. He argues for the legitimacy of "tacit" knowledge, which is intuitive, personal, experiential, and generated from practice. Decisions based on tacit knowledge, Eisner claims, "may not have a theoretical justification but nevertheless may be educationally effective and intuitively right" (1995, p. 101). A review of research on personal narrative and the growing importance of personal knowledge in research on teaching can be found in Carter and Doyle's contribution in the *Handbook of Research on Teacher Education* (1996). They assert that there is a "personal knowledge revolution" in the field (p. 122).

Aside from the growing importance of narrative research, local understandings, and tacit knowledge, the traditional researcher-teacher relationship has also been called into question. As noted above, the traditional model of knowledge generation in the profession is that researchers produce knowledge while teachers are supposed to absorb and translate that knowledge into practice. Critics of this "technical rationality" model argue that it discredits the knowledge that teachers accumulate in practice, silences teachers' voices in curriculum making and policy, and impairs their professional status. As a political movement, then, the search for the distinctive knowledge accrued by practitioners is intended to have an equalizing and empowering effect upon the teaching profession, in which researchers are viewed as engaging in a form of hegemony.

Finally, it is important to point out that the research produced at the university and stated in propositional form has often been found to be of little use to teachers (for a discussion, see Chapter 2 in this volume). Teachers, as clinicians of a sort, are interested in how to deal with individual cases. This interest is not unlike that found in all professions, including medicine, dentistry, social work, and so on. But researchers report their findings in statistical terms, such as "how much of the total variance is explained by an intervention." Researchers fully expected variance on the criterion measure within treatment groups, and gave focus to the variance between treatment groups. How to deal with individual students or specific situations was left to the teachers' own devices. And, indeed, teachers generally have relied on their firsthand experience in making decisions, rather than on research. Increasingly, experiential knowledge, or "insider" knowledge, is held to be a special quality belonging only to teachers.

In summation, all of these factors seem to deepen the field's disquiet with traditional approaches to the identification and classification of knowledge. Today, the practices of the university, and the norms on which they are based, are challenged by the epistemological foundations of narrative research. Knowledge and belief are increasingly conflated. Species of insider knowledge rest on the assertion that warrant is irrelevant to teacher knowledge. Science itself is increasingly attacked. So, it seems timely to ask, What counts as knowledge in teacher education?," both empirically and normatively. The illuminating chapters in this volume address this question from different perspectives.

In Chapter 1, Christine Sleeter reviews critiques of positivism, as well as the contributions of individuals working in alternative paradigms of educational research: qualitative researchers, teachers themselves, educators from historically marginalized groups, and post-structuralists. She suggests that it is important to learn how to "converse" across these different paradigms in the interest of advancing wisdom regarding teaching in a pluralistic society.

Mary Kennedy continues her elucidation of craft knowledge and expert knowledge in Chapter 2. She asserts that all organized activities rely on craft knowledge, but addresses the question of whether craft knowledge is sufficient for teaching. The role of schools of education is also explored.

In Chapter 3, Gregory Cizek notes the rise of narrative inquiry in educational research and the preeminence of meaning over knowledge. He offers seven explanations for why narrative research has "risen to the top of the methodological heap."

Gary Galluzo contributes a history of how the National Council for Accreditation of Teacher Education has conceived of the "knowledge base" of teaching in Chapter 4. He concludes, in part, that there is little consensus today regarding a knowledge base. He asserts that the development of knowledge to ground teacher preparation is a task that teacher education must meet, regardless of the philosophical stance of teacher educators.

In Chapter 5, the work of two narrative researchers, F. Michael Connelly and D. Jean Clandinin, is juxtaposed with several critical ethnographies of schooling. The ethnographies reveal that the vast majority of teachers, but not all, fail to question dominant ideology with respect to race, class, and gender, and accept social arrangements as they exist. It is argued that Connelly and Clandinin's work provides no means of distinguishing beliefs based on dominant ideology from those based on critical reflection.

In Chapter 6, the concepts of "subject matter knowledge" and "pedagogical content knowledge" are explicated. It is asserted that an important part of teachers' subject matter knowledge is knowledge of justification in each discipline. For example, part of subject matter knowledge for the teacher of biology is knowing how biologists justify their knowledge claims. Pedagogical content knowledge—the knowledge of how to teach content—is elaborated and illustrated with numerous examples.

Finally, in Chapter 7, Joseph Stornello discusses historical scholarship on schooling, taking the work of Elwood Cubberly as a prime example. Stornello applies the insights of critical realism to his study of history and stresses the importance of a realist ontology in the study of school and society.

We hope these essays contribute to an ongoing dialogue in the field regarding the nature of knowledge and its source. We want to thank the authors for their contributions to this volume and Ablex, our publisher, for their support.

—James Raths and Amy C. McAninch

x

REFERENCES

Carter, K. (1993). The place of story in the study of teaching and teacher education. *Educational Researcher, 22*(1), 5–12, 18.

Carter, K., & Doyle, W. (1996). Personal narrative and life history in learning to teach. In J. Sikula, T. J. Buttery, & E. Guyton (Eds.), *Handbook of Research on Teacher Education* (2nd ed.; pp. 120–142). New York: Macmillan.

Doyle, W. (1997). Heard any really good stories lately? A critique of the critics of narrative in educational research. *Teaching and Teacher Education, 13*(1), 93–99.

Eisner, E. W. (1988). The primacy of experience and the politics of method. *Educational Researcher, 17*(3), 15–20.

Eisner, E. W. (1995). Preparing teachers for schools of the 21st century. *Peabody Journal of Education, 70*(3), 99–111.

Toward Wisdom through Conversation Across Epistemologies*

Christine Sleeter
California State University, Monterey Bay

How can research help teachers to teach more effectively, and help teacher educators to assist them? On the surface, this seems like it should be a relatively simple, straightforward question to answer. However, as I will argue, it is not. One's answer depends on how one conceives of the education process and the purpose of schools (what counts as effective teaching?), the nature of teaching and teacher education (what counts as assisting someone else in teaching, learning, and learning to teach?), and research itself (what counts as knowledge and as legitimate processes of knowledge construction?). I am not the first, nor will I be the last, to attempt a useful synthesis of research on teaching and teacher education. Indeed, one can consult voluminous handbooks that have taken up this task in great detail (e.g., Sikula, Buttery, & Guyton, 1996; Wittrock, 1986). But, having worked for years as both a teacher educator and a researcher, and having read widely on the subject and engaged in many conversations at both local and national levels, I have a perspective to offer. The following story will illustrate this perspective, as well as the direction this chapter will take.

---

* I wish to express my gratitude for the helpful comments, suggestions, and points of criticism offered by several colleagues on an earlier draft of this chapter. My thanks go to Joseph Kretovics, Amy McAninch, Mark O'Shea, Thomas Popkewitz, and James Raths.

Recently, I found myself engaged in a rather heated debate in the context of a search committee for a faculty position in teacher education. A local administrator, who was a member of the committee, had a very clear image of the kind of person she believed we should hire. She wanted someone well grounded in the latest research on effective reading instruction at the primary level, citing research on the effects of teaching phonics and other word analysis skills to children. The teacher educators on the committee were interested in finding someone who could conceptualize acquiring literacy as a process of language development in a cultural context, given that a very large proportion of students in the schools locally are of ethnic minority backgrounds, the majority of whom have Spanish as their first language. They were skeptical of overly relying on reading research that had been conducted outside a bilingual paradigm. A teacher on the committee was concerned that we find a candidate with many years experience in the classroom, who could relate to the complex realities of classroom teachers. To her, research prescriptions for how to teach oversimplify the complex work teachers do.

Ultimately, our debates produced three different discourses, and not much consensus. Upon reflection, we were unable to find a "right" answer or set of common understandings because our thinking was grounded in different epistemologies, and this itself was not acknowledged. All of us were concerned about finding a teacher educator who could help beginning teachers teach literacy more effectively, but we were defining this task in epistemologically different ways.

In this chapter, I wish to tease out divergent epistemological perspectives that are embodied in the research on teaching and teacher education. Positivism has driven much of the "great conversation" about teaching and teacher education for the past 50 years (Shulman, 1986). However, critiques of it burgeoned during the 1980s and 1990s, these critiques becoming a part of that conversation. This chapter will trace the roots of these critiques—and the research paradigms they suggest—to four main sources, all of which gained power and voice during that time: qualitative researchers, teachers themselves, educators from historically marginalized groups, and poststructuralists. I am presenting these as ideal types, rather than distinct groups (e.g., one can simultaneously be a qualitative researcher and an educator from a marginalized group), in order to identify different epistemological positions about what counts as knowledge and how knowledge is produced. This chapter will illustrate the contributions that different epistemological perspectives can offer to the "great conversation" about teaching and teacher education, ultimately leading to the recommendation that we learn to converse across epistemologies, research paradigms, worldviews, and life experiences. Doing so will enable us to develop not agreement and consensus, but greater wisdom about what it can mean to teach well in a pluralistic society, and perhaps a greater capacity to converse *with* others, rather than *for* others.

EPISTEMOLOGY

Epistemology refers to the nature of knowledge and "reality," and the process of coming to know. Epistemological debates about teaching and teacher education, as in the social sciences (in broader terms), revolve around the following questions:

To what extent is reality "out there," to be grasped by gathering data in a systematic fashion? Or, on the other hand, to what extent is our knowledge of reality a product of our own minds? If reality exists "out there," apart from the knower, then knowledge is the result of the careful apprehension of that reality, and truth is judged by the degree to which knowledge can be demonstrated to approximate it. On the other hand, if knowledge is a social creation and "its existence has its base in the lives of concrete individuals, and has no empirical status apart from those lives" (Berger & Luckmann, 1966, p. 128), then truth is socially relative and contextual (Rosaldo, 1989).

What is the nature of knowledge? Kuhn (1970) elaborates on three levels of knowledge within "normal science": accumulated facts, broader theories that connect facts and guide prediction, and even broader paradigms that guide theorizing and the knowledge production process itself. Kuhn asks: "Are theories simply man-made interpretations of given data?" (p. 126). In other words, do the "facts" closely reflect "reality," but the sense we make of them reflect human subjectivity? Are the "facts" themselves also social constructions? If so, according to Foucault (1980), what is at issue is "the ensemble of rules according to which the true and the false are separated and specific effects of power attached to the true" (p. 132).

What is the nature of the knower? If reality is "out there," then the best a knower can strive for is detachment and objectivity; knowledge claims have the most validity when asserted by a knower who can verify objectivity. If reality is socially constructed, who is qualified to construct knowledge? Does one need to master certain processes for knowledge "discovery" or construction, and master certain discourse communities? Can ordinary people construct knowledge, and if so, does the everyday, common-sense knowledge that people construct "count" as knowledge (Berger & Luckmann, 1966)? Harding (1994) observes that "whoever gets to name natural and social realities gets to control how they will be organized" (p. 302); in other words, who counts as a legitimate constructor of knowledge may be a political more than an intellectual achievement. If knowledge is socially constructed, does the social location of the knower matter—the discourse communities in which the knower participates, the social power the knower occupies, the point of view of the knower from a particular social standpoint (Foucault, 1980; Harding, 1994; Rosaldo, 1989)?

These questions circulate through debates about what counts as knowledge in teaching and teacher education. The rest of this chapter is organized into five main sections, each of which presents an epistemological perspective. Each section opens by framing the central question that perspective addresses, then proceeds to a discussion of what counts as knowledge and knowledge production from that perspective.

Positivism: What Key Principles Will Enable Teachers to Teach Most Children More Effectively?

Positivist social science is rooted in the belief that reality exists apart from the knower, and can be grasped through careful processes of data collection. The scientific method—in which variables are specified and relationships among them are hypothesized, data are collected, and results are analyzed—provides guidance to the knowledge construction process. From the perspective of positivism, the main purpose of research is to seek generalizable "truths," which are assumed to be "natural laws." Campbell and Stanley (1963) argued that research, in the context of human knowledge production, serves "as the means of sharpening the relevance of the testing, probing, selection process.... It is ... a refining process superimposed upon the probably valuable cumulations of wise practice" (p. 4). In other words, through everyday observation and application, humans construct knowledge about the world, but in rather imprecise ways. Knowledge produced through science connects with informally accumulated knowledge, but is more reliable and valid, and thus, is more likely to reflect the "real" world "out there."

Following these assumptions, classical positivist research methods commonly include:

• choosing samples that represent some larger human "universe" so that findings are as "generalizable" as possible;
• using data-collection and data-analysis methods that are replicable;
• controlling for bias through various methods for validity and reliability;
• constructing studies in such a way as to differentiate between "universals" and "variables"; and
• subjecting research to review processes within the academy that ensure that published findings adhere to the above rules of the knowledge-production process.

Experimental research designs offer the most classic application of natural science research to the social sciences. The careful selection of samples, design of experimental and control conditions, and procedures for data collection and analysis represent attempts to control and manipulate variables in order to derive generalizable patterns. Other common social science research, such as survey or correlational research designs, lacks some of the controls of experimental research, but still help to generate systematic knowledge about human behavior that leads to generalizations.

The main purpose of the research process on teaching, conceptualized in this way, is to identify what effective teachers do in order to maximize student learning. Correlational studies that connect teacher behaviors with student achievement, supported by experimental research, have until recently dominated the research on teaching. In teacher education, survey research has been widely used to describe programs, and experimental research, to identify and predict characteristics of effective programs. For over 50 years, research on teaching attempted to "systematize it into discrete categories such as teacher styles, behaviors, characteristics, competencies, methods, and so forth..." (Ornstein, 1995, p. 2). In the 1970s, this research was further systematized into process-product research, in which there was an attempt to connect specific teacher behaviors (processes) with student learning performances (products). Rating scales and classification systems were developed to itemize elements of teacher and student behavior in order to describe more precisely which teacher behaviors produce the greatest student engagement and learning (e.g., Flanders, 1960; Good & Brophy, 1973). Conceived in this way, teacher education means helping novices learn to master particular behaviors associated with good teaching.

The search for key principles that will help teachers to teach children better has yielded many principles of effective teaching. Brophy and Good (1986) provide a clear synthesis of this research, summarized as follows:

> At least two common themes cut across the findings, despite the need for limitations and qualifications. One is that academic learning is influenced by amount of time that students spend engaged in appropriate academic tasks. The second is that students learn more efficiently when their teachers first structure new information for them and help them relate it to what they already know, and they monitor their performance and provide corrective feedback during recitation, drill, practice, or application activities. For a time, these generalizations seemed confined to the early grades or to basic rather than more advanced skills. However, it now appears that they apply to any body of knowledge or set of skills that has been sufficiently well organized and analyzed so that it can be presented (explained, modeled) systematically and then practiced or applied during activities that call for student performance that can be evaluated for quality and (where incorrect or imperfect) given corrective feedback. (p. 366)

Process-product research drawn from positivism provides guidance for constructing effective teaching and teacher education programs. At the same time, it can provide an illusion of certainty.

Research findings, such as those summarized above, are based on hundreds of small, individual studies. Most of the individual studies themselves have limited generalizability, although they probably have local usefulness; but at the same time, many individual studies are contradicted by other individual studies. Consider this: Ester (1994-5) wanted to find out whether there is an interaction between student learning style and teaching strategy. He divided 60 undergraduates on the basis of a measure of learning style that differentiates between concrete and abstract learners. Within each group, two different treatments were used to teach about vocal anatomy in music: computer-assisted instruction (CAI) and lecture. Ester found that concrete learners learned equally well using CAI or lecture, while abstract learners learned better through lecture than through CAI.

Of what use is such a study to the profession? Taken by itself, it has very limited use, although the findings were probably useful to the instructors involved in the study. Most teachers are not teaching vocal anatomy to undergraduates; we know almost nothing of the content being taught, nor do we know what the lectures and the computer-assisted instruction were actually like. We know very little about these 60 students, virtually nothing about the context in which the instruction took place, and nothing about the actual substance of their learning. These limitations do not render the study useless; it was probably quite useful to the context in which it occurred, particularly if the instructors were trying to determine which instructional method to use. And the study provides data that can be aggregated with other similar studies to derive general propositions about teaching effectiveness.

One can derive principles based on analysis of thousands of such studies. But one can also reach a level of abstraction that strips studies of their contexts and particulars, rendering the principles virtually meaningless. The search for principles that emerge from a large body of experimental research spawned processes of meta-analysis, developed in the 1980s. Meta-analysis synthesizes findings of related studies, and has been used to propose general principles such as those summarized by Brophy and Good (1986). A very extensive "meta-meta-analysis" of 270 research reviews and meta-analyses of student learning in schools was undertaken by Wang, Haertel and Walberg (1993) to identify which variables have the most impact on learning, based on hundreds of individual studies. Using a complex methodology, they summarized the "hard-won evidence" by recommending:

> If practitioners and teacher educators wish to enhance school learning, they must attend to proximal variables such as a) psychological variables, especially metacognition and cognition; b) classroom instruction and management, and student and teacher social and academic interactions; and c) the home environment. (p. 278)

This meta-meta-analysis can be thought of as representing the culmination of classical positivism, in its attempt to synthesize such a huge amount of research. But by isolating variables from their context, then trying to identify what is true across any and all contexts, positivism can leave us with "findings" that most people already know, and too little help in using those findings in particular classrooms of real and varied children.

Other syntheses of research that are more limited in scope, such as that by Brophy and Good (1986), offer some very helpful conclusions by showing that teachers do make a difference in student achievement, and some teaching behaviors produce higher achievement with most children than other teaching behaviors. Research based on classical positivism can also suggest conditions under which some strategies help some children consistently enough that they are worth expending the effort to learn to implement. For example, research studies and syntheses of studies by Robert Slavin and his colleagues (e.g., Slavin, 1987, 1990) have documented a fairly consistent pattern of achievement benefits of using heterogeneous grouping for several specific categories of students (such as elementary students and lower-ability students). Slavin's work does not make sweeping generalizations about heterogeneous grouping as much as it identifies where, when, or with which students it works best. His work has been extended to the Success for All model of school reform, which he and his colleagues are replicating as a treatment and comparing with control schools, finding considerable positive benefits for primary-grade children in "disadvantaged" schools (Slavin, et al., 1994).

Research such as this can help answer the question of how to teach children more effectively, not by searching for universals, but by searching for conditions under which certain strategies help certain students master certain kinds of material. It is this latter observation that helps me as an educator of teachers. If I can demonstrate to teachers that a strategy or set of strategies has a research track record supporting that it is worth learning to use, many teachers will work to add it to their repertoire, especially if they start to see it helping their own students.

However, at the same time, as a way of knowing, classical positivism has limitations. In order to construct precise measurements, broad characteristics of teaching and learning, such as generating enthusiasm or understanding a concept, are operationalized into variables that are presumed to represent these broad characteristics. Similarly, differences among children and teachers are also operationalized into specific variables that can be quantified. Distortion occurs in the process of creating precision for measurement. To get at reality that is "out there," positivism trusts training in objectivity, precise measurement, and tests of reliability and validity to counteract distortions—the distortions are outweighed by the truth that is revealed through their use. But, as Shulman (1986) points out, although research on teaching effectiveness is based on studies of effective teachers, probably no teacher does everything recommended by the research, since the research produces patterns rather than portraits of good teaching.

Other perspectives I will discuss in this chapter question the degree to which positivism actually helps us understand "reality," by questioning the nature of reality and the nature of knowledge about reality, and by questioning assumptions and perspectives of the knower. Alternative epistemological perspectives see the following limitations of positivism as a way of understanding teaching and teacher education: 1) complex instructional problems and real classrooms cannot be packaged into neat, clinical experimental designs, and studies that presume a clinical environment are too often irrelevant to classroom life; 2) reality is as much in people's heads as it is "out there," and positivism does not provide a useful way to examine people's interpretations; 3) much of what matters, including contexts and holistic portraits of individuals, is lost in the search for generalizations and attempts to isolate variables; 4) the identity, social assumptions, and social power of researchers matters; research can be understood as the process of rendering some actors' worldviews as legitimate, while excluding others; and 5) positivism is not suited to discussions of ethical or philosophical issues about what education is for, as well as what teachers and schools are trying to do. The following prescription for effective teaching of low versus high socioeconomic students (SES) masks assumptions about what the curriculum should consist of, and ethical considerations of who should have access to college preparation:

> Low-SES/low-achieving students need more control and structuring from their teachers: more active instruction and feedback, more redundancy, and smaller steps with higher success rates. This will mean more review, drill, and practice, and thus more lower-level questions. Across the school year, it will mean exposure to less material.... High-SES students are more likely to be confident, eager to participate, and responsive to challenge. They want respect and require feedback, but usually do not require a great deal of encouragement or praise. They thrive in an atmosphere that is academically stimulating and somewhat demanding. (Brophy & Good, 1986, p. 365)

If we do what these researchers recommend, we will (and do) reproduce social class and racial stratification through differential access to knowledge (Oakes, 1985), and we will not question whose knowledge gets taught in schools. Anyon's (1981) study of social class and access to school knowledge thoroughly documents this problem. The issue is not that there are no social class differences among children, but rather how the differences that teachers encounter in the classroom are framed, what questions are asked, and what questions go unasked. It has been partially in response to these limitations that alternative ways of framing knowledge about teaching and teacher education have blossomed.

Qualitative Research: What Happens When Children Try to Learn? When Teachers Try to Teach? When Teacher Educators Try to Help Teachers Teach More Effectively?

Qualitative research made its debut in education in the 1950s (Spindler, 1955), but it was not until the 1980s that one saw a dramatic unfolding of qualitative research on teaching and teacher education. Qualitative researchers saw experimental, correlational, and survey research as limited by lack of attention to context, day-to-day processes, classroom complexity, and meanings people make. For example, Jackson's 1968 book, *Life in Classrooms*, describes richly-textured patterns of life in the classroom, opening up discussion of important issues such as the "hidden curriculum" and dynamics of classrooms as crowded social spaces. Rist's 1973 book, *The Urban School: A Factory for Failure*, opened up the "black box" of the classroom to reveal daily classroom processes and teacher assumptions that led to unequal achievement on the basis of student social class. This early study turned on its head assumptions many people make about why school achievement correlates with student social class by examining daily classroom processes. Both of these ethnographies of classrooms spawned an explosion of qualitative research studies in education.

I am including in the category of qualitative research both ethnographic studies and case studies that rely primarily on qualitative data. Qualitative researchers generally approach research by asking open-ended questions rather than by stating specific hypotheses; they invite teachers and students to voice their own descriptions as opposed to asking them to respond to the categories and language generated by researchers for experimental or survey studies (Solas, 1992). Qualitative research allows the unexpected to emerge, and invites examination of richly complex patterns of human interaction. As Peshkin (1993) put it, qualitative research offers a "feast of possibilities" of purposes and outcomes, which he classified broadly as description, interpretation, verification, or evaluation. Research with an "emic" purpose seeks to capture the meanings and perspectives of teachers or children, while research with an "etic" purpose seeks to uncover patterns of behavior through observation. Both have become important in teaching and teacher education precisely because they open the door to reframing questions, examining complexity, attending to contexts, and accounting for teacher knowledge.

Loflund and Loflund (1995) explain that epistemologically, qualitative research rests on two assumptions: "(1) that face-to-face interaction is the fullest condition of participating in the mind of another human being, and (2) that you must participate in the mind of another human being (in sociological terms, 'take the role of the other') to acquire social knowledge" (p. 16). Social reality is created by people, and exists, in large part, within people's minds. Qualitative research aims to uncover how people participate in, and constitutes, social reality.

What happens when children try to learn? Wood (1996) studied how two children construct mathematical knowledge in order to gain insight about the process of learning in classrooms. The two children's thought processes differed, as well as the context of the classrooms. The study does not seek to generalize mathematical learning, but rather to help teachers and teacher educators to think more complexly about children with whom they might be working by recognizing differences among children's thinking processes, and connecting children's thinking with classroom contexts. Similarly, Jimenez, Garcia, and Pearson (1995) studied how three children constructed meaning from text, investigating relationships between language, reading strategies, and metacognitive strategies. The purpose of the study was to investigate how monolingual and bilingual students process the task of reading, primarily to understand how we might teach English language learners more effectively. The study offers rich descriptions that not only allow the authors to speculate about how children might be taught more effectively, but that also invite readers to construct teaching scenarios. As these two examples illustrate, qualitative studies of student learning provide case examples that can serve as lenses for examining the teaching-learning process, given the highly diverse nature of children who inhabit classrooms. In this regard, qualitative research tends to be "user friendly" to practitioners whose own classrooms are populated by complex and very different children. Neither study tells us (or tries to tell us) what teaching practices seem to work best; both raise questions that can help teachers think through their own practices.

What happens when teachers teach? To explore this question, numerous researchers, such as Elbaz (1981), have argued that "The single factor which seems to have the greatest power to carry forward our understanding of the teacher's role is the phenomenon of teachers' knowledge" (p. 45). Many qualitative studies—working from an emic perspective—place teachers' practical knowledge at the center of inquiry; rather than trying to predict what teachers should do, as positivist research does, qualitative research is more likely to explore what teachers already know and how they make sense of their work in the context of the classroom. For example, Elbaz examined, through open-ended interviews, an experienced teacher's underlying assumptions about content, pedagogy, students, and the school environment to attempt to understand how she makes choices and generates decisions about her work. An important conclusion of this study was that "'practical knowledge' is seen as dynamic, firmly grounded in the individual's inner and outer experience, and open to change" (p. 67). In other words, the teacher's construction of teaching was grounded in thought, reflection, and experience. Brickhouse (1990) studied three science teachers, examining how they think about what science is and how their thinking connects to their teaching. She argued that teachers construct science in the classroom purposefully, grounded in their conceptions of what science is. Similarly, Brophy and VanSledright (1997) studied three elementary teachers to find out how they understood and constructed history teaching. The teachers differed philosophically; their practice reflected their different conceptions of history. Qualitative research that focuses on what teachers know honors teachers' knowledge, and helps to clarify the dilemmas teachers face.

Qualitative studies of teaching usually frame teachers as purposeful and thoughtful; such studies illuminate the differences among teachers, the connections between what teachers do and how they think, and complex issues and dilemmas. Such studies suggest that teacher educators focus not simply on teaching particular methods with the expectation that novices will then implement them in the classroom, but rather on helping novices, as well as more experienced teachers, to clarify and develop their thinking about classroom problems.

Several qualitative researchers have explored and developed the mode of story or narrative inquiry as a way of knowing in the context of interviewing teachers. Some argue that teachers' knowledge is largely structured through stories, and that stories are epistemologically the most authentic way to understand teaching from the viewpoints of the teacher (Elbaz, 1981). Carter (1993) explained how stories construct reality in a manner that is quite different from positivism:

> Stories became a way, in other words, of capturing the complexity, specificity, and interconnectedness of the phenomenon with which we deal and, thus, redressed the deficiencies of the traditional atomistic and positivistic approaches in which teaching was decomposed into discrete variables and indicators of effectiveness. (p. 6)

Story as a form of knowledge captures the sense people make of phenomena, and the context of sense-making. Stories are not meant to describe phenomena objectively, but rather to connect phenomena and imbue them with interpretation. Teachers' narratives will be taken up later in this chapter, when I turn from knowledge constructed by researchers to knowledge constructed by teachers.

What happens when teacher educators try to help teachers teach, at the preservice and inservice level? Several qualitative studies have examined this question, largely in attempts to understand why the impact of teacher education is often quite limited. Britzman (1991) conducted case studies of two student teachers in order to find out how novices learn to teach, and why beginning teachers largely conform to existing school practices despite preparation programs that attempt to reform teaching. Britzman analyzed how these two student teachers interpreted their work over a semester. She concluded that the main problem is not that beginning teachers are ill-prepared to teach, but rather that school settings structure teaching and learning in ways that novices cannot be expected to single-handedly refashion. Elsewhere, I studied 30 teachers who were participating in a staff development project in multicultural education, to find out what they learned from it, and why they learned what they did (Sleeter, 1992). The study attempted to find out why teachers began using some strategies more than others, how the new information connected with their previous thinking and experiences, how the context of teacher work tends to reinforce many traditional patterns, and how teachers shape multicultural education to fit their prior knowledge and beliefs. Both of these studies, by examining a few cases in complex detail, tease out issues, problems, and relationships that may or may not generalize, but that help form an understanding of these cases. Both shed light on a few cases, examining social behavior up close, in order to help others raise similar questions.

Both positivism and qualitative research offer implications for teacher education, but the implications differ. Positivism offers skills and programs that promote student learning, as these variables have been operationalized for research; teacher education should help teachers acquire research-validated skills. Qualitative research on teaching offers portraits of people engaged in teaching and learning; teacher education should offer a process of supporting teachers in grappling with and thinking through the dilemmas and tensions they experience. A limitation of qualitative research, however, is that it does not necessarily evaluate what good teaching is, but is more likely than positivism to leave that evaluation to the reader. Honoring the knowledge of teachers, for example, does not necessarily lead one to ask which teachers' knowledge is more worthwhile and why.

Positivist researchers criticize qualitative research because it does not necessarily lead to generalized principles. Indeed, this is not usually its purpose. Eisner (1993) contrasted the purposes of qualitative and positivist research in relationship to his own professional background: "My encounter with the social sciences at [the University of] Chicago and my long-standing engagement in art, both as a painter and a teacher of art, forced me to confront the tension between my desire to understand and cultivate what is individual and distinctive and my wish to grasp what is patterned and regular" (p. 5). Patterns and regularities exist along with subjective meanings and complex particulars. Positivism and qualitative research foreground different kinds of phenomena, in the process giving value to different lenses for viewing education.

Qualitative research can also be critiqued on grounds similar to positivism: it represents the voice of the research community, moreso than the voices of "research subjects." In a critique of classical anthropological research, Rosaldo (1989) captured the main tenets of mainstream social science research, as applied to qualitative research:

> Once upon a time, the Lone Ethnographer rode off into the sunset in search of 'his native.' After undergoing a series of trials, he encountered the objects of his quest in a distant land. There, he underwent his rite of passage by enduring the ultimate ordeal of 'fieldwork.' After collecting 'the data,' the Lone Ethnographer returned home and wrote a 'true' account of 'the culture.' (p. 30)

As Rosaldo and several other anthropologists (e.g., Geertz, 1995) have argued, there is no truth "out there" that we can capture, except through the lenses of our own beliefs and experiences; and there is no lone researcher, but rather members of a research community. Qualitative research, to varying degrees, shares an assumption with positivism: that one must become trained in methods for creating research knowledge, and the methodology and research it produces must be legitimated by the research community. Danziger (1990), in an extensive discussion of the social history of psychology research, observed that "The fundamental issue in research is not whether the lone investigator can verify his hypotheses in the privacy of his laboratory but whether he can establish his contribution as part of the canon of scientific knowledge in his field.... It involves prior agreements about what is to count as admissible evidence and shared commitments to certain goals" (p. 3). Does the research community share biases that cannot be detached from the process of knowing, no matter how well the researcher tries either to become objective, or to contextualize his or her research? The remaining perspectives in this chapter take up this question.

Texts Written by Teachers: How Do Teachers Actually Interpret and Experience Their Own Work with Children?

Narrative inquiry, or inquiry rooted in stories about teaching and teacher education, is sometimes categorized as a subset of qualitative research (Eisner, 1988). In qualitative research on teaching and teacher education, teachers may be the research subjects. Here, I wish to differentiate texts produced by teachers, from researchers' studies of teachers' narratives. Who writes a narrative matters. Historically in educational research, researchers have had the power to construct knowledge about teaching that has become legitimated by the research community. Teachers have largely been silenced in that process, given voice mainly through qualitative researchers, who still, in the final analysis, privilege their own voices as researchers.

Gitlin (1994) argues that the "researcher/'subject' relationship" is inherently one of power imbalance, and informs the entire process of producing research knowledge, including what knowledge ends up being produced and rendered legitimate (p. 3). "Who gets to tell the educational stories" significantly affects which stories get told and which perspectives achieve the status of knowledge (Gitlin & Russell, 1994, p. 199). The same individual teacher can be (and has been) represented differently by different researchers, rendering her differently than she tells her own story, when given a chance to do so publicly (see Shulman, 1991). Voices of teachers are important to consider in their own right. As Lytle and Cochran-Smith (1992) point out, books such as the American Association of Colleges of Teacher Education *Knowledge Base for the Beginning Teacher* (Reynolds, 1989) and prescriptions for translating theory into practice assume that knowledge about teaching is something that outsiders (i.e., researchers) give to insiders (i.e., teachers), rather than something teachers are capable of producing for themselves.

A brief story will illustrate. In a graduate course I recently taught, I asked teachers to identify an issue about which they felt passionate and had some knowledge, and to write about that issue using stories from their own experience. I then helped them integrate the professional literature into their narratives, where this strengthened their arguments. The main purpose of this exercise was to help the teachers articulate their own professional knowledge in terms that made the most sense to them. Two of the teachers addressed a recent state mandate regarding the teaching of reading, which elevates phonics instruction and is requiring that coursework and inservice workshops on literacy focus on teaching word analysis. These two experienced teachers were critical of how the mandate was being implemented locally, but felt shut out of discussions because they were "only" classroom teachers, rather than policymakers or researchers. Their written narratives helped them clarify their criticisms and the basis of their own thinking; both of them explained to me that the process of writing helped them both to make visible and to articulate their own knowledge. Their narratives also helped them to critique the research being used to justify local implementation of the mandate by identifying which research had been selected and which had been omitted, and how that research differed from holistic perspectives of child development that informed their own work. One of the teachers used this exercise specifically to develop her own professional voice so that she can engage in conversations about literacy instruction with confidence, rather than submitting silently to someone else's directives.

Although texts written by teachers make up a small proportion of the literature on teaching, the quantity of such texts has been expanding. They take various forms; some examples will illustrate. Enright (1979) published an article drawing on excerpts from a diary she kept about her own teaching. She used the excerpts as a basis for reflection about the children, their experiences in her classroom, and her interactions with them. Her article extracted insights she gained about her own teaching through her diary entries. Similarly, Meyer's (1995) article presents stories involving individual children; the stories were selected to illustrate important insights he gained from observing the children. Both of these teacher-authored texts highlight the idiosyncratic experiences in their classrooms that produced significant insights about teaching children. Both were published for the purpose of grounding reflection about teaching and the stories of everyday classroom life that teachers experience.

Yennie-Donmoyer's (1993) chapter in a book about at-risk students describes Andrew, a student in her class whom she regarded as a paradox—he was a gifted child of well educated and economically successful parents, yet he was floundering in the classroom. In her chapter, Andrew comes alive as a complex and interesting person. Through spending time with him and listening to him, she came to understand why he was not achieving. By showing him that she cared enough to listen, she enabled him to begin to believe in himself, and slowly his academic work improved. Her chapter helps readers to understand Andrew, and other children like him. To teachers, classrooms are not made up of norms, averages, and generic "pupils"; they are populated by a wide array of children, and anyone who is interested in teaching must learn to attend to the unique children who actually exist in classrooms. This chapter illustrates this point well.

Waldoch (1995) describes her work with another teacher as they collaboratively reconstructed their teaching to merge special education and regular education children, in the context of their own high expectations for children's learning. She describes the origins of the "Rainbow Room," as their collaborative classroom came to be known, and how they gradually merged two different classrooms into one. Her chapter describes the thinking skills she and her colleague were teaching, and various activities and lessons they developed to teach this very heterogeneous group of elementary children. This chapter describes a practice that "works" with children, while at the same time discussing what the idea of "works" means to her in her school context.

Teacher narratives are sometimes dismissed as having less truth value than "scientific" research, but, as many writers argue (e.g., Connelly & Clandinin, 1990), the truth value of narratives is different from, not less than, the truth value of "scientific" research. Positivist research is judged on the basis of reliability, validity, and generalizability. Connelly and Clandinin (1990) propose that the truth value of teachers' narrative be judged on different criteria, such as apparency, verisimilitude, transferability, plausibility, familiarity, economy, and selectivity. In other words, the narrative should convey insight into human living through a story that "rings true." The "facts" gleaned from positivist research may be judged as reliable and valid, but to classroom teachers, they may also be so decontextualized as to be virtually useless, and the idea they support may or may not "ring true."

A narrative is a holistic piece that cannot be reduced to isolated facts without losing the truth that is being conveyed. Indeed, a narrative situates and relates facts to one another, and the essence of the truth is *how* phenomena are connected and interpreted. The narratives of classroom teachers should convey insights gleaned from practice that "ring true" to other practitioners, and that encourage reflection about teaching. Meyer (1995), a classroom teacher reflecting on his own use of narrative, observed that "stories are an important point of origin for learning about our teaching," in that classroom stories prompt reflection about one's own practice, which promotes professional growth (p. 276). Teachers' narratives often also connect ethical questions with experiences, artistry with information, solutions to problems with emergent dilemmas, and personal growth with ongoing patterns (Lyons, 1990).

There is a problem here that does not have an easy solution: that what "rings true" for some educators does not "ring true" for others. The narratives that teachers construct about teaching in a racially mixed school, for example, will likely reflect biases that those who share them regard as true, a problem that will be taken up in the next section of this chapter. However, this is not a problem just with teacher narratives, but with all research. Positivist research also is embedded within the viewpoint of the researcher and the research community, and "rings true" to those who share the assumptions and worldview of that community. But most positivist researchers, as well as many qualitative researchers, do not call into question the viewpoint or paradigm that grounds their work. To the classroom teacher who does not have a background in producing positivist research, it may not be apparent *why* a particular piece of research does or does not ring true, only that it does or does not. Qualitative research, with its more transparent narrative form, is more likely to have a voice that a teacher can identify. Teachers who are not well trained in research methodology can often follow the qualitative researcher's train of analysis and thinking, and, in the process, recognize where their own analysis might diverge from that of the researcher.

Public narration through text provides a means of engaging in dialog, and of receiving criticism, that is broader than one's informal circle of colleagues. Lytle and Cochran-Smith (1992) argue that teacher inquiry helps position teachers in relationship to their own knowledge. It helps teachers make what they know more visible, and aids them in examining the relationships between their practice and their ideas, as well as provides a means for entering into public dialog about teaching. To the extent that teacher narratives insert practitioners into public conversations about teaching, this can shift the power balance in how teachers, and teachers' knowledge, are positioned within those conversations. However, speaking publicly does not mean that one is heard; teacher narratives can still be ignored by those who believe that reality exists apart from the knower, and can be known best through social science research that strives for objectivity. This is an epistemological issue.

For some teacher educators, helping teachers to produce meaningful texts about their work is itself a valuable teaching process (e.g., Gitlin, 1994; Grumet, 1980; Hollingsworth, 1995; Lytle & Cochran-Smith, 1992; Schubert & Ayers, 1992;). Waldoch's (1995) article was a product of such work. I often have preservice teacher education students develop inquiry papers around issues or questions that matter to them, then create a textbook for the class from these papers. The students consistently report that they learn a great deal from such a project, both from creating their own texts and from reading what other students have created, because questions in their own minds are taken seriously, and they learn something of the process of constructing contextually-based knowledge and communicating it. Such texts do not substitute for their engaging with texts by researchers; both work in tandem.

From the Margins: How Can Children from Marginalized Sociocultural Communities Learn More Effectively? Why Don't They Achieve Well, Even with So Many Attempts to "Help"?

It is possible to read the research and assume that as a profession, we are getting more knowledgeable about how to help students learn effectively. National criticisms of schooling notwithstanding, the accumulated body of research on teaching, learning, and teacher education would suggest an expanding knowledge base that should lead to school improvement. From perspectives of marginalized communities, however, this is not necessarily the case, and empowering teachers is not necessarily a solution, since many teachers do not come from the same sociocultural communities as their students and may bring biases and blinders of the wider society into the classroom.

One can distinguish among several different bodies of research produced by scholars from marginalized groups, including critical race theory, culturally-sensitive research, Afrocentric research, neo-Marxist research, feminist research, socialist feminist research, queer theory[1] and gay/lesbian studies, and so forth. These research communities are quite different. However, they share common concerns and assumptions, even if they do not share the same communities of membership or interest. Research on teaching and teacher education that I categorize as coming from the margins is generally 1) conducted on students from at least one marginalized group, 2) by a researcher who is from that same group, 3) interpreted within intellectual discourse of that group, *and* 4) conducted largely for the purpose of improving education for children who are members of that community. Research conducted by mainstream scholars on students from marginalized groups, or by scholars from marginalized communities but interpreted within dominant theoretical perspectives, is not included as a part of this category.

What distinguishes this category epistemologically is its interrogation of the position of the knower within a stratified society, and the implications of that position for knowledge construction. This has been an important issue within ethnic studies, women's studies, critical theory, and gay/lesbian studies, where considerable work has been done identifying biases, distortions, and limitations of research and theory conducted by dominant communities on marginalized communities. Tetreault (1993), for example, explains that, "Positionality means that important aspects of our identity, for example, our gender, our race, our class ... are markers of relational positions rather than essential qualities" (p. 139). The knowledge that one produces is bound with one's viewpoint, which in turn is influenced by one's life experience and social position in a stratified society (Banks, 1993).

Most of the accumulated knowledge base about teaching and teacher education has been produced largely by White, male professionals. Whether acknowledged or not, from perspectives of feminist, ethnic, and critical theorists, this shared social location of so many researchers systematically shapes the knowledge base itself by consistently privileging some viewpoints while marginalizing others. This is much the same issue as that raised by teacher narratives, but, since the great majority of teachers are White, teacher narratives are largely still situated within frames of reference that make sense to White people, but not necessarily to those subordinated on the basis of race (e.g., Lipman, 1997).

The dominant paradigms for educational research originated within European and Euro-American experiences and realities. This is true of much qualitative, as well as classical, positivist research. As such, much of it has the effect of colonizing "Others," whether intended or not, through too-often unquestioned privileging of professional class European and Euro-American male experiences, in which people from marginalized communities become incorporated into someone else's view of reality. Educators of color have argued for years that mainstream research, despite claims to objectivity, is biased and almost always frames communities of color as "deficient." By attempting to incorporate everyone into its worldview and conceptual universe, Europeans and Euro-Americans developed a knowledge-construction process that at its very core is colonizing. Scheurich and Young (1997) refer to this as "civilization racism," which includes "our current range of research epistemologies—positivism to postmodernisms/poststructuralisms—[which] arise out of the social history and culture of the dominant race" (p. 8). Similarly, much of the knowledge construction process historically has silenced women. As Pagano (1990) put it, "Either we [women] are locked out or we are plagiarists. The stories that we tell are not our own. The impulse to the art of women teaching and the art of teaching women begins in that recognition" (p. 132).

Research from the margins questions universality, generalizability, and political neutrality of knowledge. Classical positivism seeks to generalize and claims objectivity; some qualitative research does the same. Research from marginalized communities explicitly does not seek to generalize outside its own community, although it may generalize within the community; nor does it claim that any knowledge is politically neutral. Rather, researchers from the margins have argued that it is highly important to explicate and develop one's cultural and historical frame of reference, and to situate one's work within one's own community, rather than presuming to produce something that generalizes to all of humanity. For example, Afrocentrism rests on the premise that people of African descent should be their own subjects of their own history rather than someone else's objects of study, and that the place of people of African descent in the knowledge production process matters epistemologically. One raises the question of place and grounding specifically to orient one to the culture, history, and cosmological frame of reference one is using. As Asante (1990) points out, all research is historically situated, "there is no antiplace" (p. 5). The problem with mainstream research is that, by claiming objectivity, researchers usually do not acknowledge the cultural-boundedness of their assumptions and findings (Gordon, 1995). This claim does not mean that members of dominant groups can never understand members of subordinant groups. But it does emphasize the history of researchers from dominant groups creating knowledge that has tended to silence or diminish voices of those from subordinant groups, and the work to be done on rewriting knowledge, from the inside.

Because mainstream research that has been done "on" marginalized communities frequently and tacitly accepts society's damaging distortions, its tenets do not necessarily have value in judging knowledge claims. For example, most mainstream research on student race or social class and achievement ends up framing students of color or students from impoverished homes in terms of what they do not do well moreso than in terms of what they can do well. The data may well be accurate, and the research deemed scientifically true. But a paradigm that leads one to foreground failure rather than strengths and successes is the wrong paradigm, and tests of validity or reliability do not assess that problem. Researchers from the margins work with and develop a different paradigm. For example, Gandara (1995) traced the biographies of 50 Chicanas and Chicanos who had obtained the highest degrees in their fields, in order to find out what factors account for their academic success, and what educational policy recommendations would follow. Soto (1997) traced the conflicts between a Puerto Rican community and the school system over bilingual education, in order to expose the politics that surround language programming, even when such programming is academically successful. Both are qualitative studies, and share assumptions with other qualitative research discussed earlier. But both also explicitly challenge interpretive frameworks within which research on their communities is conducted by outsiders; both construct an alternative interpretive framework that recognizes strengths and wisdom of Chicanos and Puerto Ricans, respectively, in the context of a racist society.

Collins (1991) argued that concrete experience should be used as a criterion of meaning, that dialogue be used in assessing knowledge claims, and that researchers should adhere to an ethic of personal accountability. Ladson-Billings's (1995) research is an excellent example of these principles. In her study of successful teachers of Black children, she identified the teachers primarily by asking for nominations from Black parents; she co-constructed knowledge about successful pedagogy with the teachers, and she reflected on her own accountability to the community in her scholarly work. By grounding her research in the community context and listening to the voice of her own experience as a Black educator, she very self-consciously worked to produce knowledge that would improve the teaching of Black children. The Black community, then, became the final arbiter of her knowledge claims.

Foster (1994) describes a similar process for judging truth. She grounded her research on Black student classroom behavior in terms of the Black community's tradition of performance, a perspective which the dominant research community has tended to ignore. Foster explains that it was only when one of the Black teachers in the study "authenticated her reliance on the Black traditions of preaching and performance and the students confirmed its significance that I felt that I had adequately captured her perspective and consequently that this theoretical perspective had merit as an analytic construct able to represent the organic intellectual tradition of contemporary African American life" (p. 144). She goes on to explain that research such as hers does not claim to speak for all communities, nor to be the only valid interpretation. But as an interpretation grounded within the intellectual frameworks of the community of which both the students and the researcher are members, it is an important interpretation that cannot be simply dismissed or ignored.

Similarly, *Women's Ways of Knowing* (Belenky, Clinchy, Goldberger, & Tarule, 1986) challenged the silence of women in the fields of psychology and education, and in the classroom. Conducted by female researchers on women of varying ages, the study sought to examine how women construct knowledge in order to help educators assist in the intellectual development of female students. Feminist teacher educators have developed these ideas relative to teacher education. Hollingsworth (1994) describes her approach to teacher education as "sustained conversation," engaging teachers in building truths by beginning with their own experiences, and her approach to research as a co-learner with teachers rather than an expert over them. Work such as hers merges feminist scholarship with teacher narrative by developing professional voices of women teachers.

Research from the margins is oriented toward practical transformation. Collins (1991) referred to this as an "ethic of caring," which to Ladson-Billings (1995) means "the articulation of a greater sense of commitment to what scholarship and/or pedagogy can mean in the lives of people" (p. 474). Indeed, much of the scholarship from the margins is oriented very explicitly toward the transformation of schools to benefit historically oppressed communities. In this way, knowledge has emancipatory power (Gordon, 1990), which challenges the colonizing function of much mainstream knowledge. Or, as Jaggar (1983) put it in an extensive analysis of feminist theory, "Feminist scholars are distinguished from non-feminist scholars precisely by their common political interest in ending women's oppression, and they see their scholarly work as contributing to a comprehensive understanding of how women's liberation should be achieved" (p. 354). As a result, mainstream scholars often charge research from the margins with "bias" and "a political agenda," to which scholars from the margins reply that mainstream research also has biases and politics, but that it masks them.

A related epistemological difference between much research from the margins and research from the mainstream concerns the origins of research questions, and subsequent selection of methodology. A purpose of research from the margins is to identify and clarify central research questions and their conceptual framing, given the history of mainstream researchers imposing questions and analytical frames on marginalized communities. Central research issues and questions from marginalized groups are rooted in the history of the community, and analytic frameworks must fit the community and its history authentically. In contrast, mainstream researchers are more likely to select a research question or propose a hypothesis based on the literature, or, as in qualitative research, determine what emerges from the data. The literature, the interests of the researcher, or the data, then become the determiners of research questions, rather than the community's needs and its history. Feminist teacher educators note the same problem in who determines the teacher education curriculum: voices of teachers and teacher education students, who are mainly women, are usually absent (Carter, 1993; Hollingsworth, 1994). Researchers from historically marginalized groups, however, look to the experiences and history of their own communities to identify and frame research issues, but at the same time must also disentangle ways of viewing educational issues advanced by the dominant society from perspectives that make sense to their own communities (Delpit, 1988; Reyes, 1992).

Research questions about teaching and teacher education generally invite an interdisciplinary perspective, although researchers themselves are generally trained within specific disciplines, such as psychology, sociology, anthropology, or linguistics. However, personal narrative and qualitative research offer more user-friendly methodologies to scholars from the margins than do experimental or survey research methodologies, primarily because narrative and qualitative research encourage exploration of complexity and sensitivity to the voices and viewpoints of those who are studied. Qualitative research, contextualized within a critique of structural oppression and oriented toward social change, has been developed as critical ethnography. Weiler (1988), for example, used feminist critical ethnography to examine 11 female teachers and administrators, working among two urban schools, in order to find out how and why they acted as progressive change agents. Her study portrays feminist teachers working for social justice in the context of teaching, and explores how teachers' biographies impacted on their definitions of their work.

The 1980s and 1990s have seen attempts to synthesize a knowledge base about teaching in order to improve teacher education. Typically, research from the margins is marginalized in mainstream syntheses. For example, the *Handbook of Research on Teaching* (Wittrock, 1986) contains separate chapters about context and special populations, but most of the chapters are written by White scholars and are based mainly on mainstream research. And embedded in much of that research are perspectives within which makes sense to recommend that teachers teach more content and offer more challenge to higher SES than lower SES children (Brophy & Good, 1986). Researchers from marginalized groups are producing compilations and syntheses, in order to recenter discussions of teaching within frames of reference that make sense to oppressed communities; the *Handbook of Research on Multicultural Education* (Banks & Banks, 1995) is the most comprehensive of such compilations.

Research from the margins clearly illustrates that all knowledge is socially created within human vantage points. Knowers are situated, and where they are situated socially matters. This does not render knowledge useless, only contingent. Research from the margins is the most explicit about its epistemological assumptions and how these differ from mainstream research, by virtue of "bumping up against" assumptions that conflict with assumptions that arise from experiences in the margins of society, and as such, it offers a critique of, and corrective to, research by dominant groups (D. Marty; personal communication, February 17, 1998). As Banks (1995) argued, "Students who have a keen understanding of how knowledge is constructed, how it reflects both subjectivity and objectivity, and how it relates to power, will have important skills needed to participate in the construction of knowledge that will help the nation to actualize its democratic ideals" (p. 24).

Postmodernism/Poststructuralism: Who Articulates What Discourses about Teaching and Teacher Education, and Whose Interests are Served by Those Discourses?

Postmodernist/poststructuralist theorists critique assumptions of modernist theory and research by questioning who constructs what narratives and theories and whose interests they embody, how ideas are codified in media and interpreted by people, and how individual subjectivity interacts with meanings generated by others. "The debates about knowledge are not only about who tells the 'truth' but about the rules on which that truth is based and the conditions in which that truth is told" (Popkewitz, 1997, p. 27). The central epistemological issue of concern to poststructuralists is not what is true, but how decisions about what counts as truth come to be made, by whom, and under what conditions. Postmodernist/poststructuralist analyses examine how pedagogical issues are framed, by whom, and what forms of discourse are foregrounded by particular framings. So far this is a small body of work in the area of teaching and teacher education, but it is an appropriate body on which to conclude this chapter. This work, like this chapter, posits multiple ways of making sense of teaching and teacher education, none of which is "correct" in some absolute sense.

For example, Tinning (1991) contrasts three ways of framing an analysis of a physical education student teaching episode: performance pedagogy (which focuses on how efficiently a teacher teaches students to perform specific skills), critical pedagogy (which focuses on how the teacher contextualizes teaching within class, gender, and race relations), and postmodern pedagogy. His discussion of postmodern pedagogy consists of identifying questions and issues, rather than analyzing the student teaching episode itself, and he concluded that, "A clear picture of what a postmodern pedagogy would look like is, at present, not available. Instead, all we have are what some would call the moral deliberations of intellectuals" (p. 14).

Cherryholms (1988) employed poststructuralist deconstruction to examine curriculum, specifically textbooks. His main argument is that, while teachers usually teach textbook knowledge and children apprehend it as a direct representation of phenomena "out there," textbook knowledge is, in fact, a social creation that gains power through the position of the textbook in schools. Similarly, research and theory on teaching is also socially created, but has power in a social context that separates theory from practice, theoreticians from practitioners, and scientific rationality from practical reasoning. His conclusion is not that there can be no curriculum, or no knowledge about teaching, but rather that none of it rests on a foundation of certitude. Uncertainty should prompt thinking and questioning; construction, deconstruction, and reconstruction of knowledge at all levels should be a continuous process.

Poststructural deconstructionists are reluctant to replace well-engrained models of pedagogy with other models that themselves can also be deconstructed, arguing that the value of poststructuralism is raising important ethical questions rather than prescribing a model of pedagogy (Capper, 1993). From the perspectives of many practitioners, that is an inherent limitation: Practitioners need to construct practice in the classroom, and research questioning the basis of practice, rather than providing guidance for practice, magnifies the uncertainty that is already a part of teaching.

At the same time, poststructuralist analyses support claims to voice by those who are not in positions of power. For example, Popkewitz (1991) examined historic and contemporary reforms in curriculum, teaching, and teacher education at the national and state levels, including parts played by philanthropic organizations and by researchers. His main argument is that, while one can identify a rich multiplicity of ideas about how schools should be—ranging from the thinking of individual teachers, to diverse ethnic and racial groups, to diverse philosophical conceptions about schooling—the reform discourses have masked multiple perspectives. Reform discourses advance singular "solutions" and often cloak them with rhetoric that suggests humanism, legitimating them through scientific justification, such as research on cognition. This process serves as a powerful form of state social control, which can be understood historically as the response of the state to social problems experienced by a highly diverse population. The result is not that deep ethical social problems are actually solved, but that they are contained.

Popkewitz's analysis is very important to this chapter, because he questions whose interests are served by the search for the "best" teaching practices for "everyone." In advancing one set of "solutions," whose voices are silenced, and what are the consequences of that silencing? As Popkewitz (1991) argued, "Educational research and its researchers are part of the political practices to be struggled over. Those who have authority to speak and what is authorized as speech are important elements in the construction and reconstructions of society" (p. 245).

CONCLUSION

I opened this chapter by suggesting that wisdom about teaching and teacher education can grow through dialogue across epistemologies. "In the end, the disagreements reside in the different vocabularies that are being used to tell different stories to ourselves and to others about research and about who we are as educational researchers." (Smith, 1997, p. 10). I do not believe it would be wise to advance one epistemology as "correct," although I certainly have my own biases regarding what questions I believe are most important, and the nature of knowledge related to those questions. But it is very important to approach our different stories as being based on truth, but a truth that is grounded differently. As researchers, we tell different stories because we start with different questions, frame them differently, and base them on various assumptions about what counts as knowledge and how knowledge is produced.

Positivism helps to uncover replicable patterns of behavior that lead to measurable student outcomes, a measure regularly employed to judge students and schools. Qualitative research helps to examine interpretations and perspectives of particular teachers and students, and complexities of school and classroom life. Teacher narratives help to frame issues in terms that connect directly to the work teachers do, and provide a means for engaging teachers in public discussions about teaching. Research from the margins frames education issues and practices directly around concerns, perspectives, and insights of historically marginalized social groups, and offers explicit critique of epistemological assumptions made by members of the dominant society. Poststructuralism helps us to examine the processes by which ideas in education arise and become accepted. These questions do not neatly fit together, and the epistemological lenses researchers have used to examine them diverge significantly. Our perspectives about what it means to teach, what counts as teaching, and what counts as knowing do differ, and those differences are reflected in our words, and our approach to defining "truth."

In other contexts, I have argued that in a pluralistic society, rather than attempting to become alike, we need to learn to talk across our differences. This is difficult, because it means learning other people's languages and viewpoints well enough to actually hear what others are saying. One need not agree, but one needs to learn to hear. In the context of this chapter, I make the same argument, and am in agreement with Shulman (1986) when he concluded that, "But when investigators have learned to speak each other's languages, to comprehend the terms of which other programs' research questions are couched, then processes of deliberation over findings can yield the hybrid understandings not possible when members of individual research programs dwell in intellectual ghettos of their own construction" (p. 33).

NOTE

[1] Some readers may be unfamiliar with the term "queer theory." The word *queer* has historically been used by heterosexuals in a pejorative way, but has been claimed and re-defined by theorists in the gay and lesbian community as a project in identity construction. The process of claiming terms that the dominant society has used pejoratively, then redefining them, is not uncommon in social movements and theories of marginalized groups (D. Marty, personal communication, February 17, 1998).

REFERENCES

Anyon, J. (1981). Elementary schooling and distinctions of social class. *Interchange, 22*, 118–132.

Asante, M. K. (1990). *Kemet, Afrocentricity, and knowledge.* Trenton, NJ: Africa World Press.

Banks, J. A. (1993). The canon debate, knowledge construction, and multicultural education. *Educational Researcher, 22*(5), 4–14.

Banks, J. A. (1995). The historical reconstruction of knowledge about race: Implications for transformative teaching. *Educational Researcher, 24*(2), 15–25.

Banks, J. A., & Banks, C. A. M. (Eds.). (1995). *Handbook of research on multicultural education.* New York: Macmillan.

Belenky, M. F., Clinchy, B. M., Goldberger, N. R., & Tarule, J. M. (1986). *Women's ways of knowing.* New York: Basic Books.

Berger, P. L., & Luckmann, T. (1966). *The social construction of reality.* Garden City, NY: Doubleday Books.

Brickhouse, N. A. (1990). Teachers' beliefs about the nature of science and their relationship to classroom practice. *Journal of Teacher Education, 41*(1), 53–62.

Britzman, D. (1991). *Practice makes practice: A critical study of learning to teach.* Albany, NY: State University of New York Press.

Brophy, J., & Good, T. (1986). Teacher behavior and student achievement. In M. C. Wittrock (Ed.), *Handbook of research on teaching* (pp. 328–375). New York: Macmillan.

Brophy, J., & VanSledright, B. (1997). *Teaching and learning history in elementary schools.* New York: Teachers College Press.

Campbell, D. T., & Stanley, J. C. (1963). *Experimental and quasi-experimental designs for research.* Chicago: Rand McNally.

Capper, C. (1993). Outcomes-based education reexamined: From structural functionalism to poststructuralism. *Educational Policy, 7*(4), 427–446.

Carter, K. (1993). The place of story in the study of teaching and teacher education. *Educational Researcher. 22*(1), 5–12.

Cherryholms, C. H. (1988). *Power and criticism.* New York: Teachers College Press.

Collins, P. H. (1991). *Black feminist thought: Knowledge, consciousness. and the politics of empowerment.* New York: Routledge.

Connelly, F. M., & Clandinin, D. J. (1990). Stories of experience and narrative inquiry. *Educational Researcher, 19*(5), 2–14.

Danziger, K. (1990). *Constructing the subject: Historical origins of psychological research.* Cambridge, England: Cambridge University Press.

Delpit, L. (1988). The silenced dialogue: Power and pedagogy in educating other people's children. *Harvard Educational Review, 58*, 280–298.

Eisner, E. W. (1988). The primacy of experience and the politics of method. *Educational Researcher, 17*(5), 15–20.

Eisner, E. W. (1993). Forms of understanding and the future of educational research. *Educational Researcher, 22*(7), 5–11.

Elbaz, F. (1981). The teacher's "practical knowledge": Report of a case study. *Curriculum Inquiry, 11*(1), 43–71.

Enright, L. (1979). Learning in my classroom. *Forum for the Discussion of New Trends in Education, 21*(3), 78–81.

Ester, D. (1994-5). CAI, lecture, and student learning style: The different effects of instructional method. *Journal of Research on Computing in Education, 27*, 129–141.

Flanders, N. (1960). *Teacher influence, pupil attitudes, and achievement.* Minneapolis, MN: University of Minnesota Press.

Foucault, M. (1980). *Power/knowledge: Selected interrviews and other writings 1972–1977.* New York: Pantheon Books.

Foster, M. (1994). The power to know one thing is never the power to know all things. In A. Gitlin (Ed.), *Power and method* (pp. 129–146). New York: Routledge.

Gandara, P. (1995). *Over the ivy walls.* Albany, NY: State University of New York Press.

Geertz, C. (1995). *After the fact.* Cambridge, MA: Harvard University Press.

Gitlin, A. (Ed.). (1994). *Power and method.* New York: Routledge.

Gitlin, A., & Russell, R. (1994). Alternative methodologies and the research context. In A. Gitlin (Ed.), *Power and method* (pp. 181–202). New York: Routledge.

Good, T., & Brophy, J. (1973). *Looking in classrooms.* New York: Harper & Row.

Gordon, B. M. (1990). The necessity of African-American epistemology for educational theory and practice. *Journal of Education, 172*(3), 88–106.

Gordon, E. W. (1995). Culture and the sciences of pedagogy. *Teachers College Record, 97*(1), 32–46.

Grumet, M. R. (1980). Autobiography and reconceptualization. *Journal of Curriculum Theorizing, 1*, 155–158.

Harding, S. (1994). Is science multicultural? Challenges, resources, opportunities, uncertainties. *Configurations, 2*, 301–330.

Hollingsworth, S. (1994). *Teacher research and urban literacy education.* New York: Teachers College Press.

Jackson, P. W. (1968). *Life in classrooms.* New York: Holt, Rinehart & Winston.

Jaggar, A. M. (1983). *Feminist politics and human nature.* Totowa, NJ: Rowman & Allanheld.

Jimenez, R. T., Garcia, G. E., & Pearson, P. D. (1995). Three children, two languages, and strategic reading: Case studies in bilingual/monolingual reading. *American Educational Research Journal, 32*, 67–97.

Kuhn, T. S. (1970). *The structure of scientific revolutions.* Chicago: University of Chicago Press.

Ladson-Billings, G. (1995). Toward a theory of culturally-relevant pedagogy. *American Educational Research Journal, 32*(3), 465–492.

Lipman, P. (1997). Restructuring in context: A case study of teacher participation and the dynamics of ideology, race, and power. *American Educational Research Journal, 34*(1), 3–37.

Loflund, J., & Loflund, L. H. (1995). *Analyzing social settings: A guide to qualitative observation and analysis* (3rd ed.). Belmont, CA: Wadsworth.

Lyons, N. (1990). Dilemmas of knowing: Ethical and epistemological dimensions of teachers' work and development. *Harvard Educational Review, 60*(2), 159–180.

Lytle, S. L., & Cochran-Smith, M. (1992). Teacher research as a way of knowing. *Harvard Educational Review, 62*(4), 447–474.

Meyer, R. J. (1995). Stories to teach and teaching to story: The use of narrative in learning to teach. *Language Arts, 72*, 276–286.

Oakes, J. (1985). *Keeping track.* Princeton, NJ: Princeton University Press.

Ornstein, A. C. (1995). Beyond effective teaching. *Peabody Journal of Teacher Education, 70*(2), 2–23.

Pagano, J. A. (1990). *Exiles and communities: Teaching in the patriarchal wilderness.* Albany, NY: State University of New York Press.

Peshkin, A. (1993). The goodness of qualitative research. *Educational Researcher, 22*(2), 23–29.

Popkewitz, T. S. (1991). *A political sociology of educational reform.* New York: Teachers College Press.

Popkewitz, T. S. (1997). A changing terrain of knowledge and power: A social epistemology of educational research. *Educational Researcher, 26*(9), 18–29.

Reyes, M. (1992). Challenging venerable assumptions: Literacy instruction for linguistically different students. *Harvard Educational Review, 62*(4), 427–446.

Reynolds, M. C. (Ed.). (1989). *Knowledge base for the beginning teacher.* Oxford, England: Pergamon Press.

Rist, R. C. (1973). *The urban school: A factory for failure.* Cambridge, MA: MIT Press.

Rosaldo, R. (1989). *Culture and truth.* Boston: Beacon Press.

Scheurich, J. J., & Young, M. D. (1997). Coloring epistemologies: Are our research epistemologies racially biased? *Educational Researcher, 26*(4), 4–17.

Schubert, W., & Ayers, W. (1992). *Teacher lore: Learning from our own experience.* New York: Longman.

Shulman, L. S. (1986). Paradigms and research programs in the study of teaching: A contemporary perspective. In M. C. Wittrock (Ed.), *Handbook of research on teaching* (pp. 3–36). New York: Macmillan.

Shulman, L. S. (1991). Ways of seeing, ways of knowing: Ways of teaching, ways of learning about teaching. *Curriculum Studies, 23*(5), 393–395.

Sikula, J., Buttery, T. J., & Guyton, E. (Eds.). (1996). *Handbook of research on teacher education* (2nd ed.). New York: Macmillan.

Slavin, R. E. (1987). Ability grouping and student achievement in elementary schools: A best-evidence synthesis. *Review of Educational Research, 57,* 347–350.

Slavin, R. E. (1990). Achievement effects of ability grouping in secondary schools: A best-evidence synthesis. *Review of Educational Research, 60*(2), 471–499.

Slavin, R. E., Madden, N., Dolan, L. J., Wasik, B. A., Ross, S. M., & Smith, L. J. (1994). Whenever and wherever we choose. *Phi Delta Kappan, 75*(8), 639–647.

Sleeter, C. E. (1992). *Keepers of the American dream.* London: The Falmer Press.

Smith, J. K. (1997). The stories educational researchers tell about themselves. *Educational Researcher, 26*(5), 4–11.

Solas, J. (1992). Investigating teacher and student thinking about the process of learning using autobiography and repertory grid. *Review of Educational Research, 62*(2), 205–225.

Soto, L. D. (1997). *Language, culture, and power.* Albany, NY: State University of New York Press.

Spindler, G. D. (Ed.). (1955). *Education and anthropology.* Stanford, CA: Stanford University Press.

Tetreault, M. K. T. (1993). Classrooms for diversity: Rethinking curriculum and pedagogy. In J. A. Banks & C. A. M. Banks (Eds.), *Multicultural education: Issues and perspectives* (2nd ed.; pp. 129–148). Boston: Allyn & Bacon.

Tinning, R. (1991). Teacher education pedagogy: Dominant discourses and the process of problem solving. *Journal of Teaching in Physical Education, 11,* 1–20.

Waldoch, J. S. (1995). Student success: A matter of compatibility and expectations. In B. B. Swadener & S. Lubeck (Eds.), *Children and families "at promise"* (pp. 224–237). Albany, NY: State University of New York Press.

Wang, M. C., Haertel, G. D., & Walberg, H. J. (1993). Toward a knowledge base for school learning. *Review of Educational Research, 63*(3), 249–294.

Weiler, K. (1988). *Women teaching for change.* South Hadley, MA: Bergin & Garvey.

Wittrock, M. C. (Ed.). (1986). *Handbook of research on teaching* (3rd ed.). New York: Macmillan.

Wood, T. (1996). Events in learning mathematics: Insights from research in classrooms. *Educational Studies in Mathematics, 30,* 85–105.

Yennie-Donmoyer, J. (1993). Andrew: The story of a gifted at-risk student. In R. Donmoyer & R. Kos (Eds.), *At-risk students* (pp. 135–152). Albany, NY: State University of New York Press.

2

Ed Schools and the Problem of Knowledge

Mary M. Kennedy
Michigan State University

In 1997, the University of Chicago closed its education department. The news was greeted with dismay by faculty in other education departments throughout the country, largely because the University of Chicago's education department has played such a visible and important role in our history. But it is not clear whether anyone else noticed, or at least cared. These other responses, of people outside of education departments, are more important, for they indicate the extent to which education is considered to be a legitimate field of study in higher education.

A central issue in arguments about whether education programs should exist is whether they provide warranted and useful knowledge. Like most programs in higher education, education programs are maintained under the premise that they provide a body of knowledge that is (a) empirically justifiable, and (b) valued by someone—in this case, it should be valued by education practitioners. Consistent with this premise, education faculty members are encouraged to conduct research, findings from research are codified into textbooks, and courses for a wide range of education practitioners are organized and offered to students—indeed, required of students. All of this occurs under the assumption that there is a justified knowledge base that can be articulated and transmitted to students and, further, that this knowledge base can contribute to their future practice.

So we have built a huge enterprise, called education, that is based on a set of assumptions that many people, including teachers, doubt. Some 1,200 institutions of higher education participate in this enterprise. They have departments, schools, or colleges of education, all offering programs of study that include program participation standards, completion requirements, and so forth. All 50 states participate in this system of education, outlining courses and curricula that they require for certification. Textbook publishers participate in this system by publishing the texts that are used in all these courses. Funding agencies, both public and private, participate in this system, sponsoring research that they expect to be added to the knowledge base and to be ultimately of value to practitioners.

And yet, despite the size, complexity, and expense of this undertaking, despite the widespread commitments of foundations, state agencies, textbook publishers, and colleges and universities, and despite the apparently entrenched, institutionalized, and embedded nature of education programs, there have always been skeptics raising questions about the need, value, or merit of these programs. Apparently, the University of Chicago was skeptical. And apparently, the justifications put forth by education professors have not been adequate, for the skeptics never go away.

One opinion about the University of Chicago's decision is particularly telling, for it was written by a teacher who was, at the time, attending a graduate school of education (Bassett, 1997). This teacher said he would not miss the University of Chicago Education School—that it didn't really offer much to teachers like himself. He further claimed that education schools which are cut off from practice become arcane and irrelevant, that a good teacher education program acknowledges the importance of clinical faculty, and that a good education school recognizes that *teaching is a craft, not a science.* "They respect and rely on the knowledge, judgement, and experience of practicing master teachers" (p. 35).

This is an interesting argument. If it is the case that teaching is a craft, rather than a science, and if it is the case that it is best learned from clinical faculty rather than from academic faculty, then one can reasonably ask why the subject of education should be included in a higher education curriculum at all, or be the subject of research at all. One can ask why teachers must obtain a credential before entering teaching, rather than learning their craft in doing, as craft knowledge is typically learned. When we think of craft knowledge, we think of knowledge that is kinesthetic—knowledge of touch and feel, weight and balance, timing and nuance. We think of it as knowledge that develops from repeated experiences working with a particular kind of material, gaining a sense for its responsiveness to different kinds of actions. Crafts are not learned by reading books. They are learned from experience and with guidance from a master.

Bassett's (1997) column gives us one way of understanding the nature of the continuing debate about the merits of teacher-education programs. His argument that teaching is a craft, and therefore does not rely on research, is fundamental to debates about whether education programs can make a genuine contribution to teaching, or to any other education pursuits such as counseling, administering, curriculum developing, or policymaking. Are all of these activities crafts? Do they not benefit from the kind of formal knowledge generated from research and transmitted in textbooks?

If Bassett (1997) is right, then it is indeed fair to ask what value is added by this huge enterprise. Why should we continue to study teaching, learning, and child development, for instance, and why codify our knowledge in textbooks for prospective educators, if knowledge from research is unrelated to the craft knowledge educators actually need and use in their practice?

To address this question, I focus on the practice of teaching and examine the nature of knowledge generated by research and codified in textbooks on teaching with the nature of knowledge that Bassett (1997) claims is used in teaching. Let us call the knowledge that is produce by researchers *"expert"* knowledge, always retaining the quotes to indicate that this is the *ostensible* knowledge of experts. Let us also refer to the kind of knowledge that derives primarily from clinical experiences, as *craft* knowledge, following Bassett. In the pages that follow, I examine each of these kinds of knowledge. I then introduce a third kind of knowledge, which I call *expertise*, and which I put forth as a blend of "expert" knowledge and craft knowledge.

THE NATURE OF "EXPERT" KNOWLEDGE

"Expert" knowledge is the product of research. As such, it has a number of important features. Probably the most salient of these features is that "expert" knowledge is *propositional*. That is, we can say in sentences all the things that have been learned from research. We can put this knowledge into encyclopedias, textbooks, how-to manuals, guidebooks, and handbooks. We can list it in bullet form, or we can elaborate on it if we wish. Propositional knowledge is very different from, say, *kinesthetic* knowledge, which feels as if it is held in the muscles rather than in the brain. Teachers know how to move about in their classrooms, for instance, and how to posture themselves to maintain a certain persona, yet they cannot lay out this knowledge in sentences. It is only with great difficulty that experienced teachers can tell novices how to quiet a classroom simply by their posture. Knowledge about the movements of teaching—*kinesthetic* knowledge— is an important kind of knowledge that is used every day, but is not definable in sentences; it is not propositional.

That "expert" knowledge is propositional also means that it is public, rather than private. Because we can say it and write it down, we can share it and discuss it with others. We can refer to encyclopedias to settle disputes among ourselves. This public nature of "expert" knowledge makes it different from, say, *experiential* knowledge, the large stores of knowledge each of us has accumulated from our own experiences. Experiential knowledge is private: it is retained from our own private point of view, each of us having a unique collection of experiences. And, of course, we draw on our experiential knowledge virtually all the time to help us make sense of new experiences. Each time we meet someone new, for instance, and want to assess that person's trustworthiness, we form our judgment by contrasting this person with analogous people we have known in the past. Teachers can sense when a class is getting restless, and what the consequences of that might be, because they have seen these signs many times before. Yet each teacher might be receptive to different cues, based on the particulars of his or her own experiences.

So "expert" knowledge is different from experiential knowledge because it is public, and different from kinesthetic knowledge because it is propositional. This public, propositional nature of "expert" knowledge also means that it is testable and contestable. If I were to claim that, say, fourth-grade children frequently hold misconceptions of photosynthesis, thinking that plants obtain food from the soil rather than making it themselves, you may challenge me on this proposition. You might ask what evidence I have, or where and how I determined this. You may test the proposition yourself, by quizzing a group of fourth graders, and comparing your results to mine. If you tell me that children across the nation are performing more poorly in science than children in other countries, I may choose to contest that point. Even if we don't have the resources needed to directly assess children nationwide, we can seek other written material, such as journal articles or research reports, to learn what others say about this proposition and to learn what evidence they have used to draw their conclusions. So "expert" knowledge is testable and contestable, in part because of its propositional and public nature.

Finally, "expert" knowledge is developed through procedures, such as research, that are themselves public. Research is an activity that is governed by canons of evidence, procedures, and warrants. Like elementary arithmetic students, researchers must show their work. They must show their readers how they derived their findings. And they must be prepared for readers to argue about the appropriateness of these methods, to contest the conclusions that derive from these procedures, and to devise their own procedures to test the conclusions for themselves. Their results, in turn, are public, so that the entire community may enter into this debate if they desire.

Everything about "expert" knowledge, then, is public. Not only are the findings public by virtue of being propositional, but, in addition, the procedures are public, the canons regarding the procedures are public, and the canons regarding the reporting of procedures are public. That all these aspects of "expert" knowledge are public means that all of them are also open to dispute. Just as we can challenge the procedures used by any one individual, so can we challenge the canon itself, so that over time, not only does "expert" knowledge change, but so do community standards for how "expert" knowledge is justified.

All of these features of "expert" knowledge—the fact that it is propositional, public, testable and contestable, and is based on procedures that are public and contestable—are important. Because "expert" knowledge has these characteristics, it is also *group* knowledge. It is shared knowledge. It is distinctly different from the vast stores of kinesthetic and experiential knowledge that each of us privately holds, and that each of us uses everyday.

There is one final aspect of "expert" knowledge that is also important: The problems people try to solve when they produce "expert" knowledge are also public. They are shared, group problems, and efforts to solve these problems are group efforts rather than individual efforts. Even though particular researchers may work in isolation, they compare their progress with that of others and are interested in learning about the progress of others. If one researcher solves the problem entirely, there is no need for others to solve it again; just as the problem was a public, shared, group problem, so the solution is a public, shared, group solution. If one researcher makes progress on understanding adolescent alienation, all researchers can profit from this finding. Everyone can learn and possess this new knowledge.

This shared quality of "expert" knowledge makes it quite different from kinesthetic and experiential knowledge, which are necessarily private. When an individual teacher sees a problem of adolescent alienation, the problem she is trying to solve is a private problem, not a shared problem. She identifies it through her own private experiences with this particular adolescent, and she strives to solve it by further analyzing these experiences. To the extent that other teachers also are troubled about alienated adolescents of their own, we may say that their problems are *common* problems, but they are still separate, private problems, for each teacher faces a particular manifestation of the problem and interprets it in a unique way, based on his or her own configuration of experiential knowledge. Common problems, then, are families of analogous private problems that many people face, but that must be solved privately by each individual, whereas *shared* problems belong to groups and can be solved together. With this distinction, we can now characterize "expert" knowledge not only as propositional and public, not only as deriving from public canons of evidence and warrants, and as testable and contestable, but also as organized around problems and solutions that are shared rather than common.

"Expert" knowledge is an essential ingredient in all of higher education, for the entire organization of higher education is based on the assumption that there is a substantial body of public, propositional knowledge whose validity has been tested and which can be summarized in textbooks and lectures for students. Few doubt that such knowledge exists, nor that it is important, nor that it contributes to the quality of our lives in a wide range of ways. At the same time, few would argue that expert knowledge is the *only* kind of knowledge that is useful in our daily pursuits. Both kinesthetic and experiential knowledge are important and legitimate forms of knowledge. Like "expert" knowledge, these other forms of knowledge are learned, they are retained in memory, and they are recalled and applied in new situations.

But many doubt that "expert" knowledge has a substantial contribution to make to the field of teaching. Many critics of teacher education either believe that teachers are born, rather than made, or that teaching is a self-evident line of work, the sort of thing that can only be learned in the doing. Because teachers' knowledge is invisible—as virtually all knowledge-in-use is—and because teaching seems in so many ways to be analogous to parenting, it is easy to conclude that the most important knowledge about teaching is experiential and kinesthetic, not propositional. Indeed, most parents, policymakers, and other observers of education consider themselves to be experts in education because of their own experiential knowledge of schooling (Cooper, 1996; Kaestle, 1992). Consequently, we can probably expect skeptics to continue to be part of discussion and debate in the field of education.

What makes the contemporary version of this debate unusual, though, is that the salience of "expert" knowledge to teaching is also being challenged by education faculty themselves, not just by people outside the field (see, for instance, Carter, 1993; Doyle, 1997). That is, people who actively and willingly participate in this enormous, complex, and expensive enterprise, whose professional work consists of producing "expert" knowledge and/or of transmitting that knowledge to college students, whose incomes depend on these activities, and who are knowledgeable about teaching and have an intense personal interest in it, are questioning the value of propositional "expert" knowledge from educational research and are praising the wisdom of teachers' craft knowledge. Though the education professorate as a whole is accustomed to living with skeptics from outside the field, and of having to defend itself and its work against them, it is unaccustomed to having to defend its work against its own membership. Because this membership is far more informed than many external skeptics, it is important to understand these new arguments and to consider their merits.

THE NATURE OF CRAFT KNOWLEDGE

Two lines of thinking have contributed to this new and vital interest in teachers' craft knowledge. One of these lines is interested in finding ways to make "expert" knowledge more accessible to teachers—in bridging the chasm between public propositional knowledge and private experiential knowledge. The other is more interested in establishing the validity of teachers' craft knowledge, *sans* "expert" knowledge. Both of these lines of thought picked up steam in the early 1980s, motivating the current interest in the nature of teachers' craft knowledge.

The first line of thought developed as researchers began to extend their methodology to include case studies and interviews. As they did, they found a need to articulate the form of "expert" knowledge they thought they were generating. Stake (1978), for instance, noted that case study findings were in an epistemological form that was more in harmony with readers' experiences. Then, in 1983, Bolster elaborated on the compatibility argument. He noticed that teachers tended to have little regard for "expert" knowledge, and suggested that a particular set of disparities between "expert" knowledge and teacher's craft knowledge contributed to this apparent impasse. One disparity Bolster noticed was in the way each kind of knowledge was formulated or discovered. Teachers do not learn through formal, public experiments that can be critiqued by their peers, as researchers do, but instead through a continuous, private process of predictions and outcomes—in other words, through experience. As they work in their classrooms, teachers constantly adjust their predictions based on what has happened on previous occasions.

Bolster (1983) outlined other differences as well. For instance, teachers' experiential knowledge is context dependent, dynamic, and particularistic. All of these features derive from the fact that teachers' knowledge is built from their own experiences. Experiential knowledge is inherently private and idiosyncratic, since it is derived from the unique configuration of each individual's experiences. And since teachers' experiential knowledge is built from specific experiences in particular schools and communities, it often requires substantial change when teachers relocate.

These features of teacher knowledge contrast with the kind of knowledge Bolster (1983) thought researchers aimed to produce, for example, propositions about universal regularities ("Children move from pre-operational to operational thinking at about age eight"). To make research more valuable, understandable, and useable to teachers, Bolster argued that researchers should generate a kind of "expert" knowledge that better matched the form of knowledge held by teachers. Instead of conducting formal experiments and searching for universal truths, for instance, Bolster argued that educational researchers should conduct ethnographic studies which would illuminate the multiple causes and interactive influences that characterize classroom life. Such studies would yield a form of knowledge closer to the kind of knowledge teachers seem to hold—particular, context-sensitive, narrative, and multifaceted—and would be, by virtue of its compatibility, more understandable to, and useable by, teachers.

Bolster's (1983) argument reflected a major methodological shift that was already well under way in educational research, and has continued since. Today, it is safe to say, formal experiments constitute only a small fraction, and case studies constitute a very large fraction, of the corpus of contemporary educational research. Bolster's argument also anticipated a continuing debate about the relative contributions of different forms of knowledge to teaching, and a continuing interest in the tenuous relationship between "expert" knowledge and teaching practice. Michael Huberman (1985; 1993), for instance, has carried Bolster's argument a few steps further by suggesting not only that (a) teachers' knowledge is particularistic, but also that (b) teachers develop their instructional repertoires through an inherently idiosyncratic process, (c) there is little they can learn from others, and (d) their "truth tests" for new ideas do not rest on empirical evidence, but rather on "craft validation": that is, an idea is worth trying if another teacher vouches for it or if it fits intuitively into the teacher's own past experience. Huberman's argument is that teachers have *common* problems, not *shared* problems. Consequently, each teacher must devise her own solution to her own version of the problem, and "expert" knowledge offers very little help.

Central to this general line of reasoning is that, even though "expert" knowledge and experiential knowledge differ, there is still a role for "expert" knowledge. These analysts are not suggesting that "expert" knowledge has no value for practitioners, but rather that it could have more value, if only it were altered in important ways. They claim, for instance, that past research has been overly positivist when it should be interpretive (Barone, 1990), or that it has yielded propositional knowledge when it should yield narrative knowledge (Olson, 1995), or that it has been done objectively when it should have been done subjectively (Wolfe, 1989), or that it has been done independently of teachers when it should have been done collaboratively (Huberman, 1990). What holds these various arguments together is the observation that the knowledge teachers draw on—much of which is necessarily experiential— is fundamentally different from the formal, propositional "expert" knowledge that is developed by educational researchers, and that if we want teachers to rely more on "expert" knowledge, we must find ways to help them incorporate it into their experiential knowledge.

The second line of thought, initiated at around the same time, was stimulated in part by Donald Schon's (1983, 1987) studies of professional practice and professional learning. Schon distinguished the reasoning and methods used to generate "expert" knowledge from those used by practitioners, calling the former *technical rationality* and the latter *reflection-in-action*. He has since been criticized for forcing a dichotomy between these two modes of knowing (Fenstermacher, 1988; Shulman, 1988), but the distinction has remained, nonetheless, stimulating a new generation of research that aims to understand the nature and nuances of teacher knowledge and teacher thinking, quite apart from whether research knowledge does, or could, contribute to teaching.

This second line of work differs from the first not only in its lack of interest in the real or potential role of "expert" knowledge, but also in its political overtones. Much of it aims not only to document the character of teachers' experiential, or craft, knowledge, but also to celebrate how unique and valuable teachers' knowledge is. An example of such work is that of Clandenin and Connelly, who have devoted themselves to defining what they call teachers' "personal practical knowledge" (Clandinin, 1986; Clandinin & Connelly, 1991; Connelly & Clandinin, 1985; Connelly, Clandenin, & He, 1997). These authors focus on the flow of events in classrooms and in how teachers' knowledge is embodied in this flow. They characterize teachers' knowledge as experiential, and as consisting of such things as images, rhythms, metaphors, and routines—all of which form a narrative unity that extends over time, so that today's experiences in the classroom are tied to last year's experiences, and together these experiences form a coherent whole. These authors eschew the kind of categories and analytic accounts of teaching that generally accrue from public, propositional "expert" knowledge, claiming that such accounts necessarily do an injustice to the real thing (Connelly & Clandinin, 1985).

Other authors have examined the kinds of reasoning teachers use (Brown & McIntyre, 1993) the kinds of metaphors they use (Russell & Munby, 1991; Russell, Munby, Spafford, & Johnston, 1988), the kinds of routines they devise (Doyle, 1986; 1990), the case-based or narrative form of their knowledge (Thomas, 1994), and the situated nature of that knowledge (Yinger & Hendricks-Lee, 1993). In nearly all these cases, the authors are struggling to identify the special character of teachers' craft knowledge and the features that distinguish it from "expert" knowledge.

Rather than seeking rapprochements between different forms of knowledge, this second line of work tends to distinguish them, emphasizing the inherent incompatibilities between craft knowledge on one side, and "expert" knowledge on the other.

Because these arguments frequently challenge the authority of traditional "expert" knowledge, Thomas (1994) has referred to them as *treasonable* texts. Hargreaves (1996) characterizes this second line of research on teacher knowledge as a whole by saying that it has

> focused on its personal and practical nature, has celebrated rather than dismissed its idiosyncrasies, has sometimes embraced its emotional and intuitive qualities as well as more usual rational and reflective ones, has valued rather than demeaned the narrative forms of storytellling and case examples through which teachers discuss their practice, and has generally sought to represent the wisdom of teachers' practical knowledge and experience in a full and favorable light. (1996, p. 107)

The central argument of these numerous studies is that the kind of knowledge that enables teachers to function in the classroom is fundamentally different from the kind of knowledge researchers are generating, and the differences are so great as to suggest that perhaps educational research does not, in fact, have a viable role to play in the improvement of teaching.

Often, this literature seems to reflect a craving for freedom from any kind of constraints. Diorio (1982), for instance, suggests that the possession of "expert" knowledge restricts one's professional autonomy, presumably because it forces one to comply with the "expert" prescriptions. Similarly, Webb (1996; Webb & Blond, 1995) argues that policies that impose standards on teaching, such as teacher evaluation systems, student assessments, or curriculum frameworks, inherently deny teacher knowledge, presumably because teachers know what to teach and know whether they are doing a good job. These authors seem to believe that any references to "expert" knowledge automatically challenges the validity of the teachers' craft knowledge. Casey (1995) finds these arguments to be essentially narcissistic, and speculates that they express an emotional response to the alienation of a postmodern world.

What is missing from much of this second line of work is the idea that, even if craft knowledge is important, it might also benefit from "expert" knowledge, and it is the potential for complementarity that I now want to address. The central argument I want to make is that the existence of situated, strategic, narrative knowledge—that is, craft knowledge—does not mitigate the need for public, justified, propositional "expert" knowledge. To do so, I now introduce yet a third kind of knowledge, *expertise*. Expertise is governed both by "expert" knowledge and by craft knowledge, as children are governed by two parents, each bringing a unique perspective to the upbringing.

THE NATURE OF EXPERTISE

Let us return for a moment to the teacher's editorial that stimulated this paper. Bassett (1997) argues that "expert" knowledge has little to offer teachers because "expert" knowledge derives from science, whereas teaching is a craft *rather than* a science. The implication of such a statement is that there are only two ways of conceptualizing teaching. If teaching is a science, then every move teachers make must be based on "expert" knowledge. If, on the other hand, it is a craft, then every move is based on experience, and "expert" knowledge has nothing to offer.

But there are other ways of conceptualizing professional knowledge, and one in particular that I want to examine is the notion of professional *expertise*. Cognitive researchers have been examining professional expertise for several years now, and are beginning to have a good sense for what it is and how it functions. Expertise appears to develop from an optimal combination of "expert" knowledge and craft knowledge.

The character, content, and source of expertise has been studied in many different fields, beginning with expertise in closed systems, such as chess, and then moving into more open, but disciplinary systems, such as medicine and physics. A number of important findings are beginning to emerge from this work. These findings are important to the ongoing arguments in education, for they give us a broader perspective from which to view our own provincial turf. And it is in these studies of expertise that we learn whether or how "expert" knowledge fits with craft knowledge.

One thing that is clear about expertise is that there is a great deal of craft in it. People with expertise are able to monitor their own behavior. They can judge their actions with their senses—gauge the look and feel of their work and sense the timing for it. They can recognize signs of success and signs that might be worrisome because they have seen these signs before and have seen what happens next before. This is craft knowledge, built from extensive experience. It is dynamic, situated, private, and frequently kinesthetic—and much of it tacit as well. Experts may be very adept at accurately judging their own actions and at accurately recognizing signs of success or of potential problems and yet still have difficulty articulating this knowledge to an apprentice.

But another important feature of expertise is that it is voluminous. Experts are people who can bring a richly detailed body of both propositional knowledge and experiences to bear on any given situation. This knowledge, in turn, gives them a way of interpreting and understanding new situations—called pattern recognition—which enables them to recognize a situation as similar to other situations and to know, through this recognition, what their options are for response (Bereiter & Scardamalia, 1993). Chess players, for instance, recognize configurations of pieces on the board because the configurations have meaning for them and because they have seen most of them before. Once meaningful patterns are recognized, options for action are also recognized. Physicians recognize patterns of symptoms, wine experts recognize nuances of flavor, and teachers recognize and interpret patterns of student errors. The importance of pattern recognition cannot be over-emphasized, in part because it has been found so frequently in studies of expertise, in part because pattern recognition is often tacit, and in part because something like pattern recognition is frequently observed in studies of teacher knowledge.

But pattern recognition is not made possible simply by having had experiences. Experts are able to retain large stores of knowledge because of the way in which their knowledge is organized. Experts are able to retain more details from their own experiences, and to see more details in a new situation, because they can store the information in larger, more meaningful chunks than nonexperts can. The ability to organize information into large, meaningful chunks allows them to retain more of it and to automate many chunks of behavior, thus freeing up mental energy to attend to other things. "Expert" knowledge frequently provides the concepts and principles that enable experts to organize and retain their experiential knowledge. Without "expert" knowledge, it would be possible for people with very similar experiences to organize, chunk, and retain their experiential knowledge in very different ways, so that what they have learned from their experience seems remarkably different. With "expert" knowledge, even people whose experiences are different have the potential to organize their experiences according to shared concepts and principles.

The most important feature of expertise, then, is that it is *grounded in principled knowledge*—that is, in "expert" knowledge (Bereiter & Scardamalia, 1993). Physicians, for instance, have a body of knowledge that is tightly organized around the principles of pathology (Christensen & Elstein, 1991). The propositions they have learned enable them to classify their experiences and to store their experiential knowledge in a way that reflects "expert" knowledge. Practitioners with expertise may draw on experiential knowledge to recognize patterns in situations, but they can also, when called upon to do so, justify their thinking and their actions with reference to the "expert" knowledge in their field. This is the aspect of expertise which is often overlooked when researchers examine the craft of teaching.

Consider again, for instance, the problem of alienated adolescents. Numerous teachers may encounter this type of problem in their secondary classrooms, and may struggle to find ways to engage these students in academic material. English teachers may seek literature that addresses adolescent issues, and biology teachers may try to organize their content to address adolescent concerns. The solutions they devise will surely depend on their particular contexts and the particular observations of the students they face. But the patterns they see in their own experiences, the symptoms they recognize, and their interpretations of these patterns and symptoms, depend on concepts and principles that derive from "expert" knowledge— knowledge of the symptoms of alienation, of how and why it develops in adolescents, and so forth. Different teachers may try different approaches to engaging their students, but the teacher with expertise will be able to justify her solution by appeal to the body of public, tested knowledge; whereas the teacher with craft knowledge can only justify her approach by saying that her private experience motivated her to try this approach. We cannot challenge her rationale, for we have no access to her store of craft knowledge.

This difference is subtle but important. Moreover, to the outside observer, expertise is easy to miss, for as expertise develops, propositional knowledge is reorganized, transformed into experiential knowledge, and frequently becomes tacit

(Dreyfus & Dreyfus, 1986). It becomes what Brown, Collins, and Duguid (1989) call *situated* knowledge. Teachers may learn about adolescent alienation in textbooks, for instance, but their understanding of this concept will change as they encounter different specific examples of it. Similarly, they may study the kind of misconceptions in science that fourth graders are likely to develop, and then elaborate this knowledge of student misconceptions as they see numerous examples of them in their practice. Their propositional knowledge about student misconceptions has become situated—embellished through experience—so that they now have a much more detailed and elaborated understanding of the general phenomenon. That their knowledge is situated, however, does not mean that the original concept of student misconceptions no longer exists in a propositional form. On the contrary, the "expert" knowledge has facilitated the teacher's ability to organize her experience of children's learning so that she sees more than she otherwise would have noticed, and can retain more than she otherwise would.

All professional expertise, then, begins with propositional knowledge, which eventually becomes converted into a dynamic, situated, and experiential form. In fact, this is true not only of professional expertise, but of any proposition *which is acted upon*. For to act upon a proposition is to understand it's meaning in the context of a specific situation. The proposition that "fourth-grade children hold misconceptions about scientific phenomena" does not automatically enable teachers to recognize those misconceptions, nor to design activities that will correct them. These events can only occur once the teacher has translated the proposition into its situated meaning.

One thing that happens when propositions are translated into experience is that they become the property of the individual, rather than of the group. It is through this process that public knowledge becomes relevant to private problems. I have argued elsewhere that even such compelling research evidence as that regarding the health hazards of smoking has rarely directly influenced anyone's practice. When someone decides to stop smoking, they do so not because the research says smoking is unhealthy, but instead because they have translated that proposition into a set of experiences. They have become aware of events that they may not have noticed before—shortness of breath or a nagging cough—and it is this pattern of experience that they respond to (Kennedy, 1989). When propositional knowledge is translated into experiences, we are able to see patterns that we may not have noticed before, or to interpret familiar patterns in new ways.

Expertise, then, represents what happens to "expert" knowledge when it is transformed into experiential knowledge. Expertise enables us to recognize and define our private experiences, and to notice and interpret its patterns. One teacher may know what a "cooperative group" is, for instance, because she has read an article about cooperative groups, and another may know because she has seen many instances of cooperative groups. It is easy to conclude that the former teacher has "expert" knowledge, while the latter teacher has craft knowledge, but such a conclusion would be mistaken. The latter teacher's understanding is highly situated because she has many specific cases on which to base her knowledge. But the *concept* itself derives from "expert" knowledge and can be defined verbally if need be. Because this situated knowledge is grounded in "expert" knowledge, it is more than craft knowledge—it is expertise.

"EXPERT" KNOWLEDGE, CRAFT KNOWLEDGE, AND THE FUTURE OF EDUCATION

One of the primary arguments against the need for education programs in colleges and universities is that teaching is a craft rather than a science, and that the kind of formal, propositional knowledge that is developed and taught in education programs does not, and cannot, contribute to the dynamic, situated, and idiosyncratic practices of teaching. This argument gains salience in part because observers of teaching, and even teachers themselves, may not be able to see the "expert" knowledge once it becomes incorporated into teaching routines.

Still, there are real and legitimate differences between "expert" and craft knowledge, and the differences are striking enough to wonder whether the two can ever marry. "Expert" knowledge derives from formal investigations, in which one's methods are explicit and one's reasoning is subjected to peer review. It is knowledge that is agreed upon by the community at large, based on argument and on inferences from evidence. The results of "expert" knowledge can be described in sentences—propositions—that describe how we think one thing relates to another. Because "expert" knowledge can be stated in sentences, it can also be pulled together into textbooks and encyclopedias, enumerated and summarized in a number of ways. It is this quality of "expert" knowledge that causes it to sometimes be labeled as *static* in order to distinguish it from craft knowledge and expertise, both of which are situated and dynamic.

Craft knowledge differs from "expert" knowledge in almost every dimension. It is private rather than public, dynamic rather than static, tied to actions and developed through active experiences rather than through public procedures, is frequently tacit, and is difficult to describe in sentences. A great deal of our knowledge is craft knowledge—not just our professional knowledge, but the knowledge we use every day in our interactions with our families, in our management of our personal business, and in our daily routines and habits. All of these activities depend heavily on experiential knowledge, and we probably could not do much of anything without this knowledge. Without experiential knowledge, we could not drive to the store, get dressed, prepare a meal, or do any of the other activities that we routinely do.

The question of interest here, though, is whether craft knowledge is inherently incompatible with the kind of knowledge embodied in "expert" propositions. After examining these two kinds of knowledge separately, I introduced the notion of expertise as a blend of "expert" propositions and craft knowledge. Expertise differs from both "expert" knowledge and craft knowledge in important ways. It differs from "expert" knowledge in that it is dynamic, tied to actions, and developed through active experiences. But it differs from craft knowledge in that it can be justified with propositions and its merits can be evaluated by publicly-shared standards of practice. While there is plenty of room in expertise for personal style and personal judgment, it is not as private, tacit, or idiosyncratic as craft knowledge seems to be.

I doubt that anyone would argue that professional knowledge can or should consist solely of "expert" propositions. Teaching clearly is not a science, and we can never expect the practice of teaching to be entirely governed by "expert" knowledge. In fact, *no organized activity or practice can occur without craft knowledge.* The question that demands an answer, therefore, is not whether craft knowledge has a role in teaching, but whether "expert" knowledge has a role in teaching. And the answer to that question depends on whether teaching is built entirely on craft, or instead, is built on expertise.

A lot is at stake in answering this question. The entire enterprise of education is built on the assumption that teaching, and other forms of educational practice, should not be based solely on craft knowledge, but that they demand expertise. Education schools are formed under the assumption that "expert" knowledge has an important role in teaching. Education faculty engage in research on teaching and learning under this assumption, textbook publishers compile research findings under this assumption, and states require education programs for certification under this assumption. Millions of dollars are expended by governments, textbook publishers, and students to assure that these propositions find their way from dusty research journals to the hearts and minds of aspiring young teachers. All under the assumption that this knowledge can be translated into action and can provide the basis for teaching expertise.

But having established that expertise exists in other fields does not mean that it exists, or should exist, in teaching. Moreover, even if we found, through examination, that expertise existed in *some* teaching, we would not know that it existed in all teaching. The ideas I have outlined here simply clarify the terms of the debate, they do not resolve it. In fact, two hypotheses are still possible from this examination of expertise. One is that those who have extolled the virtues and intricacies of teachers' craft knowledge are missing the importance of "expert" knowledge in teaching. Like adoring relatives of a newborn who only see traits from their side of the family in the infant, these researchers have, in their zeal to recognize the importance of situated knowledge and accumulated experiences, neglected the equally important role of "expert" knowledge. They have noticed the craft—one side of the family lineage—but not the "expert" knowledge, which blends with craft to form expertise. If this is our hypothesis, then we can still envision a role for colleges of education, for research in education, for textbooks in education, and for the degree and certification requirements that currently outline teacher preparation programs.

But the other hypothesis is that teachers do not, in fact, either have *or want* the kind of expertise that is recognized and valued in other professions. Teachers may prefer to sustain their field as one in which privately-accumulated idiosyncratic experience—craft knowledge—is all they need. There is some merit to this idea. Many teachers, as well as many parents, view teaching as an extension of parenting: It is something learned in the doing, not something one formally prepares for, and it is driven largely by one's own value system. We expect parents to be idiosyncratic in their styles, values, and tactics. Perhaps this is what we should expect from teachers as well. But if teaching depends solely on craft knowledge, rather than on expertise, then there is indeed no role for educational research, no need for courses in education, and no need for education departments altogether.

REFERENCES

Barone, T. E. (1990). Using the narrative text as an occasion for conspiracy. In E. W. Eisner & A. Peshkin (Eds.), *Qualitative inquiry in education: The continuing debate* (pp. 305–325). New York: Teachers College Press.

Bassett, J. (1997, November 12). The University of Chicago will not be missed. *Education Week*, 35.

Bereiter, C., & Scardamalia, M. (1993). *Surpassing ourselves: An inquiry into the nature and implications of expertise.* Chicago: Open Court.

Bolster, A. S. J. (1983). Toward a more effective model of research on teaching. *Harvard Educational Review, 53*(3), 294–308.

Brown, J. S., Collins, A., & Duguid, P. (1989). Situated cognition and the culture of learning. *Educational researcher, 18*(1), 32–42.

Brown, S., & McIntyre, D. (1993). *Making sense of teaching.* Philadelphia: Open University Press.

Casey, K. (1995). The new narrative research in education. In M. W. Apple (Ed.), *Review of research in education* (Vol. 21, pp. 211–253). Washington, DC: American Educational Research Association.

Carter, K. (1993). The place of story in the study of teaching and teacher education. *Educational Researcher, 22*(1), 5–12, 18.

Christensen, C., & Elstein, A. S. (1991). Informal reasoning in the medical profession. In J. F. Voss, D. N. Perkins, & J. W. Segal (Eds.), *Informal reasoning and education* (pp. 17–35). Hillsdale, NJ: Lawrence Erlbaum.

Clandinin, D. J. (1986). *Classroom practice: Teacher images in action.* Philadelphia: The Falmer Press.

Clandinin, D. J., & Connelly, F. M. (1991). Narrative and story in practice and research. In D. A. Schon (Ed.), *The reflective turn: Case studies in and on educational practice.* New York: Teachers College Press.

Connelly, F. M., & Clandinin, D. J. (1985). Personal practical knowledge and the modes of knowing: Relevance for teaching and learning. In E. Eisner (Ed.), *Learning and teaching the ways of knowing: Eighty-fourth yearbook of the National Society for the Study of Education, part II* (pp. 174–198). Chicago: National Society for the Study of Education.

Connelly, F. M., Clandenin, D. J., & He, M. F. (1997). Teachers' personal practical knowledge on the professional knowledge landscape. *Teaching and Teacher Education, 13*(7), 665–674.

Cooper, H. (1996). Speaking power to truth: Reflections of an educational researcher after 4 years of school board service. *Educational Researcher, 25*(1), 29–34.

Diorio, J. A. (1982). Knowledge, autonomy, and the practice of teaching. *Curriculum Inquiry,* *12*(3), 225–282.

Doyle, W. (1986). Classroom organization and management. In M. C. Wittrock (Ed.), *Handbook of research on teaching* (3rd ed.; pp. 392–431). New York: Macmillan.

Doyle, W. (1990, April). *Teachers' curriculum knowledge.* Paper presented at the annual meeting of the American Educational Research Association, Boston.

Doyle, W. (1997). Heard any really good stories lately? A critique of the critics of narrative in educational research. *Teaching and Teacher Education, 13*(1), 93–99.

Dreyfus, H. L., & Dreyfus, S. E. (1986). *Mind over machine: The power of human intuition and expertise in the era of the computer.* New York: The Free Press.

Fenstermacher, G. D. (1988). The place of science and epistemology in Schon's conception of reflective practice? In P. P. Grimmett & G. L. Erickson (Eds.), *Reflection in teacher education* (pp. 39–46). New York: Teachers College Press.

Hargreaves, A. (1996). Transforming knowledge: Blurring the boundaries between research, policy, and practice. *Educational Evaluation and Policy Analysis, 18*(2), 105–122.

Huberman, M. (1985). What knowledge is of most worth to teachers? A knowledge-use perspective. *Teaching and Teacher Education, 1*, 251–262.

Huberman, M. (1990). Linkage between researchers and practitioners: A qualitative study. *American Educational Research Journal, 27*(2), 363–391.

Huberman, M. (1993). The model of the independent artisan in teachers' professional relations. In J. W. Little & M. W. McLaughlin (Eds.), *Teachers' work: Individuals, colleagues, context* (pp. 11–50). New York: Teachers College Press.

Kaestle, C. F. (1992). *Everybody's been to fourth grade: An oral history of Federal R&D in education* (Report No. 92-1). Madison, WI: Wisconsin R&D Center.

Kennedy, M. M. (1989). Studying smoking behavior to learn about dissemination. *Knowledge: Creation, Diffusion, Utilization, 11*, 107–115.

Olson, M. R. (1995). Conceptualizing narrative authority: Implications for teacher education. *Teaching and Teacher Education, 11*(2), 119–135.

Russell, T., & Munby, H. (1991). Reframing: The role of experience in developing teachers' professional knowledge. In D. A. Schon (Ed.), *The reflective turn: Case studies in and on educational practice* (pp. 164–187). New York: Teachers College Press.

Russell, T., Munby, H., Spafford, C., & Johnston, P. (1988). Learning the professional knowledge of teaching: Metaphors, puzzles, and the theory-practice relationship. In P. P. Grimmett & G. L. Erickson (Eds.), *Reflection in teacher education* (pp. 67–90). New York: Teachers College Press.

Schon, D. A. (1983). *The reflective practitioner: How professionals think in action.* New York: Basic Books.

Schon, D. A. (1987). *Educating the reflective practitioner.* San Francisco: Jossey-Bass.

Shulman, L. S. (1988). The dangers of dichotomous thinking in education. In P. P. Grimmett & G. L. Erickson (Eds.), *Reflection in teacher education* (pp. 31–38). New York: Teachers College Press.

Stake, R. E. (1978). The case study method in social inquiry. *Educational Researcher, 7*(2), 5–8.

Thomas, D. (1994). Treasonable or Trustworthy text: Reflections on teacher narrative studies. *International Analyses of Teacher Education,* 231–249.

Yinger, R., & Hendricks-Lee, M. (1993). Working knowledge in teaching. In C. Day, J. Calderhead, & P. Denicolo (Eds.), *Research on teacher thinking: Understanding professional development* (pp. 100–123). Washington, DC: The Falmer Press.

Webb, K. M. (1996). I have left my classroom. Why? Systematic denial of teachers' knowledge. *Teachers and Teaching: Theory and Practice, 2*(2), 299–313.

Webb, K. M., & Blond, J. (1995). Teacher knowledge: The relationship between caring and knowing. *Teaching and Teacher Education, 11*(6), 611–625.

Wolfe, A. (1989). *Whose keeper? Social sciences and moral obligation.* Berkeley, CA: University of California Press.

3

The Tale Wagging the Dog: Narrative and Neopragmatism in Teacher Education and Research

Gregory J. Cizek
University of Toledo

> For the great enemy of the truth very often is not the lie—deliberate, contrived, and dishonest—but the myth—persistent, persuasive, and unrealistic.
> —John F. Kennedy, commencement address at
> Yale University, June 11, 1962

The question considered by a panel of education scholars at a symposium during a recent annual meeting of the American Educational Research Association was: "Should a novel count as a dissertation in education?" That question, perhaps better than any other, illustrates the ascendant role of the narrative in teacher education and research.

Two presenters debated the question and their positions were questioned by a panel of discussants. One of the presenters, Howard Gardner, rejected the proposition, saying: "I don't understand how a novel can possibly ever be accepted as research. Essentially, in a novel you can say what you want, and you are judged by how effectively you say it without any particular regard to the truth value. And it seems to me that *the essence of research is effort ... to find out as carefully as you can what's happening and then to report it accurately*" (emphasis added; qtd. in Donmoyer, et al., 1996, p. 403). Elliot Eisner, favoring the proposition, argued that "the issue here has to do with the form in which one has learned to write, the virtues of that form for addressing the particular problem that one wants to address, *and the kind of understanding that one wants to foster*" (emphasis added; qtd. in Donmoyer, et al., 1996, p. 407).

In the course of framing their concerns as they did, the presenters pointed to a more fundamental question than whether a novel should "count" as a dissertation. They reflected upon a profound disagreement about what counts as knowledge in teacher education. Looking even deeper, the disagreement concerns the more essential, unspoken question: Is knowledge even the proper aim of educational research?

BATTLE OF THE GALACTIC TITANS: KNOWLEDGE VERSUS MEANING

As alluded to by Gardner, the aim of science has been to uncover and refine truths— properties of, or relationships between, elements or actions that occur with predictable regularity in specified contexts. For example, in medicine, penicillin was discovered to be antibiotic in nature—an uncovered truth. Its antibiotic effect is reduced in certain resistant strains of viral organisms—a refined truth. In educational psychology, Yerkes and Dodson (1908) described the now-familiar, U-shaped relationship between anxiety and performance—an uncovered truth. Another uncovered truth is that memory aids, such as mnemonic techniques, are useful for enhancing learning (Yates, 1966). However, Gross and Mastenbrook (1980) demonstrated that low-anxiety students perform better without a memory aid than when such an aid is provided—a refined truth.

Whether in basic or refined form, scientists regard these findings as *knowledge*. A collection of basic and refined truths is, in a discipline, called its *knowledge base*. A discipline exists to the extent that a collection of these basic and constantly refined truths is pursued on a continuing basis. When the pursuit of knowledge within it stops, a discipline perishes.

An alternative pursuit is the search for *meaning*. Carter (1993) described narratives as central to meaning: "[S]tory is a mode of knowing that captures in a special fashion the richness and nuances of meaning in human affairs" (p. 6). To repeat Eisner: "The issue here has to do with ... the kind of understanding that one wants to foster" (qtd. in Donmoyer, et al., 1996, p. 407). Eisner has also asserted that narratives and other "images" are necessary for helping both producers and consumers of research to become aware of aspects of the educational world that they may not have noticed before.

However, Eisner's images are not necessarily true to life; in fact, he expressly encourages them to be larger than life, in order to convey meaning that may not be adequately conveyed otherwise. Accordingly, he recommends strategies that seem contrary to traditional notions of good science. For example, when describing an educational phenomenon, Eisner advocates tapping emotions, which are "absolutely essential to understand some things," and "constructive neglect," which he defines as knowing which facts or details to leave out in order to be better able to make a point (qtd. in Donmoyer, et al., 1996, p. 408). From Eisner's perspective, apparently knowledge ain't all it's cracked up to be. The continuing viability and progress of education as a discipline hinges on reduced reliance on traditional modes of inquiry, which are focused on generating knowledge and increased movement toward alternative forms of representation designed to enhance the construction of meanings.

What have been called "the paradigm wars" (Gage, 1989, p. 4), which frequently centered on qualitative and quantitative research methods, can now be seen as merely skirmishes. The larger context suggests that the real clash involves two epistemological titans: Currently, it would appear that Meaning rules over Knowledge. On the front lines, metaphor trumps meta-analysis.

There is, however, some support for such a position. Constructivist philosophers and postmodern educational writers reject the very possibility of objective empiricism, suggesting that all knowledge is personal, socially mediated, and humanly constructed and reconstructed (see, for example, Berger & Luckmann, 1966; Geertz, 1988). In an applied sense, Peshkin (1993) has also suggested that research methods—which are theory-driven, hypothesis-testing, or generalization-producing—are insufficient to meet the goals of meaning and understanding to which modern science should aspire. In practice, this position requires its adherents to use quotation marks around the word *truth*, to denote its ephemeral, personal, and even mythical, nature. In rhetorical terms, it suggests serious discussion of questions such as: "Should we abandon traditional distinctions between fact and fiction, truth and falsity entirely?" and "Should we reject truth as the principal criterion for assessing the worth of scholarship?" (Eisner, qtd. in Donmoyer, et al., 1996, p. 406).

THE ASCENDANCE OF THE NARRATIVE

If meaning transcends knowledge, it follows that traditional ways of conveying knowledge may be inadequate for conveying meaning. As I have previously suggested, that the narrative has already supplanted other forms as the method of choice for communicating scholarly ideas. In an article that considered the tensions between qualitative and quantitative methods, I described the pervasive professional expectation that any scholarly writing will not simply present the design and results of a study in quantitative terms, but would add to (or replace) quantitative presentation with a description that addresses the situation, characters, and contextual concerns— an engaging narrative that conveys richer *meaning* (Cizek, 1996).

To illustrate the expectation, I recalled an event in the life of a fellow faculty member involved in preparing beginning teachers:

> A colleague of mine in educational psychology told me of some research she had recently submitted for publication. The manuscript dealt with the different ways that

teachers collaborate with student teachers. The reviewers reacted favorably to the manuscript, but the journal editor suggested that it be revised and resubmitted. The problem? "The results of the regression analysis are presented in terms that are too 'black and white.' We need to get to *know* these teachers."

> The editor's wording was deliberate. Saying that "we need to get to know these teachers" is an encrypted message. My colleague understood the code though, and emended the manuscript to include snippets of the student teachers' conferences with their supervisors, exchanges between the student teachers and the students in their classroom, and rich, full description of the classroom context. The colleague further ensured that the revised manuscript would be accepted by adding material in the introduction that described her perspective (this is called "situating yourself"), and by restating her conclusions so that they didn't sound so conclusive (qualitative research deals with phenomena that are "emerging"). (1996, p. 228)[1]

The expectation does not exist, as has been asserted by some, because qualitative and quantitative methods are complementary, but because narratives are superior for communicating meaning. This belief in the superiority of narratives is often not baldly asserted, but can easily be gleaned. For example, Carter (1993) reported that researchers "have been telling stories about teaching and teacher education *rather than simply reporting correlation coefficients or generating lists* of findings" (emphasis added; p. 5). She continued by noting that "Stories [have] *redressed the deficiencies* of the traditional atomistic and positivistic approaches" (emphasis added; p. 6).

Other educational researchers have recognized the hegemony of the narrative and have urged caution. For example, Duncan Waite, himself an ethnographer, stated at a recent annual meeting of the American Educational Research Association that "ethnography, specifically, and qualitative research, in general, have fallen victim...to a type of groupthink that has valorized one type of method—interview, narrative, and the so-called emic perspective—to the exclusion of all others" (1994, p. 4). He called for researchers to redress the problem of the "privileged position of the narrative" in social science research.

I also identified the growing press for qualitative representation as "the hegemony of the narrative" (1996, p. 227). However, I did not foresee that the press for more personal meaning would overturn the criterion of accuracy. It is worthwhile at this point to recall Eisner's beliefs about what constitutes what he calls an "artistically crafted" narrative:

> In writing, especially in writing that is artistically crafted, there is something that I'd like to think of as constructive neglect—knowing what to leave out in order to be better able to make the point that's telling and to give a certain kind of form, and shape, and coherence. There is a very selective process going on. And that selectivity, I think, is instrumental to the generation of insight, and to the development of awareness. (qtd. in Donmoyer, et al., 1996, p. 408)

The selective process to which Eisner referred apparently need not be constrained to factual information. He would allow for a narrative form that would select from among fictions for its grist, so long as meaning is conveyed. According to Eisner, "we would say that what one wants out of all these fictions, so to speak, is a deeper, and more complex, and more interesting conversation" (qtd. in Donmoyer, et al., 1996, p. 415). As Berliner (1992) has reminded us, "stories, even when not true, are extremely persuasive" (p. 151). But Berliner goes further, exhorting educational researchers to recognize the human mind's preference for stories: "[T]he findings and concepts of our discipline are not seen as possessing verisimilitude.... To do better, we must learn to tell stories about our research" (p. 143).

Thus, as we approach the end of the 1900s, a story that conveys a certain *je ne sais quoi* regarding life in classrooms is preferable to a presentation of the "properties of, or relationships between, elements or actions that occur with predictable regularity in specified contexts." A fictitious, though engaging and compelling, narrative is preferred over a factual, though stodgy and unstimulating, monograph. It appears that the quest for meaning through narrative expression has supplanted the quest for knowledge. In teacher education and research, the tale now wags the dog.

VARIETIES OF STORY

Before beginning to speculate about why narrative forms have supplanted other forms of representation, it is appropriate to differentiate between the various ways that stories are used in support of claims in education. At least three varieties exist.

One variety of story is that which purports to be, more or less, an unvarnished,[2] scientific account of "what is." Early ethnographic studies in the field of education, such as Wolcott's (1973) *The Man in the Principal's Office* or Cusick's (1973) *Inside High School*, might qualify as exemplars of this variety. Specific claims or generalizations regarding the contexts or phenomena under study are not usually asserted by the authors of such works. Instead, narratives of this variety are probably intended to stimulate acceptance of an (implicit) claim of universality of relationships or, at minimum, to induce a belief in the verisimilitude of the narrative, if only by the sheer weight of the description.

A second rhetorical approach is to advance a claim and proceed to offer a story as evidence that the claim is plausible. For example, a parent might dispute the very existence of what is called Attention Deficit Hyperactivity Disorder (ADHD) in the following way: "There's no such thing as ADHD. I know because our doctor diagnosed our daughter, Tiphany, as having that disorder. But we just had her quit drinking Mountain Dew and Surge and her teacher says she's just fine in class now." This variety of story—like the testimonial in advertising—is especially powerful to hearers who are similarly situated (i.e., who have children with behavioral difficulties) and who have some relationship with the storyteller.

A third approach is simply to use narrative events as illustrative support for a claim. In such cases the narrative is not offered as proof of a claim. For example, Doyle (1986, 1997) has claimed that teachers experience pressure from students to reduce the cognitive complexity of an assignment. This pressure might be observed in students asking otherwise innocent questions of the teacher, such as "How many pages do you want?," or "How many references are needed?," or "Can you give an example of what you want?" These questions could easily be fleshed out in narrative form by adding details that describe the setting and the teacher, elaborating on the students' questions, reflecting on the teacher's disappointment with the level of the students' questions, and so on. The resulting narrative would not be meant to prove the claim related to pressures to reduce the complexity of tasks, but simply to give meaning to the claim. The story—a realistic, contextualized account of student questioning and teacher disappointment—would obviously not carry evidentiary weight and would not support the validity, or "truth value," of the claim. Unfortunately, an artistically crafted narrative of this variety can inebriate to such a degree that readers can fail to recognize it as merely illustrative and (incorrectly) leap to the tempting inference that it constitutes proof of the claim.

SEVEN SPECULATIONS REGARDING THE NARRATIVE NISUS

The preeminence of meaning over knowledge and the prominence of the narrative as the research method of choice in education are clearly related phenomena. Insight into this relationship can be gleaned from examining potential explanations of *why* the narrative has risen to the top of the methodological heap.

One rationale for the ascendance of the narrative is that narratives—stories, verbalizations, affective accounts, and so on—represent a better fit to the information-processing styles of an increasingly feminine educational research enterprise. On the surface, this explanation has some appeal. As of 1997, women now hold the majority of the faculty positions in colleges of education; according to the National Center for Education Statistics, 51% of full-time instructional faculty and staff in institutions of higher education are females (USDOE, 1997). Complementing this fact is an increasingly popular, professional literature that proposes unique cognition, epistemology, and modes of representation for women (see, e.g., Belenky, 1986; Lather, 1991). Increasing attention to feminist pedagogy and research attest to the fact that these fairly recent ideas have been rapidly translated into educational practice and scholarship.

So, then, the *prima facie* case can be made. Put coarsely: Women think differently and there are more of them doing educational research. However, the *prima facie* case is unsatisfactory for several reasons. For one, it does not explain the ascendance of narratives in fields other than education in which females do not hold the majority of the faculty or research positions; equally vital feminist literatures can be seen in fields such as medicine, mathematics, physics, and so on. Clearly, the coarse explanation does not even fully capture the complexity of why narrative now occupies a preeminent position in teacher education and research. The remaining sections of this chapter suggest seven other possible explanations which may explain—more likely in combination, as opposed to singly—the phenomenon more completely.

Getting Real

A first possible explanation for the dominance of the narrative in teacher education and research is that the narrative can project an appearance of high fidelity with the realities of teaching and learning. A narrative can be crafted that elicits a strong sense of authenticity.

Eisner (1997) described two characteristics—particularity and dimensionality—that he proposes as necessary conditions of something "being real" (p. 8). These attributes are not only important for narratives, but for all forms of research reporting as a means of conveying reality. According to Eisner: "One function of all forms of data representation is to confer a sense that what is being portrayed is real. Authenticity is not a bad quality of research of any kind to have" (p. 8). Others (see, for example, House, 1991) concur that realism is essential in both research and in the relationship between research and practice.

If the goal of research is to promote meaning in the sense of promoting greater understanding of different realities, then various forms of representation might facilitate that end. Coles (1989) has suggested that narratives constitute perhaps the best means of conveying understanding of the lives of others. Eisner (1997) has argued that the narrative is uniquely qualified to represent some realities, with the qualification that different modes of representation—such as readers' theater, still photography, film, journals, and video—might well represent other realities.

Narrative: The Lingua Franca of Teaching

A second possible explanation for the rise of the narrative lies in the role of narratives in the construction of knowledge. Research on the practice of teaching has revealed that narratives are commonly used by teachers as a way of thinking and knowing (Connelly & Clandinin, 1985, 1990, 1991). Carter (1993) has asserted the "centrality of the story to the organization of knowledge and the processes of comprehension and thinking" in teachers (p. 7), citing the concurring comments of Elbaz (1991, p. 3):

> Story is the very stuff of teaching, the landscape within which we live as teachers and researchers, and within which the work of teachers can be seen as making sense. This is not merely a claim about the aesthetic or emotional sense of fit of the notion of story with our intuitive understandings of teaching, but an epistemological claim that teachers' knowledge in its own terms is ordered by story and can best be understood in this way.[3]

The strategy of using narrative to structure cognition, when viewed from a behavioristic perspective, can be seen as simply a logical response. After all, narratives serve to reduce the complexity of ill-structured knowledge domains, of which teaching, replete with myriad uncertainties, is clearly an example. To the extent that narratives reduce the associated ambiguities, they can also be negatively reinforcing.

On the other hand, it is troubling when one considers the potential effect of these claims regarding teachers cognitions on the status of teaching as a profession—a status that is currently, and oftentimes, described as lowly. Substituting claims about the centrality of stories and the primacy of narratives for traditional notions of a knowledge base seems only to reduce further the status of teaching as a profession. Perhaps in the future preparation for professional practice in education will be said—more appropriately—to be derived from a "meaning base."

Just as it is hypothesized that teachers' thinking and knowledge is structured in terms of narratives, it has been suggested that narratives provide a powerful means for promoting and structuring students' understandings. Such a pedagogy has been used effectively in the medical, legal, and business fields for some time, and more recently has been applied to other primary, secondary, and post-secondary contexts. For example, Sykes and Bird (1992) have promoted the use of what are called *case methods*; and Shulman (1992) and McAninch (1995) have described the use of case methods in teacher education.

More Powerful than the Other Leading Brand

A third potential explanation for the ascendance of the narrative is its association with affective response. Affect commonly overrules cognition in a variety of situations. As evidence of this phenomenon, it is necessary only to view any local news broadcast: In time, there is certain to be a story about a homeowner who, despite a raging blaze, runs into a burning structure to rescue the family cat. Advertisers surely have long known that emotions are a powerful key to promoting sales of a product or service. They are trading on the principle that, for example, the glamorous feeling associated with driving a new vehicle will override information such as the vehicle's poor safety record, low fuel efficiency, and high maintenance and repair costs. Politicians, like advertisers, ply the same principle to their advantage. It is common for each side in a debate to present testimony—in the form of intensely personal accounts—from persons with a specific story to tell about how legislation would affect them. As the political advertisements of the health care debate of the early 1990s illustrated, it is not even necessary that the testimony come from real persons retelling actual events. The advertisements included highly effective, televised narratives in which a married couple fretted about how health care changes would affect an elderly parent. Televised programs of current events are no longer said to be broadcasting news, but news *stories*.

A well-crafted story possesses the potential to form opinion or stimulate action in a way that is much more powerful than a staid presentation of indices. The work of Nisbett and Ross (1980) illustrated the strategies and shortcomings of human inference. They suggested that "people's inferences and behavior are so much more influenced by vivid, concrete information than by pallid and abstract propositions of substantially greater probative and evidentiary value" (p. 44). The reasons for the power of such things as firsthand observation, anecdotes, and narratives, according to Nisbett and Ross, lie in their *vividness* and *concreteness*. Greater impact on behavior is attained also by proximity of the evidence to the individual. Abstract statistical summarizations of thousands of events (e.g., means and standard deviations) are far removed from lived experiences and are considerably less powerful than a single, vivid, concrete narrative of a classroom event related by a colleague.

Similarly, in scholarly inquiry in the field of education, rare is the scientifically adequate research report, consisting of the familiar Background, Objectives, Methods, Analysis, and Discussion that could be termed "moving." On the other hand, a novel that lacks the ability to move its reader has little chance of finding a publisher. Referring to a novel as a form of narrative representation that is useful for conveying meaning, Eisner has stated: "I think that the development of a story that is coherent and that is told within a form that is moving is another important function that a novel performs. I think narrative form can promote empathic participation in the lives of others" (qtd. in Donmoyer, et al., 1996, p. 408).

However, the narrative is not more powerful simply because it can promote the kind of affective response to which Eisner referred. It derives much power also from the fact that it redresses a known deficiency in traditional modes of representation—the problem of multiple interpretations.

The products of traditional data analytic techniques—including recent advances such as meta-analysis and hierarchical linear modeling—are particularly susceptible to differing, even opposite, interpretations. The problem is easy to illustrate by considering nearly any of the important educational issues of the day. For example, a series of articles have appeared in *Educational Researcher* on topics such as the academic achievement of American students compared to students in other countries, and the effects of spending on student achievement. In the case of international comparisons, authors such as Baker (1997), Bracey (1996, 1997), and Stedman (1994, 1997), have arrived at markedly different conclusions, in spite of the fact that such studies are frequently based on the same data sets. Regarding the impact of educational spending, the same situation can be seen in the published debates between Hanushek (1989, 1994) and Hedges, Laine, and Greenwald (1994a, 1994b). The numerical presentation and quantitative precision mask the fact that traditional data analytic techniques are simply not capable of producing an unequivocal and broadly compelling picture, nor is that their purpose.

On the other hand, narratives are specifically constructed for such a purpose: To convey a specific interpretation and elicit a specific reaction from a reader. Carter (1993) has described stories as consisting of "events, characters, and settings arranged in a temporal sequence *implying both causality and significance*" (emphasis added; p. 6). Further, according to Carter, in constructing stories "authors attempt to convey their intentions using a variety of cultural tools, and by *selecting incidents and details [and] arranging time and sequence*" (emphasis added; p. 6). Carter cites the caution proffered by Smith, who put the matter baldly: "We may assume that every narrative version has been constructed in accord with some set of purposes or interests" (1981, p. 215). This fact means, *a fortiori*, that a narrative is more likely to accomplish its intended purpose of conveying meaning than a traditional analysis is to overcome its inherent deficiency.

Neo-Neo-Romanticism

Romanticism has long been a philosophy with strong, recurring ties to education. One familiar example is the work of Rousseau (1858/1979), who outlined the contours of romantic philosophy in the specific context of education and whose work continues to influence educational theory and practice in the United States. Also, the many writings of Dewey (e.g., 1902, 1938/1963), though not easily classified, are nonetheless both influenced by romantic philosophy and greatly influential in modern educational thought. Interestingly, Dewey holds the distinction of being the only person to whom a special interest research group within the American Educational Research Association is dedicated. Certainly, romantic philosophies have had a long and lingering influence on American education, spanning early attention to child-centered teaching (see Rugg & Shumaker, 1928) to more current notions of child-centered learning and whole-child education, embodied in the writings of, for example, Montessori (1914/1966) and Hendrick (1988), respectively.

In my own experience, I find manifestations of a tacit adherence to romantic philosophy in my interactions with the teachers who are my students at the university, and in whom preconceptions about recognizing the innate goodness of students and honoring the experiences of teachers are deeply ingrained. The following example is illustrative of this.

I frequently teach an introductory graduate course in educational assessment. As might be expected, one segment of the course provides thorough coverage of the concepts of reliability and validity as they apply to traditional measures of student achievement, such as standardized tests. Whatever my students' feelings about such tests, they uniformly agree that *whatever* information is yielded by the measures ought to be dependable (i.e., reliable) and related to the kinds of decisions that a teacher might make about students (i.e., valid).

Also included in the course is extensive attention to how these same principles of reliability and validity can be generally applied to observations. That is, although these psychometric conceptions usually connote contexts involving No. 2 pencils, they can also profitably be applied to the situations in which teachers evaluate student products, performances, or portfolios. Whether we are observing how a student responds to a multiple-choice item on a reading test or how a student responds to a knotty walnut blank when turning a table leg on a lathe, we recognize that our observations are fallible. At least they are fallible in the sense that they are inconsistent because of a variety of factors we cannot control and usually do not understand. In addition to this inconsistency (i.e., lack of reliability), our observations are also frequently inaccurate. That is, we form inappropriate conceptions about students, which can result in poor decisions about the student's understanding, the need for further instruction, appropriate placement, and so on.

I remember one particular class discussion that occurred as we approached the end of our consideration of the fallibility of our observations. I had asked a question about which of two standardized tests would be preferable for use: Test A, which had a reliability coefficient of .70 or Test B, which had a reliability coefficient of .90. Assuming other things to be equal, such as the appropriateness of the test, my students had no hesitation in selecting Test B because it yields more dependable information about students.

I then asked them to compare two teachers, for whom information was available regarding the reliability of their observations about students' performances. Teacher A showed a reliability of .30, and Teacher B showed a reliability of .50. Again, invoking various assumptions about the comparability of the observation protocols, etc., my students did not hesitate to choose Teacher B as the preferred observer, due to the fact that Teacher B's observations were more dependable.

For me, the surprise came when I combined these two situations. "Suppose that both Test B and Teacher B are designed with a common purpose and are supposed to be observing the same thing," I said. That is, they are both trying to measure the same aspect of student performance. "Let's choose the most dependable test—Test B, with a reliability of .90—and the most dependable teacher—Teacher B, with a reliability of .50. Which of these 'information-gathering tools' would be preferable?" I asked. "The teacher," they responded. I only dimly perceived at the time that their response revealed a strong, Romantic preference for giving air to the teacher's voice in decision making.

Although the recurring influence of romantic philosophy on American educational theory and practice is easily recognized, the influence of romanticism is only recently being recognized in educational research. Hargreaves (1996) has observed that "the concern with *voice* has come to have special relevance for the place teachers occupy and the role they play in school restructuring and reform; and in how research knowledge about teachers and their work is generated" (original emphasis; p. 12). He notes that, in the discourse of teacher education, research, and practice, "the teachers' voice has often become unduly romanticized" (p. 12), explaining that:

> [T]he discourse of the teacher's voice has tended to construct it in a particularly 'positive' way against a background of silence in which it had previously been trapped by policy and research. This discourse works by selectively appropriating particular empirical voices of predominantly humanistic, child-centred teachers, then condensing them into a singular voice, *the* teacher's voice, which becomes representative of *all* teachers. This generic voice is given a particular and positive moral loading... (original emphasis, p. 13)

At an even larger level than Hargreaves concern is the romanticization of voice in any form. Some advocates of narrative forms might recoil at the proposition that an account which boasts of the prominency of "voice" is not automatically meritorious. It seems heretic—or at least judgmental—to assert that some voices are better than others. In vocal music, however, voices are trained in the standards of quality accepted by other professionals (e.g., pitch, clarity, rhythm, and so on) before they are deemed suitable for public display. There do not appear to be similar standards for voice in educational displays. Certainly there are no accepted standards of quality for voice or prerequisite training in the educational context: All voices are honored and affirmed merely by virtue of the fact that they are voices.

The presence of, and concerns about, romanticization of voice are especially pronounced in narrative modes of inquiry, which are the context of Hargreaves's observations. With the current technology of educational research, narratives provide one of the most feasible methods for representing the characteristic of voice to which Hargreaves referred. It is possible that the increasing appeal of narrative modes of inquiry is related to the enduring influence of romanticism in American educational research and practice.

Refraction Is Where the Action Is

A fifth potential reason for the ascendance of the narrative in teacher education and research is its tractability. Stories provide a medium for translating objective experience into subjective understandings. Traditionally, one aim of research generally has been to attempt to represent objective experience as faithfully as possible. Loosed from these moorings by constructivist thought, narrative forms of inquiry represent conscious attempts to alter objective experience in such a way as to maximize the meaning of events in the eyes and minds of readers. This shift in aim has resulted in a representational form that is not only more relevant and accessible to its audience (as described earlier in this chapter), but is also in a more tractable form from the viewpoint of the research producer. This characteristic makes the narrative more useful as a tool for disseminating meaning to a wider audience.

Cushman (1991) has suggested that scientists are predestined to represent themselves in the conduct and reporting of their research, because human beings are inseparable from the powerful forces of the cultural ethos and historical epoch in which they live. In researching us, researchers unknowingly reproduce us. To illustrate this position, an article by Cushman presents a case of research on child development, embodied in a treatise on the subject produced by Stern (1985). Cushman argues that Stern's research on child development produced a

> marvelous infant: masterful, bounded, interior, full of feelings, eager to share its subjectivity—relentlessly relational. Stern pictured the infant as a bounded, cohesive, independent, continuous Western self who is preoccupied with relating to others. Even heretofore strictly physiological activities such as eating, sleeping, and defecating were

depicted by Stern as being performed within and to some extent in order to facilitate the holding container. This image is extremely appealing to modern Western readers. Why? Because it *is* them. It describes so well who they are, what they are interested in, what is most vital to them. One might well say that this concept of infancy is irresistible to them. (p. 208)

Along these lines, it is interesting to draw a parallel between the changes in perspective of cognitive psychologists and the emergence of narrative forms in educational research. Previous generations of educational psychologists may have perceived the human mind as a passive, information processing machine. However, in describing how the discipline of educational psychology has changed over the past three decades, Calfee (1992) asserts that today "one can imagine the mind looking for connections between present events and previous memories, searching for purpose and value in the world about itself, actively altering the raw data to achieve 'meaning'" (p. 166). Although Calfee's characterization describes current thinking about human cognition in general, it also provides an accurate description of the process educational researchers use in producing narratives, including Eisner's (1997) accommodation for fictions, selectivity, and the constructive neglect of data in artistically crafting a powerful narrative for promoting meaning.

Malleability of the raw data as hypothesized standard-cognitive-operating procedure is paralleled also in the language and process of crafting narratives in educational research. One particularly prevalent example of this lies in the ubiquitous use of "the lens" in narrative inquiry. Classroom events can be scrutinized in many ways, although increasingly, they are viewed through the lens of feminist theory, or constructivist philosophy, or gender politics, and so on. The metaphor of the lens has been invoked frequently and in many contexts, but consideration of the epistemological significance of the metaphor has been overlooked. It's a "not seeing the forest for the trees" kind of thing, to use a metaphor.

Obviously, a lens can have a beneficial purpose; as in the device used in eyeglasses, it can improve visual perception for an individual with reduced acuity. It is such a purpose that is the foundation for the use of the lens metaphor in educational research. Purportedly, when viewed through several competing corrective lenses, objective social phenomena can be perceived more accurately by their viewers. Of course, one problem with the metaphor is that only one lens is truly corrective. Having a touch of myopia myself, I know that lenses which corrected for hyperopia would certainly provide me with a different perspective on the world, though not necessarily a helpful one. In the same way, viewing social phenomena—especially those in the field of education—through various lenses begs the question of whether the resulting acuity is improved or worsened.

The metaphor of the lens is also problematic from another perspective. There is a glaring contradiction inherent in the use of the lens metaphor by those who espouse constructivist philosophy. In technical terms, the sole purpose of a lens is refraction. As a physical process, refraction is really just distortion, in that incoming stimuli (e.g., light) are contorted in such a way as to make resulting images more appealing to the person using the refracting device—the lens. The contradiction is that the metaphor of the lens presumes the existence of objective phenomena upon which the lens acts.

To illustrate the contradiction, it is insightful to consider the familiar fable of the six blind men and the elephant, which is often cited as highlighting the value of multiple perspectives. The first verse of a 19th-century poem by American poet John Godfrey Saxe, based on a centuries-old Indian fable, is reproduced below.

It was six men of Indostan
To learning much inclined,
Who went to see the Elephant
(though all of them were blind),
That each by observation
Might satisfy his mind.

The remaining verses describe how the first blind man stumbled into the side of the elephant and concluded that it was like a wall; the second blind man, feeling the elephant's tusk, concluded that an elephant is like a spear; the third blind man, grasping the animal's trunk, perceived the elephant to be like a snake, and so on. Saxe summarizes the scene with the moral that disputes are often sustained by people with only limited knowledge of the bigger picture. However, one thing is sure: The power of the poem presumes the existence of an objectively *real* elephant. Similarly, use of the metaphor of the lens presumes the objective existence of realities that can be transformed by viewing them though refractive processes.

The final phrase of the verse shown earlier ties together several elements of this potential explanation for the increasing use of narrative forms of inquiry in teacher education and research. The appeal of the narrative can be seen in its malleability and in its power to refract experience through the lenses of our choosing and produce compelling, artistically crafted stories. And, as Cushman (1991) claims, narratives may also provide the means by which we are able to reproduce our own visions as the products of scientific research.

Neo-Pragmatism

Pragmatism—the philosophical belief that meaning and truth are inexorably bound to consequences of thought and actions—was introduced in the United States near the beginning of the 20th century by Peirce (1903/1997). As a philosophical system, it flourished briefly. However, the themes of pragmatism may be recurring at the beginning of the 21st century, as educational researchers eschew the necessarily messy work of gathering data in favor of the (comparatively) fairly tidy enterprise of crafting narratives.

One problem with "the raw data" alluded to in Calfee's (1992) description of cognitive processing is that, in educational research, there is so little of it. This paucity of data may also help explain a burgeoning interest in narrative forms of representation. Everyday life is particularly fecund in its ability to engender an infinite number of "research reports" in the form of narratives. On the other hand, well-conceived, rigorous, and suitably controlled empirical work is eminently more limited. Thus, from a purely pragmatic perspective, narratives present a mother load of data.

Proponents of qualitative research methods have often, and justifiably, criticized the artificiality of traditional experimental research designs. In the process of designing a study, there is almost always a tradeoff between two competing ends: The gains accrued by measuring adequately operationalized variables, controlling experimental conditions, and promoting strong internal validity on the one hand; and the desirability of accurately capturing the range of human behavior, viewing it in naturally occurring contexts, and enhancing strong external validity on the other. The perfect study—one that completely satisfies both of these aims—cannot be conducted. With increasing costs of doing research and attention to the rights of those being studied, the likelihood of conducting a good study—one that satisfies either aim—is being reduced.

A testament to the trend of decreasing availability of good new data is the proliferation of studies in education that rely on good *old* data. For example, there is increasing attention to analysis of large scale data sets (e.g., High School and Beyond; National Education Longitudinal Study, National Assessment of Educational Progress), especially those collected by an entity possessing the financial wherewithal to gather the data, such as the federal government. In addition to the nearly limitless research questions that can be addressed by these massive data collections, there is certainly a pragmatic reason to prefer a few large data collections supporting nearly infinite analyses and broad conclusions over infinite data collections yielding narrower, more parochial conclusions.

Across social science and even physical science disciplines, there has also been much more attention given to using existing data as input for new research—the methodology known as meta-analysis. Criticism of meta-analysis on substantive grounds notwithstanding, the technique has proven to be a powerful and practical means of generating new knowledge, without the need for administering yet another treatment, survey, or questionnaire under increasingly difficult research conditions.

Getting the Job Done

The final, and perhaps most likely, explanation for the ascendance of the narrative to a place of dominance in teacher education and research is that it holds the potential to be more efficacious in influencing educational policy. As described earlier in this chapter, the narrative possesses the ability to elicit affective response in a way that traditional representations of data do not. Beyond that, it also possesses the power to support advocacy and compel educational policymakers to a degree that has eluded educational researchers whose aim it has been to translate research findings into governmental policy and classroom practice.

The fact that educational research has been comparatively impotent has been chronicled by educational policy researchers. For example, Kaestle (1993, p. 23) bemoaned "The Awful Reputation of Education Research" in the title of an article on that topic. Numerous authors have suggested reasons for the reputation. A sampling of these might begin with Silberman (1970), who postulated that the pervasive sense of crisis in American education at the time was due, among other things, to the incomparability of expectations across disciplines. The so-called "hard sciences" had demonstrated that the public's expectations for monumental accomplishments promised by its leaders (such as traveling to the moon) could be achieved. In the social sciences, similar expectations about monumental achievements (such as universal literacy or elimination of poverty) were not fulfilled.

Kennedy (1997) has developed four hypotheses to account for the lack of influence of educational research on classroom practice. Kennedy's hypotheses include the possibilities that: a) poorly designed or conducted research is not sufficiently persuasive or authoritative; b) some research is not sufficiently relevant to practice or amenable to practical implementation; c) research findings are frequently not disseminated in ways that are accessible or comprehensible to teachers; and d) even if reliable, powerful, practical, and comprehensible innovations were identified, education as a system is either too inherently unstable for innovations to "take," or is so mammoth and monolithic, that it is inherently unable to change. Kennedy's second hypothesis is similar to what Doyle and Ponder have called the *practicality ethic*, which they define as "teachers' perceptions of the potential consequences of attempting to implement a change proposal in the classroom" (1977/1978, p. 6).

Similarly, Kleine and Greene (1992, p. 187) suggested other "factors contributing to the irrelevancy of educational research," which included the hypotheses that: a) communication about research is primarily a closed, academic discourse; b) practitioners lack the specific knowledge that is necessary for interpreting some research findings; and c) research is often not extended to the point of observing its application in actual practice. In a followup to Kaestle's 1993 article, Sroufe (1997) offered his suggestions for improving the awful reputation of educational research.

The real issues appear to be advocacy and efficacy. Educational researchers are increasingly perceiving themselves as lacking the dimension of advocacy which might make their suggested reforms for educational practice more efficacious. David Berliner, a former president of the American Educational Research Association (AERA), identified advocacy as a key missing element in the organization's activities. He opined that "AERA has failed to be an advocate for creating the conditions under which our knowledge could possibly affect the lives of children" (Berliner, et. al., 1997, p. 12).

Berliner has carefully laid out the interconnections between this advocacy role and the use of narratives. He first notes, as other writers have, that educational researchers suffer "a lack of influence on people and policies in the educational field" (1992, p. 157). Second, he asserts that the very "nature and mission of educational psychology is to provide...data and concepts to create sensible, persuasive, and powerful stories" (p. 143). Third, he recognizes the unique power of narratives, observing that:

> Educational psychologists often fail to contextualize and particularize their research. But context-free and universal findings, derived from internally and externally valid logicodeductive research will probably not be attended to unless those findings can be embedded in authentic stories of practice. (p. 154)

Berliner then ties these elements together in a remarkably frank prescription for making educational research more efficacious through narratives:

> ...we should take our ideas to school sites and then try to (a) weave sensible, persuasive, and powerful stories, (b) that refer to real humans, in real situations, (c) that evoke emotions and a sense of reality, (d) so that we can influence people in the ways that we want. (1992, p. 158)

Berliner's assertion that a narrative is simply "what works" in influencing educational policy is interesting in its own right. However, it also represents a conception of educational research as baldly political activity in a way heretofore unstated, or at least understated. In an evaluation of publications titled, coincidentally, *What Works* (USDOE, 1986, 1987), Glass commented on the political aspects of reports of research findings. He observed that "groups of people who formulate policies use research to advance their causes," and "the mere doing of research, regardless of what it shows, legitimizes political positions" (1987, p. 9). Although Glass specifically excluded basic, theory-based research from this stinging assertion, Berliner's (1992) prescription for what works in educational policymaking would not appear to do so.

In such a world of educational research and policymaking, where the goal is to influence people in the ways that we want, powerful stories may indeed provide more punch than sound data. Kennedy (1997) has lamented that, in the deliberations about American education, "our influence [as educational researchers] in the ongoing debate sometimes seems to depend more on our advocacy than on our evidence" (p. 10). Narratives may now provide an efficacious tool for getting a job done that evidence could not.

CONCLUSION

Narrative description of educational phenomena is not new. Pre-service teachers and graduate students are enculturated to education as a profession and to educational research via intricate observations of ordinary life in classrooms (e.g., Jackson, 1968) and detailed descriptions of extraordinary life outside of classrooms (e.g.,

Willis, 1977). The pervasive use of the narrative in teacher education has had predictable results that reflect the superordinate status of meaning over knowledge. For example, it is likely that a far greater number of teachers are familiar with the meaning of labeling and the potency of expectations from the rich description of *Pygmalion in the Classroom* (Rosenthal & Jacobson, 1968) than have knowledge about the hows, whys, and magnitudes of teacher expectancy effects from meta-analytic research (see Raudenbush, 1984).

What is new are claims of superiority of meaning over knowledge and of narratives over other modes of representation. There are numerous possibilities that may explain, individually or in combination, why narratives have achieved a position of prominence in educational inquiry. The possibilities include: their grounding in perceptions of reality; their relevance to classroom life and accessibility to teachers; their ability to evoke emotional response; their appeal to romantic philosophy; their malleability; and practicality. Perhaps most of all, however, narratives have recently been discovered to be an important tool for wielding power in educational politics. Over 30 years, the ascendance has been remarkable. In the 1960s, Jackson's *Life in Classrooms* provided a melange and analysis of real events with the stated aim "neither to damn schools nor to praise them, nor even, necessarily, to change them" (1968, p. vii). In the 1990s, researchers advocate the production of artistically crafted fictions, for the expressed purpose of changing the people and institutions they wish to influence.

Unquestionably, the narrative is both a powerful tool for conveying meaning and an efficacious instrument for influencing people in the ways that we want. However, it is not inconsistent to acknowledge, as Glass (1987) implied, that research has always had a political dimension and has been put to political uses, while also lamenting (and resisting) the notion that such use is, as Berliner (1992) has asserted, a primary function. It can be hoped that 30 more years will reveal whether satisfactory rules of evidence for the use of narratives will be developed, and whether the use of narrative influences what really matters: student learning. For now, it is too early to tell if reliance on the narrative as a mode of representation and a weapon of political warfare will belie the title of this book or match its promise as an advance in teacher education.

NOTES

[1] Reviewers of this chapter have remarked about the irony of using stories (such as the one retold in here and one in a subsequent section describing the romantic philosophy of some graduate students) to make certain points, in a chapter devoted to the ascendance of narrative ways of conveying meaning. Such use was intentional. In fact, the material cited in this chapter from the Cizek (1996) article dealing with pressures to include more narrative in research reporting, was followed in that article by the following tongue-in-cheek comment: "I suppose that I've just succumbed to the pressure by relating *this* incident!"

Though ironic, the use is not contradictory. It is one thing to recognize the importance and power of narratives (as is accomplished in the retelling of stories in this chapter). It is quite another to recognize narratives or fictions as legitimate forms of—or substitutes for—educational research.

[2] The term *unvarnished*, as used in this sentence, represents a desperate attempt to avoid using the term *objective*.

[3] Connelly and Clandinin (1985, 1990, 1991) and Elbaz (1991) both appear to use the term *knowledge* to refer to teachers' *understandings*, despite the fact that the two terms are not synonymous. Carter (1993) does not seem to worry about the distinction either, although she does not equate the terms as the others have done. At the risk of oversimplifying her position, it appears that Carter views narratives not as knowledge or understandings in themselves, but as useful mechanisms by which knowledge and experience are organized in human cognition.

REFERENCES

Baker, D. P. (1997). Good news, bad news, and international comparisons: Comment on Bracey. *Educational Researcher, 26*(3), 16–18.

Belenky, M. F. (Ed.). (1986). *Women's ways of knowing: The development of self, voice, and mind.* New York: Basic Books.

Berger, P. L., & Luckmann, T. (1966). *The social construction of reality.* New York: Doubleday.

Berliner, D. C. (1992). Telling the stories of educational psychology. *Educational Psychologist, 27*(2), 143–161.

Berliner, D. C., Resnick, L. B., Cuban, L., Cole, N., Popham, W. J., & Goodlad, J. I. (1997). "The vision thing": Educational research and AERA in the 21st century. Part 2: Competing vision for enhancing the impact of educational research. *Educational Researcher, 26*(3), 12–18, 27.

Bracey, G. I. (1996). International comparisons and the condition of American education. *Educational Researcher, 25*(1), 5–11.

Bracey, G. I. (1997). On comparing the incomparable: A response to Baker and Stedman. *Educational Researcher, 26*(3), 19–26.

Calfee, R. (1992). Refining educational psychology: The case of the missing links. *Educational Psychologist, 27*(2), 163–175.

Carter, K. (1993). The place of story in the study of teaching and teacher education. *Educational Researcher, 22*(1), 5–12, 18.

Cizek, G. J. (1996). The hegemony of the narrative: Reflections on the contours of social science research. *Review of Higher Education, 19*, 227–236.

Coles, R. (1989). *The call of stories: Teaching and the moral imagination.* Boston: Houghton Mifflin.

Connelly, F. M., & Clandinin, D. J. (1985). Personal practical knowledge and the modes of knowing: Relevance for teaching and learning. In E. W. Eisner (Ed.), *Learning and teaching the ways of knowing* (pp. 174–198). Chicago: University of Chicago Press.

Connelly, F. M., & Clandinin, D. J. (1990). Stories of experience and narrative inquiry. *Educational Researcher, 19*(5), 2–14.

Connelly, F. M., & Clandinin, D. J. (1991). Narrative and story in practice and research. In D. Schon (Ed.), *The reflective turn: Case studies in and on educational practice* (pp. 258–281). New York: Teachers College Press.

Cushman, P. (1991). Ideology obscured: Political uses of the self in Daniel Stern's infant. *American Psychologist, 46*(3), 206–219.

Cusick, P. A. (1973). *Inside high school: The student's world.* New York: Holt, Rinehart, and Winston.

Dewey, J. (1902). *The child and the curriculum.* Chicago: University of Chicago Press.

Dewey, J. (1963). *Experience and education.* New York: Collier Books. (Original work published 1938)

Donmoyer, R., Eisner, E., Gardner, H., Stotsky, S., Wasley, P., Tillman, L., Cizek, G., & Gough, N. (1996). Viewpoints: Should novels count as dissertations in education? *Research in the Teaching of English, 30,* 403–427.

Doyle, W. (1986). Classroom organization and management. In M. C. Wittrock (Ed.), *Handbook of research on teaching* (pp. 392–431). New York: Macmillan.

Doyle, W. (1997). Heard any good stories lately? A critique of the critics of narrative in educational research. *Teaching and Teacher Education, 13,* 93–99.

Doyle, W., & Ponder, G. A. (1977/1978). The practicality ethic in teacher decision making. *Interchange, 8*(3), 1–12.

Eisner, E. W. (1997). The promise and perils of alternative forms of data representation. *Educational Researcher, 26*(6), 4–10.

Elbaz, F. (1991). Research on teachers' knowledge: The evolution of a discourse. *Journal of Curriculum Studies, 23,* 1–19.

Gage, N. L. (1989). The paradigm wars and their aftermath: A "historical" sketch of research on teaching since 1989. *Educational Researcher, 18*(7), 4–10.

Geertz, C. (1988). *Works and lives: The anthropologist as author.* Stanford, CA: Stanford University Press.

Glass, G. V. (1987). *What Works:* Politics and research. *Educational Researcher, 16*(3), 5–10.

Gross, T. F., & Mastenbrook, M. (1980). Examination of the effects of state anxiety on problem-solving efficiency under high and low memory conditions. *Journal of Educational Psychology, 72,* 605–609.

Hanushek, E. A. (1989). The impact of differential expenditures on school performance. *Educational Researcher, 18*(4), 45–51.

Hanushek, E. A. (1994). Money might matter somewhere: A response to Hedges, Laine, and Greenwald. *Educational Researcher, 23*(4), 5–8.

Hargreaves, A. (1996). Revisiting voice. *Educational Researcher, 25*(1), 12–19.

Hedges, L. V., Laine, R. D., & Greenwald, R. (1994a). Does money matter? A meta-analysis of studies of differential school inputs on student outcomes. *Educational Researcher, 23*(3), 5–14.

Hedges, L. V., Laine, R. D., & Greenwald, R. (1994b). Money does matter somewhere. A reply to Hanushek. *Educational Researcher, 23*(4), 9–10.

Hendrick, J. (1988). *The whole child: Developmental education for the early years.* Columbus, OH: Merrill.

House, E. R. (1991). Realism in research. *Educational Researcher, 20*(6), 2–9, 25.

Jackson, P. W. (1968). *Life in classrooms.* New York: Holt, Rinehart, and Winston.

Kaestle, C. F. (1993). The awful reputation of educational research. *Educational Researcher, 22*(1), 23–31.

Kennedy, M. M. (1997). The connection between research and practice. *Educational Researcher, 26*(7), 4–12.

Kleine, P. F., & Greene, B. A. (1992). Story telling: A rich history and a sordid past. *Educational Psychologist, 28*(2), 185–190.

Lather, P. A. (1991). *Getting smart: Feminist research and pedagogy with/in the postmodern*. New York: Routledge.

McAninch, A. R. (1995). Case methods in teacher education. In L. W. Anderson (Ed.), *International encyclopedia of teaching and teacher education* (pp. 583–587). Oxford, England: Pergamon.

Montessori, M. (1966). *The secret of childhood* (M. J. Costelloe, Trans.). New York: Ballantine Books. (Original work published 1914)

Nisbett, R., & Ross, L. (1980). *Human inference: Strategies and shortcomings of social judgment*. Englewood Cliffs, NJ: Prentice-Hall.

Peshkin, A. (1993). The goodness of qualitative research. *Educational Researcher, 22*(2), 23–29.

Peirce, C. S. (1997). *Pragmatism as a principle and method of right thinking: The 1903 Harvard lectures on pragmatism*. Albany, NY: State University of New York Press. (Original work published 1903)

Raudenbush, S. W. (1984). Magnitude of teacher expectancy effects on pupil IQ as a function of the credibility of expectancy induction: A synthesis of findings from 18 experiments. *Journal of Educational Psychology, 76*(1), 85–97.

Rosenthal, R., & Jacobson, L. (1968). *Pygmalion in the classroom*. New York: Holt, Rinehart & Winston.

Rousseau, J. J. (1979). *Emile* (A. Bloom, Trans.). New York: Basic Books. (Original work published 1858)

Rugg, H. O., & Shumaker, A. (1928). *The child-centered school*. Yonkers-on- Hudson, NY: World Book Company.

Shulman, J. H. (1992). *Case methods in teacher education*. New York: Teachers College Press.

Silberman, C. E. (1970). *Crisis in the classroom*. New York: Random House.

Smith, B. (1981). Narrative versions, narrative theories. In W. J. T. Mitchell (Ed.), *On narrative* (pp. 209–232). Chicago: University of Chicago Press.

Sroufe, G. E. (1997). Improving the "awful reputation" of education research. *Educational Researcher, 26*(7), 26–28.

Stedman, L. C. (1994). Incomplete explanations: The case of U.S. performance in the international assessments of education. *Educational Researcher, 23*(7), 24–32.

Stedman, L. C. (1997). International achievement differences: An assessment of a new perspective. *Educational Researcher, 26*(3), 4–15.

Stern, D. (1985). *The interpersonal world of the infant: A view from psychoanalysis and developmental psychology*. New York: Basic Books.

Sykes, G., & Bird, T. (1992). Teacher education and the case idea. In G. Grant (Ed.), *Review of Research in Education, 18* (pp. 457–521). Washington, DC: American Educational Research Association.

United States Department of Education. (1986). *What works: Research about teaching and learning*. Washington, DC: U.S. Government Printing Office.

United States Department of Education. (1987). *Schools that work: Educating disadvantaged children*. Washington, DC: U.S. Government Printing Office.

United States Department of Education, Office of Educational Research and Improvement, National Center for Education Statistics. (1997). *Digest of education statistics, 1997*. Washington, DC: U.S. Government Printing Office.

Waite, D. (1994, April). *Ethnography's demise: What's next for the narrative?* Paper presented at the annual meeting of the American Educational Research Association, New Orleans, LA.

Willis, P. (1977). *Learning to labor: How working class kids get working class jobs*. New York: Columbia University Press.

Wolcott, H. F. (1973). *The man in the principal's office: An ethnography*. New York: Holt, Rinehart, & Winston.

Yates, F. A. (1966). *The art of memory*. London: Routledge and Kegan Paul.

Yerkes, R. M., & Dodson, J. D. (1908). The relation of strength of stimulus to rapidity of habit formation. *Journal of Comparative Neurology and Psychology, 18*, 459–482.

4

Consensus and the Knowledge Base for Teaching and Teacher Education[1]

Gary R. Galluzzo
George Mason University

As recently as 15 years ago, one could attend the "invisible college for research on teaching," quietly held in conjunction with the annual meeting of the American Educational Research Association (AERA), and hear passionate, academic discussions led by the prominent researchers of the time. Upon entering these meeting rooms, one would have heard these researchers asking whether the rapidly growing body of research at the time was leading the *study* of teaching to our first-ever *theory* of teaching. These were exciting times, with the best minds in the field offering their opinions in debates on conducting classroom-based research. Researchers of teaching conducting seminal work—including David Berliner, Bruce Biddle, Jere Brophy, Mick Dunkin, Carolyn Evertson, Tom Good, Greta Morine-Dershimer, Lee Shulman, Jane Stallings, Barak Rosenshine, Claire Weinstein, Bob Soar, Fred McDonald, and Nate Gage, perhaps the leading scholar on teaching at the time—weighed in on the question of whether we were approaching a theory of teaching. They brought their graduate students to listen, and to share what they were reading as well.

These were heady times, for the study of teaching was building from a field without a study into a viable field of inquiry, grounded in the systematic observation of classroom dynamics and classroom processes. Supported by Medley and Mitzel's (1963) pioneering analysis of the contributions of direct observation of classrooms, and Flanders's (1960) groundbreaking work in conducting reliable and valid observations of classroom interactions, the study of teaching was finally beginning to approach a view of teaching that was divorced from the personality of the teacher and the implementation of curriculum or methods (Medley, 1979). For perhaps the first time, the field of teaching was approaching what could be speculated to be a theory of teaching and teacher effectiveness that could be taught to preservice teachers to ground them in a systematically-derived knowledge base (Dunkin & Biddle, 1974; Good & Brophy, 1996; Rosenshine, 1979, 1986).

The 1970s and early 1980s are particularly prominent as the decades in which the field of teaching was approaching what might look like a theory of teaching. With thanks to the then United States Office of Education for its generous funding of classroom observation research—with specific attention to studies of teacher behaviors that correlated with higher levels of student achievement in lower socioeconomic second and fifth grade reading and mathematics classes—researchers were rapidly transforming our understanding of how teachers behave to increase the likelihood of student achievement (Denham & Lieberman, 1980). The Beginning Teacher Evaluation Studies, inspired additionally by Carroll's (1963) "model of school learning," were actually a broad series of studies which sought to correlate teacher behavior with student achievement, thereby earning the label "process-product research." The processes—for example, the frequency of specific teaching behaviors in the classroom—were correlated with student performance on standardized tests (products) in selected settings and subject areas (Berliner, 1979).

Optimistically titling this research "effective teaching," practitioners and students of teaching were encouraged to rely on the collection of propositions about teaching that were grounded in the process-product research literature. It was intended that these findings would inform the numerous decisions teachers make daily. It was also intended that reasoned use of these "effective" teacher behaviors would increase the likelihood of student achievement, thereby validating a theory of teaching against student performance. In 1986, these studies were characterized in a publication from the United States Department of Education entitled *What Works*.

Back at the invisible college meetings, processes were beginning that were intended to prepare the next generation of researchers. One could observe the presentation of syllabi for classes for graduate students devoted to immersing them in this literature. One could also hear discussions of how this knowledge could be and should be disseminated to school-level practitioners. Whole issues of journals were devoted to "direct instruction," as the name of this line of research came to be known, borrowing on one dimension in the Flanders Interaction Analysis System. Symposia on effective teaching dominated the appropriate divisions and special interest groups at the annual meetings of AERA and the American Association of Colleges for Teacher Education (AACTE).[2] Over the next decade, books were written in which leading researchers codified the process-product literature for all to read, study, and critique (Reynolds, 1989; Smith, 1983; Wittrock, 1986). Methods textbooks began to appear that translated this research into essential teacher knowledge regarding what happens in the classroom (Anderson, 1989; Arends, 1988,

1992; Cooper, 1980; Dill, 1990; and Kindsvatter, Wilen, & Ishler, 1988, among many others) so that beginners would be able to study classrooms and their own growth within the context of effective teaching. Many teacher educators around the country began incorporating this literature into their coursework for preservice and practicing teachers. State departments of education employed research summaries of the process-product literature (e.g., in Florida and in Kentucky) in an effort to bring more focus to the preparation and induction of new teachers into the profession. In so many ways, the fields of teaching and teacher education were approaching a unity between them. It was the kind of unity that contributes to the development of a profession through a body of research-informed practice that could be accepted as the definition of good practice. Teaching was developing its own version of the medical profession's foundational text, *Gray's Anatomy*, and in short order, and due in no small part to the inclusion of the term "knowledge base" in the new standards for accreditation from the National Council for Accreditation of Teacher Education (NCATE), this expression was widely used to capture what this new research evidence had become, the knowledge base for teaching and teacher education. Perhaps for the first time in the history of teaching and teacher education did the field approach a "scientific basis" (Gage, 1978, 1985) for teaching (Medley, 1977, 1979; Wang, Haertel, & Walberg, 1993).

Thus, a grand vision for the study of teaching, initially explicated collectively in the first edition of the *Handbook of Research on Teaching* (Gage, 1963), was now accessible in many formats, including presentations at annual research conferences, special conferences, journal articles, books, televised videotapes, protocol materials, and much more. In fact, at least two presidencies of AACTE were devoted directly to codifying the research on teaching so that it would serve as the foundation for the new profession of teaching and teacher education (Shulman, 1987). The presidencies of David Smith, in 1982, and William Gardner[3], in 1986, intended to place the process-product research at the center of the resurrection of the decried public schools across the country. In essence, Smith and Gardner called for the use of the knowledge base for teaching as the foundation for reform in teaching and teacher education, as well as urged the field of researchers to continue to conduct further investigations into the gaps in the research to improve practice in classrooms. For all intents and purposes, the fields of teaching and teacher education had a knowledge base in the same tradition of logical- positivism that characterized the knowledge base in other fields. In the case of teaching, it was argued that it was possible to identify more or less effective instruction based upon teachers' use of these behavioral correlates of student achievement, and therefore, the knowledge base was about specific behaviors teachers used in the classroom that correlated with student performance. It was hailed as a knowledge base that could be taught to others.

The path to "the" knowledge base took decades. It was fixed on course by the prevailing views of what mattered most in the classroom. As such, the researchers over this century concentrated on the personality of the teacher, or the methods the teacher used, or, more recently, on the curriculum that was used to teach students, and whether any of these made a difference in student achievement. As Medley (1979) notes, each of these perspectives on effective teaching was found wanting. Neither teacher personality, instructional methods, nor curriculum mattered much. However, armed with the ability to peer into classrooms as Flanders (1960) initiated, researchers could examine what teachers did that correlated with student achievement. The search for the scientific basis for teaching and its results became "the" knowledge base for teaching and teacher education.

ALTERNATE VIEWS

To be fair, the debates at the "Invisible College" also included its share of those who found this definition of teacher effectiveness too narrow to serve as a theory of teaching. For the many analyses that concluded the field was close to a theory of teaching, there was a critic who would stop the presenter in mid-sentence and offer a counterargument. The challenges were broad and varied, as they should be; and they were immediate. For example, in the same volume in which Medley, Rosenshine, Berliner, and others were extolling the gains made in understanding teaching, Peterson (1979) was sounding cautionary tones regarding the overgeneralization of the findings and the exclusivity of their perspective. As she writes, "the picture of direct instruction seems not only grim but unidimensional as well. It assumes that the only important educational objective is to increase student achievement and that all students learn in the same way and thus should be taught in the same way" (p. 66). Her critique is fair, and while it did not necessarily set a tone for forthcoming analysts and critics of the logical-positivist orientations of the knowledge base found in process-product research, the juxtaposition of her critique amidst advocates for this research tradition certainly suggested caution. Peterson spoke to a fuller definition of teaching and of the research knowledge needed to support it. As will be seen later in this chapter, she may not know she had many kindred spirits in the community of scholars.

An entire issue of the *Review of Educational Research* was devoted to examining the extant knowledge base as described by Wang, Haertel, and Walberg (1993). Across the remainder of the journal issue, scholars of teaching analyzed important questions of epistemology, empiricism, methodology, the applicability of "the" knowledge to practice, applications to policy, and others. These remain salient issues on the way to a theory of teaching that attends to the contexts in which teaching occurs. Many of the comments in response to Wang, Haertel, and Walberg are concerned with the "decontextualized" aspects of a theory of teaching. This forum advanced our thinking about a knowledge base for teaching and teacher education at the same time it obfuscated the political arena in which education policy is made and teaching is conducted. By the end, the knowledge base was merely a continuous discussion among academicians, thus moving us farther from the consensus view of teaching needed as one dimension of a profession.

These 10 years saw the acceptance of the process-product research as important to understanding teaching, providing its relative narrowness was taken into account. Increasingly, researchers and scholars developed the context within which the knowledge base had to be considered. The works of others—including Calderhead (1987), on teacher thinking; Clandinin and Connelly (1992) and Duckworth (1987), on teachers's epistemologies; Fosnot (1989), on the application of constructivism to teacher education; Goodlad, Soder, and Sirotnik (1990), on the moral aspects of teaching; Schon (1983) on reflective practitioners; and Zeichner and Gore (1990), on teacher socialization—placed the process-product research into a portrait in which both its significance and relative insignificance could be assessed. Alternative themes of teaching challenged the purported knowledge base along the lines of these scholars. The general view of teaching as something more than "behaving" or "acting" underwent, and continues to undergo, serious scrutiny and challenge. Scholars who advocated this broader view of teaching did not necessarily argue against the need for "a" knowledge base, however, there was a general concern that the extant view of teaching drawn from the process-product literature painted a mechanistic image of teaching, and an image of teachers that could be labeled as anti-intellectual. The literature during these years, in many ways led by the rise of cognitive perspectives on teaching and alternative pedagogies grounded in more varied views of humans, spoke of the teacher as a reflective practitioner in the Deweyan sense, demonstrating a caring for students in a more holistic way. In the case of the cognitive perspective, the behaviors, so important to the process-product research, were actually the manifestations of teachers' thoughts, and that these behavior manifestations could only be understood by examining those thoughts (Borko, Cone, Russo, & Shavelson, 1979; Peterson, Marx, & Clark, 1978). In order to assess the veracity of these alternate perspectives on effective teaching, researchers tested and employed new data-gathering methods—for example, stimulated recall (McNair & Joyce, 1978; Yinger, 1986)—to try and capture what teachers thought during instruction, or "plan aloud" activities, to learn more about how teachers planned (Clark & Peterson, 1986). In essence, the argument went, the "processes" part of process-product research were controlled by teachers' mental images of their lessons and how well they felt those lessons were proceeding. In other words, teacher behaviors were predicted, or controlled, by teacher thoughts. The definition of teaching was changed. The word "effective" slowly disappeared as a widely accepted modifier of the term "teaching." Within the research community, the notion that effective teaching was the use of behaviors that correlated with student achievement was assailed at the same time it gathered momentum. The introduction of the person into the process-product equation changed our view of teaching, and in fact, of learning to teach (Carter, 1990). In sum, the more holistic view of teaching was generally accepted that teachers' decision-making processes influenced their behaviors to an unpredictable degree, and the extent to which those thoughts did influence their behaviors had to be taken into account in the research, as well as in the preparation of future teachers. By the mid-1990s, another volume on the knowledge base for teaching and teacher education appeared in which one could find many authors writing more expansively and inclusively of teaching (Murray, 1995).

THE NEED FOR A KNOWLEDGE BASE

As is its proper role, the research community continues to push the definition of teaching even further. In many ways, the context in which the process-product research was placed brought more attention to various aspects of the contexts in which teachers practice as centrally important to their effectiveness. It becomes a bit dangerous to name those contexts, but the neophyte who asks, "Well, whatever happened to the research on teaching?" would have to look in new places, as the notion of generic skills has given way to context-dependent analysis of effectiveness. One very profitable place to look is in the subject matter disciplines. Shulman's powerful AERA Presidential Address (1986), which posited that the discipline is essential in understanding knowledge in teaching, launched a movement into research on teaching in the disciplines that essentially is grounded in the perspective that there are some aspects of teaching that are generic, and that while some behaviors/practices are generalizable, there is just enough nuance within each discipline to examine it separately for its uniqueness (Grossman, 1990; McDiarmid, 1987; Wilson, 1990; Wineburg, 1994). This research line is invaluable in the development of teaching as a profession for two reasons. First, it acknowledges that there are routines in teaching to which all teachers must attend. Second, it says that the discipline, and the nature of the content within it, affects those routines and requires teachers to be more thoughtful and analytic about effectiveness and student achievement. There is no doubt a need for the continuing expansion of the knowledge base for teaching and teacher education in the research community. At the same time, there is a need for codifying something that can be shared with beginners and practitioners that grounds their thought processes, the decisions they make, and the behaviors they employ to affect student achievement. That codification—sought by Smith (1983) and Gardner (see Reynolds, 1989) during their AACTE presidencies—is elusive and is not in sync with the more practical demands of education's external audiences, who believe the improvement of schooling for all children is within reach and is not happening fast enough, and who perceive it is caught up in the scholarly community's internal squabbles of what effective means. Agreement on a knowledge base with attendant research would facilitate public relations for a field sorely in need of a better image.

A separate and specific example of the need for a knowledge base for teacher education can be found in the redesign of the standards for accreditation promulgated by the NCATE (1987, 1992, 1995). Long criticized as ineffective, the NCATE underwent a highly publicized, politically charged, and seemingly reasonable effort to redesign both its standards and procedures for accreditation. The critics of the

NCATE argued against its historic emphasis on inputs and its penchant for compliance with its old standards by verifying that courses were in the curriculum. The NCATE, through the leadership of key educators, emerged as a new body of corporate members requiring that curricular matters be placed in the hands of the institution's faculty. With the inclusion of the new *Standards for Accreditation* (1987), requiring that the unit's programs are grounded in a knowledge base, NCATE removed itself from requiring a collection of courses and moved toward requiring accredited units to have a sequenced and coherent curriculum. The implication was quickly derived that teacher education faculty would teach "the knowledge base," as found in the process-product research so visible at the time of the redesign of the NCATE. Thus, the knowledge base was needed to facilitate the important task of accrediting education units on campuses that prepare education professionals. The fact that the process-product knowledge base was questioned for its validity seemed to lay outside the more immediate concern of moving many aspects of teacher education forward. Professional accreditation required program faculty to explicate a knowledge base that was grounded in current and established research. This has proven a taller order than originally anticipated for reasons apparent already and more explicit, of which are discussed later in this chapter.

KNOWLEDGE BASE AND KNOWLEDGE BASES

Amidst the energy devoted to establishing the findings from process-product research as "the" knowledge base for teaching and teacher education, the strong, longheld view that it painted an insufficient picture of teaching gained momentum. Perhaps it was the philosophical challenges to the tradition outlined above, or the attempt to establish the process-product research as the prevailing view of teaching. Perhaps the skepticism was based in latent and unresolved conflicts about the multiple definitions of good teaching held by nonresearch-oriented practitioners, or in the significant philosophical work of scholars who minimized the contribution of research to understanding teaching in a deeper and/or moral sense. Or perhaps it was based in the declining performance of schools, or in a more passive, but nonetheless resistant, rejection of the generic definition of teaching. Each of these, alone or in multiple combinations and permutations, could be viewed as contributing to the fact that in 1998, there is no widely accepted knowledge base for teaching and teacher education that is grounded in research. Most views today, once again, return to perspectives individuals hold about schools, schooling, children, and learning. Shortly after the publication of *The Knowledge Base for Beginning Teachers* (Reynolds, 1989), one could hear both praise and criticism of the concept of "the" knowledge base. The author heard, on many occasions, the argument that the idea of a teacher-centered classroom was a fundamentally flawed view of good teaching.

The reaction against, and in some quarters the outright rejection of, "the" knowledge base was little more than a re-igniting of age-old arguments on the purpose of education. The reticence on the part of many teacher educators to accept "NCATE's knowledge base" was an indication of the widely held belief that there is no one way to teach, and their general reluctance to adopt one model that might, through lack of scientific or philosophical rigor, exclude any children from receiving an equal education.

My reference for this observation comes from having an article published on the essential attributes of a program knowledge base (Galluzzo & Pankratz, 1990). While an article alone rarely generates much interest, this particular piece, as well as some work on the reform of a teacher education program, afforded us dozens of opportunities to work with faculty members in schools, colleges, and departments of education across the nation seeking NCATE accreditation, most of whom were grappling with the "knowledge base" standard. In our earliest attempts to help teacher educators prepare their response to the standard, we followed the intent of the times, to prepare teachers who understood the findings from the process-product tradition. It was less than a year into some large-scale, jointly-sponsored, AACTE/NCATE national workshops that backlashes against this literature emerged. Many teacher educators at these national workshops seemed less interested in the knowledge base than in being able to gain accreditation. Slowly over time, criticisms could be heard, faintly echoing Peterson (1979), that the process-product research failed to grasp fully what really goes into teaching. Arguing with less precision than Peterson, many faculty in these workshops denied the existence of "a" knowledge base for teaching and teacher education, or at the least, of this particular knowledge base.

This was all a bit confounding to someone ostensibly on the campus to help the faculty prepare for accreditation. The search for a research-informed profession, along the lines Gage (1963) proposed and Medley (1979) described, was not nearly as important to many rank- and-file teacher educators. Faced with a high-stakes accreditation that required all program faculty to be "on the same page," with regard to the fundamental principles that guide their teaching in the program, was a daunting task from which relief was sought. Arguing for multiple knowledge bases appeared as one solution to the "one way to accreditation" approach in a field so historically emergent as research on teaching.

The Purposes of Education as Knowledge Bases

In many ways, the call for multiple knowledge bases could be traced to the more philosophical traditions from which teacher education grew. Quite often, discussions among program faculty as they were planning their NCATE knowledge base statement were grounded in analyses of the purpose of education and perspectives on what schools are for, what schools should become, and in what domains children should be learning. These discussions of philosophical perspective brought faculty members together to share their innermost feelings about the role and purpose of education, as they tried to find what grounded their program in what could be called a knowledge base.

Matters became a bit more complicated when it came time to address the NCATE standard completely. The NCATE standard includes a statement requiring the faculty to document their knowledge base with "current and established research." In the case of the process-product knowledge base, addressing this standard was a relatively easy task. In those instances where that literature was rejected, the knowledge base for the program would be supported with scholarship, sometimes of a high level, but without any research (in the traditional sense of the term) on the effectiveness of the practices associated with this philosophical orientation to promoting student achievement in any domain (cognitive, affective, social, emotional, etc.). In essence, "knowledge base" no longer meant process-product research. It now included philosophical treatises on the image of teaching that research connoted, as well as alternatives to the extant research. The definition of a knowledge base might have been expanded, but it was not necessarily strengthened, primarily due to the lack of research findings to support the validity of the championed perspective.

Over the years of conducting campus-based workshops, we watched faculty members prepare a knowledge base statement that would satisfy the needs of NCATE and which had fidelity with a view of teaching that reflected and accommodated the diverse membership of the faculty at the institution. To the credit of many of these teacher educators, we witnessed some rich discussions of teaching, and some inventive statements of principle to which the faculty would commit. We also came to see the struggle within the faculty as the negotiation of philosophical views on the purpose of education, and as one might surmise, these views were incredibly diverse, strongly held, and often taught in the collection of courses that characterized the teacher education program at the institution. The perspectives became so intriguing over time that we collected them as a way of thinking about the development of a program knowledge base. The following list of topics could be read in many ways, but perhaps it is easiest to look upon it as what professors of education around the country think the various purposes of education are and which could simultaneously serve as the knowledge base for a program, but certainly not as "the" knowledge base.

Examples of Purposes of Education

- Subject matter mastery
- Critical thinking/problem-solving skills
- Social participation skills
- Transmission of (multi)cultural values
- Development of self-esteem
- Development of creativity/imagination
- Preparation of the workforce
- Technology mastery
- Social justice
- Emancipation

- Perpetuation of a democracy
- Understanding the global community
- Knowledge navigation skills

This is a truncated list, but it captures what we heard on campuses around the nation of what could constitute knowledge bases for a professional education program. Simply restated, most teacher educators with whom we worked did not subscribe to the idea that a knowledge base for teacher education begins with an analysis of the research. Rather, it starts with a philosophy and a view of the child, the teacher, learning, and the school in the larger societal domain. The criticism we heard most often in the rejection of the process-product tradition is that the teacher is in charge, the learners are passive, and the school concentrates first and foremost (and we guess they mean *exclusively*) on improving standardized test scores. More often than not, this view was rejected for one of the other "knowledge bases" listed above as examples, or those found in one of the few compilations of knowledge base statements (Hall, et al., 1994). One can only wonder whether the lack of consensus, which this list represents, serves as evidence in support of the recent report by the Public Agenda (1997) that called professors of education "out of touch" with the realities of schools, or whether professors of education are fully cognizant of the shortcomings in contemporary schools and are posing alternative perspectives and preparing future teachers in these knowledge bases.

If the foregoing is a reasonably accurate portrayal of what happened on the way to a knowledge base for teacher education is at all accurate, then we can conclude that the concept of a "knowledge base," as practiced in preparation for NCATE accreditation, relies less on traditional research than it does on perspectives on the purpose of education. If this portrayal is reasonably accurate, then we also have to assess where we are as a field, what is achievable, what passes for knowledge, and what we should expect of ourselves.

THE PRESENT AND THE FUTURE

The Present

As this chapter began, it has been only 15 years since a body of knowledge on teaching that could be taught to others was codified. It was within that same amount of time that this literature was challenged for its narrow scope within the logical-positivist research tradition. But all that has occurred in the last 15 years should neither surprise nor frustrate us. It should remind us that the world outside the research community moves at a faster pace than it can respond. It should also remind us that too few education professors are researchers/scholars of that which they teach. Both of these are causes for concern and have implications for determining what passes for knowledge in teacher education.

The research which led to "the" knowledge base conducted in the 1970s, and perhaps best characterized by the Beginning Teacher Evaluation Studies mentioned earlier in this chapter, derived its energy from the Great Society movement of the period. The need to discover how to teach reading and math to second and fifth graders in lower socioeconomic schools was an important national goal. Moreover, it was argued that if we know how to help the children for whom learning is often difficult, then we could apply those findings to all children. Because of this single-minded purpose, little consideration was given to other purposes of education. Raising the floor for our most disadvantaged was the purpose and the foundation for the research. Other purposes of schools, such as critical thinking, social participation, technology, imagination and creativity, social justice, and the others listed above, were themes not central to this more pragmatic and utilitarian research agenda. The error in trying to generalize from these studies to all children has turned out to be as fatal as Freud generalizing to all people from a sample of middle-class women in Vienna. The researchers had the right instincts and the right intentions, and good data, but failed to consider the social context of knowledge and the limitations it creates on the dissemination of research. In this instance specifically, little consideration was given to the audience waiting to hear the results. What passes for knowledge in teacher education seems not to start with the research. It instead begins with the views of those who translate the broader array of professional knowledge for their students. The process-product research, while sound in some very fundamental ways, was found wanting because it failed to consider other purposes that education serves in society.

The failure of "the" knowledge base to survive a decade can also be attributed to other factors besides philosophical orientation. At the end of the 20th century in the United States, the rise of individualism, widely documented in both scholarly journals and the popular press, may have convinced professors of education that research ostensibly promoting generic teaching skills fails to see the teacher as an individual who constructs his/her own understandings of teaching. In my experience in working with teacher educators, this was a common theme paraphrased as, "with the proper experiences, our students will come to understand teaching." This view is particularly problematic because a profession is based on a body of accepted knowledge and skills. The process-product research uncovered some rather refined teacher behaviors that, it can be argued, shaped the study of teaching and informed teacher decision- making. The constructivist view of learning to teach questions the validity of these behaviors at best, and perhaps allows for them never to be constructed and built into teacher repertoire, at worst. This is a conundrum of enormous proportions, as it speaks directly to whether the social responsibility of demonstrated student achievement that accompanies teaching is exchanged for individualistic understandings of teaching that may have little to do with student achievement. It is possible, under this view, for a teacher education candidate to construct an image of teaching that lacks a well-developed conception of the power of classroom interactions and their relationships to student achievement. While this is problematic, the constructivist approach to learning to teach awaits some high quality empirical studies that capture the full effects of such a program. This is a challenge to all teacher educators who believe the process-product research was too narrow and who believe a more constructivist approach will educate well-prepared teachers.

Finally, the failure of "the" knowledge base to survive a decade may also attribute to the fact that as a profession teaching is in a period where research knowledge on teaching is undergoing a redefinition. It is not a drastic redefinition, such as the shift from the dominant view of effective teaching being based in the personality of the teacher to instructional materials and methods. It is a quieter, but richer, edefinition, from general knowledge to context-sensitive knowledge about teaching effectiveness. The particular challenge facing the research community is the identification of research methods that are more than idiosyncratic (mis)applications of proven methods, which capture the redefinition of teaching, and which remain focused on the social responsibility with which teaching is naturally beset. We seem a distance away from much-needed research methods. The most recent research concentrated on subject matter understanding is adding to a knowledge base for teaching that considers the contexts in which teaching occurs and the various purposes of education. While research on discipline-based teaching is an improvement over earlier and more general process-product research, it is insufficient in developing knowledge about teaching applicable to teacher education in the more rounded definition of teaching implied by the purposes of education above. From my perspective and experiences in the last 15 years, I conclude that we have momentarily lost our consensus definition of teaching and teacher education. It will take a great deal of effort to create the next one, although it is not impossible. It will, however, ask teacher educators and education researchers to work in ways they have not in the past. In fact, it will ask them to become one community of scholars, rather than two, which currently exist.

The Future

With regard to the future, I propose that in order for the research community and the teacher education community to achieve a measure of success vis-à-vis the world of practice, some longstanding practices will have to change.

First, the circle of practicing researchers will have to expand. The platitude that "20% of the people produce 80% of the scholarship" will have to change. The group that makes up the 20% joined that group by adopting the narrow views of teaching that predominated and set the agenda. This means that the rank-and-file teacher educators who rejected "the" knowledge base will be obligated to conduct research on their philosophical views regarding the purpose of education, holding it up to the public scrutiny of peers. It is insufficient to teach future teachers to behave in certain ways without validated research findings to support their position.

Second, widening the circle of active researchers presupposes well-articulated statements on the purpose of education that ground the preparation program. As noted briefly above, more often than not, "the" knowledge base was rejected because of its narrowness and its prescriptive nature. It was not rejected, in the experience of this author, because there were more compelling data elsewhere representing a more profound purpose of education, and in the community of scholars, this condition is unacceptable. The argument could be made that the worst side of scholarship in education schools was exposed by NCATE's inclusion of the knowledge base standard. In the world of scholarship, the decision should be based on the weight of the argument, and not because one or two faculty members resist the accreditation standard because they hold opposing philosophical orientations. A well-articulated knowledge base, along with a clarifying statement of its shortcomings *should*, in the world of scholars, provide the outline for faculty research and program development.

Third, we need to reinsert the measurement of student achievement, in all its forms, into all research on teaching. Along with the demand for clearly articulated philosophical perspectives and faculty who are themselves researchers, the need for studying the effectiveness of the practices derived from various views must be the focus of the research. This point is influenced by the external expectations to which education and education research must attend. University-based teacher education is under attack, and as a field, the scholarly community has mounted little evidence of its importance in the preparation of teachers. The general public wants to know whether university-based teacher education makes a difference. The devotees of "knowledge bases" are obligated to understand and make public their practices and their effects in educating educators. Arguing that "imagination" or "critical thinking" cannot be measured does not advance the creation of a profession or the growth and development of a professional practitioner. Nor does it strengthen the social contract for students who are well-educated upon high school graduation.

Finally, and perhaps this sums up the three preceding points, we must be ever mindful of the fact that society's demands for highly qualified teachers outruns the ability to provide them with the readiness to practice successfully as novices. The kinds of teachers implied in *What Matters Most* (National Commission on Teaching and America's Future, 1996) are knowledgeable of their disciplines and how to teach it to others. They are also thoughtful and analytic of their students as well as themselves. These are not new themes; they have been in the pages of journal articles, books, and handbooks over the last 10 years, and hundreds of authors have outlined what needs to be done next. The creation of knowledge to guide the education of teachers is a task teacher educators must take up regardless of philosophical persuasion. It is a part of the social contract.

In sum, there currently is no consensus on a knowledge base for teaching and teacher education. The process-product research tradition, for all its important contributions, was not accepted as the knowledge base. It was argued in this paper that the lack of consensus results from forces within the profession that are historic, for example, the inability to agree upon the purpose of education, and from general social forces that question the political nature of all knowledge and how it was derived. There are, however, opportunities to advance the profession of teaching and teacher education within what some might characterize as a "culture war," but real-

izing them will necessitate changes in the research community and among practitioners. The research community will need to expand, and it will need much clearer
articulations of good teaching than have been available heretofore. It will also have
to continue to attend to the importance of context in studying teaching and learning
in classrooms. Finally, the development of a knowledge base will require practicing
teacher educators to attend much more to an agenda of research that validates the
power of the philosophical persuasions they hold and teach to their future teachers.

NOTES

[1] In this essay, I am looking at the issue of the knowledge base for teaching as it affected
a teacher educator who was prepared in the late 1970s, was immersed in the process-product
traditions, and who continually adjusts to the changing definitions of teaching found in the literature. The citations are intentionally global and general to illustrate my experiences and,
hence, my argument.
[2] Terms like "effective teaching" and "teacher effectiveness" can be found in large number
throughout the subject indexes and proceedings of the annual meetings of AERA and AACTE,
thereby suggesting the mounting interest in establishing a body of knowledge on which the
profession could be built.
[3] William Gardner's presidency of AACTE had as the theme for its annual conference,
"What We Know and What We Need to Know." The intent here was to establish "the" knowledge base in the minds of practicing teacher educators, as well as the agenda for continuing
research to develop the knowledge base more completely.

REFERENCES

Anderson, L. W. (1989). *The effective teacher*. New York: Random House.
Arends, R. I. (1988). *Learning to teach*. New York: Random House.
Arends, R. I. (1992). *Learning to teach* (2nd ed.). New York: McGraw-Hill.
Berliner, D. C. (1979). Tempus educare. In P. Peterson & H. Walberg (Eds.), *Research on teaching* (pp. 120–135) Berkeley, CA: McCutchan.
Borko, H., Cone, R., Russo, N. A., & Shavelson, R. (1979). Teachers' decision making. In P. Peterson & H. Walberg, (Eds.), *Research on teaching* (pp. 136–160). Berkeley, CA: McCutchan.
Calderhead, J. (1987). *Exploring teachers' thinking*. London: Cassell.
Carroll, J. (1963). A model for school learning. *Teacher College Record, 64*, 723–733.
Carter, K. L. (1990). Teachers' knowledge and learning to teach. In W.R. Houston (Ed.), *Handbook of research on teacher education* (pp. 291–310). New York: Macmillan.
Clandinin, J., & Connelly, M. (1992). Narrative and story in teacher education. In T. Russell & H. Munby (Eds.), *Teachers and teaching: From classroom to reflection* (pp. 124–137). Washington, DC: Falmer Press.
Clark, C. M., & Peterson, P. L. (1986). Teacher and student cognitions. In M. C. Wittrock (Ed.), *Handbook of research on teaching* (3rd ed., pp. 255–296). New York: Macmillan.

Cooper, J. (Ed.). (1980). *Classroom teaching skills* (4th ed.). New York: D. C. Heath

Denham, C., & Lieberman, A. (Eds.). (1980). *Time to learn*. Washington, DC: National Institute of Education.

Dill, D. D. (1990). *What teachers need to know*. San Francisco: Jossey-Bass.

Duckworth, E. (1987). *The having of wonderful ideas*. New York: Teachers College Press.

Dunkin, M., & Biddle, B. (1974). *The study of teaching*. New York: Holt, Rinehart, & Winston.

Flanders, N. (1960). *Interaction analysis in the classroom: A manual for observers*. Minneapolis, MN: University of Minnesota College of Education.

Fosnot, C. (1989). *Enquiring teachers, enquiring learners*. New York: Teachers College Press.

Gage, N. L. (1963). Paradigms for research on teaching. In N. L. Gage (Ed.), *Handbook of research on teaching* (pp. 94–141). New York: Rand McNally.

Gage, N. L. (1978). *Scientific basis for the art of teaching*. New York: Teachers College Press.

Gage, N. L. (1985). *Hard gains in the soft sciences*. Bloomington, IN: Phi Delta Kappa.

Galluzzo, G., & Pankratz, R. (1990). Essential attributes of a program knowledge base. *Journal of Teacher Education, 41*(4), 7–14.

Good, T. L., & Brophy, J. E. (1996). *Looking in classrooms* (7th ed.). New York: Harper & Row.

Goodlad, J. I., Soder, R., Sirotnik, K. A. (Eds.). (1990). *The moral dimensions of teaching*. San Francisco: Jossey-Bass.

Grossman, P. L. (1990). *The making of a teacher: Teacher knowledge and teacher education*. New York: Teachers College Press.

Hall, G. E. (Ed.). (1994). *Analysis of teacher education knowledge base statements: The foundation for advancing teacher education into the 21st century*. Cedar Falls, IA: TECSCU.

Kindsvatter, R., Wilen, W., & Ishler, M. (1988). *Dynamics of effective teaching*. New York: Longman.

Medley, D. M. (1977). *Teacher competence and teacher effectiveness*. Washington, DC: American Association of Colleges for Teacher Education.

Medley, D. M. (1979). The effectiveness of teachers. In P. L. Peterson & H. Walberg (Eds.), *Research on teaching* (pp. 1–11). Berkeley, CA: McCutchan.

Medley, D., & Mitzel, H. (1963). Measuring classroom observation by systematic observation. In N. L. Gage (Ed.), *Handbook of research on teaching* (pp. 247–328). New York: Rand McNally.

McDiarmid, W. (1987). Why staying one chapter ahead doesn't work: Subject-specific pedagogy. In M. C. Reynolds (Ed.), *Knowledge base for beginning teachers* (pp. 193–205). Elmsford, NY: Pergamon.

McNair, K., & Joyce, B. R. (1978). *Teachers' thoughts while teaching: The South Bay study*. (ERIC Document Reproduction Service No. 191 979)

Murray, F. B. (Ed.). (1995). *The teacher educator's handbook*. San Francisco: Jossey-Bass.

National Commission on Teaching and America's Future. (1996). *What matters most*. Washington, DC: Author.

National Council for Accreditation of Teacher Education (1987, 1992, 1995). *Standards for accreditation*. Washington, DC: Author.

Peterson, P. L. (1979). Direct instruction reconsidered. In P.L. Peterson & H. Walberg (Eds.), *Research on teaching* (pp. 57–69). Berkeley, CA: McCutchan.

Peterson, P., Marx, R., & Clark, C. (1978). Teacher planning, teacher behavior, and student achievement. *American Educational Research Journal, 15*, 417–432.

Public Agenda. (1997). *Different drummers.* New York: Author.

Reynolds, M. (Ed.). (1989). *Knowledge base for beginning teachers.* Elmsford, NY: Pergamon.

Rosenshine, B. V. (1979). Content, time, and direct instruction. In P. L. Peterson & H. Walberg (Eds.), *Research on teaching* (pp. 28–56). Berkeley, CA: McCutchan.

Rosenshine, B. V. (1986). Teaching functions. In M. C. Wittrock (Ed.), *Handbook of research on teaching* (3rd ed., pp. 376–391). New York: Macmillan.

Schon, D. (1983). *The reflective practitioner: How professionals think in action.* New York: Basic Books.

Shulman, L. (1986). Those who understand: Knowledge growth in teaching. *Educational Researcher, 15*(2), 4–14.

Shulman, L. (1987). Knowledge and teaching: Foundations of the new reform. *Harvard Educational Review, 57,* 1–22.

Smith, D. (Ed.). (1983). *Essential knowledge for beginning educators.* Washington, DC: American Association of Colleges for Teacher Education.

United States Department of Education. *What works: Research about teaching and learning* (1986). Washington, DC: U.S. Government Printing Office.

Wang, M. C., Haertel, G. D., Walberg, H. J. (1993). Toward a knowledge base for school learning. *Review of Educational Research, 63*(3), 249–294.

Wineburg, S. S. (Ed.). (1990). The teaching and learning of history. *Educational Psychologist, 29*(2).

Wilson, S. M. (1990). The secret garden of teacher education. *Phi Delta Kappan, 72*(3), 204–209.

Wittrock, M. (Ed.). (1986). *Handbook of research on teaching* (3rd ed.). New York: Macmillan.

Yinger, R. (1986). Examining thought in action: A theoretical and methodological critique of research on interactive teaching. *Teaching and Teacher Education, 2*(3), 263–282.

Zeichner, K. L., & Gore, J. Teacher socialization. In W. R. Houston (Ed.), *Handbook of research on teacher education* (pp. 329–348). New York: Macmillan.

5

What Do Critical Ethnographies of Schooling Tell Us About Teacher Knowledge?

Amy C. McAninch
University of Missouri, Kansas City

Over the last 15 years, conceptions of teaching and teacher knowledge have shifted dramatically "from a view of teachers as the recipients and consumers of research to the current view of the teacher as producer or mediator of knowledge" (Richardson, 1994, p. 5). Richardson adds that research on teaching has likewise shifted from a focus on teacher behavior to the study of "how teachers make sense of teaching and learning" (p. 5). Narrative research, for example, reflects this new emphasis and frequently involves intensive study of a teacher's practice within the context of his or her life history (Carter, 1993; Elbaz-Luwisch, 1997). Perhaps the most influential work of this kind has been conducted by Clandinin (1985, 1989) and Connelly and Clandinin (1985, 1987, 1988, 1991), who engage in a form of classroom ethnography that roots teachers' curricular activities in a "narrative of experience" (1987, p. 495). In a highly collaborative and dialectic effort, Clandinin and Connelly work with individual teachers to construct a meaning-giving account of the teacher's curricular practices. The findings of this research—descriptions of teachers' personal practical knowledge—have been widely cited, even providing the rationale for curriculum innovation in teacher education.

One of the criticisms of Clandinin and Connelly's work is that the analysis and interpretation of teachers' personal practical knowledge is truncated. Commenting specifically on their work, Willinsky (1989) points out that their focus "on the individual's actions ... conceptually isolates the teacher's practice from their inescapable institutional element" (p. 251). Clandinin and Connelly's research, in other words, does not examine the broader social and institutional context within which teachers work as an object of inquiry. Thus, we cannot learn from their research if teachers' personal practical knowledge corresponds to their social and institutional realities or what the consequences of their personal practical knowledge are.

For this reason, it is useful to examine critical ethnographies of schooling for their contribution to our understanding of teacher knowledge. Because ethnographies can provide highly detailed information regarding teachers' understandings, as well as social and institutional facts, they provide an opportunity to complement the findings advanced by narrative researchers who give emphasis to life history and who see meanings as the object of study. To the extent that social structure and ideology may shape teachers' activities and understandings in ways that they do not fully understand, critical ethnographies of schooling may provide additional insight into teacher knowledge.

The significance of this investigation is twofold. First, ethnographies have been understudied for this purpose. Although rich ethnographic literature has developed parallel to teacher educators' interest in teacher knowledge and thinking, ethnographic studies have not been placed in juxtaposition with the characterization of teacher knowledge that has emerged from Clandinin and Connelly's work. Second, I believe an analysis of these studies will yield findings regarding teacher knowledge distinct from Clandinin and Connelly's studies. This examination will make clear the need for a theory or model of teacher knowledge and thinking that incorporates both social structure and biography in a more integrative manner than has previously been the case.

In this chapter, Clandinin and Connelly's work will be briefly explicated and their conception of teacher's personal practical knowledge will be reviewed. Their work, as a case of narrative research, illustrates well some of the strengths and weaknesses of this research genre. Next, critical ethnographies by Fine (1991), Grant and Sleeter (1996), Mehan, Hertweck, and Meihls (1986), Page (1991), and Wells and Crain (1997) will be examined. These leading ethnographies represent a variety of school contexts, including inner city, working class, and special education settings. Furthermore, they rely on different theoretical perspectives for the interpretation and analysis of findings. Also in this chapter, conclusions regarding the nature of teacher knowledge will be induced from these works and then compared to Clandinin and Connelly's findings. Finally, this chapter will conclude with a discussion of the implications of this work.

A CASE OF NARRATIVE RESEARCH: CONNELLY AND CLANDININ ON PERSONAL PRACTICAL KNOWLEDGE

Clandinin and Connelly seek to describe the knowledge teachers hold and manifest in practice. Personal practical knowledge is defined by Clandinin in the following way:

By "knowledge" in the phrase "personal practical knowledge" is meant that body of convictions, conscious or unconscious, which have arisen from experience, intimate, social and traditional, and which are expressed in a person's actions.... Personal practical knowledge is knowledge which is imbued with all the experiences that make up a person's being. (1985, p. 362)

Relying on Polanyi's (1958) work, Clandinin (1985) asserts that personal practical knowledge is neither propositional knowledge nor is it simply practical knowledge. Instead, it is a combination of both kinds of knowledge, blended by the teacher's own experiences and personality and expressed in teaching practice:

It is assumed that knowledge so defined is not found in lists of the contents of teacher education textbooks, workshop outlines, or teacher task analysis. These matters, of course, all have their part but such lists, with their categories of concepts, theories, facts, tasks, properties, and skills, do not define a teacher's personal practical knowledge. These lists of objective and definable content are leavened by one's personal and practical experience, subsumed, as Polanyi would say, in one's "subsidiary awareness" (Polanyi, p. 88). It is this personal and existential matrix that makes up what the teacher "knows" about teaching. (Clandinin, pp. 362–363)

In other words, personal practical knowledge has its source in experience and because it is largely tacit, it is "revealed through interpretations of observed practices over time and is given biographical personal meaning through reconstructions of the teacher's narratives of experience" (p. 363). Personal practical knowledge, in other words, is generated from, and embodied in, the actions of the teacher.

It should be clear from this description of personal practical knowledge that the term "knowledge" is not being used in the conventional sense. Fenstermacher (1994) has pointed out that Clandinin and Connelly are using the term "knowledge" here as a "grouping term," referring to a mix of cognitive, affective, and intuitive processes, a usage quite distinct from the traditional philosophical conception of knowledge as justified true belief. In other words, the term "knowledge" is applied as a catch-all label to subsume a wide variety of thinking/feeling outcomes, without a concern for justification. Indeed, Clandinin's (1985) interest is in capturing teachers' understandings of their own practice within the context of biographical narrative; she is not seeking "objective" truth or testable propositions. Thus, the elements of personal practical knowledge, discussed below, carry with them this special usage.

A key to understanding Clandinin and Connelly's work lies in the concept of "image," a component of personal practical knowledge. Based on Lakoff and Johnson's (1980) work on metaphor, Clandinin and Connelly maintain that teachers hold images that guide them in their future work. These images are derived from their personal and professional biographies, from a "narrative of experience" or their "narrative unity," and are used to interpret, and make sense of, future experiences. Clandinin (1985) emphasizes again that "image" does not refer to conceptual knowledge. Rather, "images are embodied and enacted. Their embodiment entails emotionality, morality, and aesthetics and it is these affective, personally felt and believed, meanings which engender enactments" (p. 363). Images are part of a larger narrative and are uncovered through careful observations and interviews with the teacher over time.

Clandinin and Connelly's methodology is highly collaborative, as the researcher and teacher work together, through a dialectic process, to construct and reconstruct the teacher's narrative unity. Narrative unity is another important concept in this work and has its source in the work of McIntyre (1981). As Connelly and Clandinin (1987) explain, "The notion of narrative unity is not merely a description of a person's history but a meaning-giving account, and interpretation of one's history and as such provides a way of understanding the experiential knowledge of classroom participants" (p. 131). Clandinin (1985) further explains:

> What we mean by unity is the union in a particular person in a particular place and time of all that he has been and undergone in the past and in the past of the tradition which helped to shape him. The notion of narrative unity is not merely a description of a person's history but a meaning-giving account, an interpretation, of one's history. We can see within the history of an individual a number of narrative unities. The notion of narrative unity allows us the possibility of imagining the living out of a narrative as well as the revision of ongoing narrative unities and the creation of new ones. (p. 365)

Clandinin (1985) illustrates the concept of "image" through her description of an elementary teacher named Stephanie. Through extensive observation and interviews, Clandinin inferred that Stephanie held an image of the "classroom as home" and that her curriculum activities could be interpreted as its manifestation. This image, Clandinin asserts, is derived from Stephanie's prior experience in school, where she herself felt alienated, from later experience as a teacher candidate and teacher, and from her personal life. Specific curriculum activities can be interpreted as corresponding with Stephanie's image and, according to Connelly and Clandinin (1985), illustrate the moral and emotional nature of personal practical knowledge. Thus, according to this research, teaching is in large part a living out of one's narrative unities. These narrative unities make teaching coherent and continuous for the teacher— they give meaning to the teachers' activities and indeed are how they "know" their classroom situation.

Aside from the images teachers hold, Clandinin and Connelly (1985) assert that teachers also know their classrooms through rhythms and cycles of the school year: "We use the term rhythm in the commonplace sense of something occurring repetitively, perhaps cyclically, and which has an aesthetic quality as performed" (p. 189). In Stephanie's case, cultural holidays lent a cyclic quality to the curriculum, as the class would be engaged in preparation for one holiday and then the next.

Finally, before moving on to an examination of ethnographies of schooling, it is useful to look at Clandinin and Connelly's rationale in developing this line of research. Clandinin specifically cites two reasons for her work. First, she notes that teachers are typically cast in a role in which they have been asked to carry out someone else's intentions, while their own intentions have been overlooked (1985, p. 364). Clandinin and Connelly write:

> We hope, thereby, to counteract in some small way those administrative, policy, and research traditions which deny a central voice for teachers in curriculum and instruction. Our intention is ... to enhance teachers' sense of authority amidst a predominantly prescriptive administrative, policy, and research environment. (1988, p. 269)

Therefore, their approach is deliberately *uncritical*. As they see it, their research task is to reconstruct the biographical meaning of curriculum acts from the standpoint of the individual teacher, rather than to evaluate or judge. They maintain a partial stance toward classroom practice, focusing solely on the problem of what the meaning of the event for the actor is and how those meanings constitute a form of knowledge. In fact, the categories "error" and "belief" are theoretically excluded from this theory of teacher knowledge (see Fenstermacher, 1994).

Second, citing Lortie (1975), Clandinin (1985) writes that there is a "popular belief that teachers as professionals do not possess a body of knowledge" (p. 364). For this reason, she avers, teaching does not enjoy the status of a full-fledged profession. Uncovering and documenting teachers' personal practical knowledge is a means to counter this stereotype of teachers. Thus, this research is in large part a repudiation of not only the traditional university researcher/teacher relationship, but also of the view of teaching as a profession without specialized knowledge. The idea that this conception of teacher knowledge is ultimately empowering to teachers will be discussed at the conclusion of this chapter.

In summary, through this mode of research, Clandinin and Connelly see personal practical knowledge as dynamic and evolving, rather than static. This knowledge is embodied and tacit, rather than explicit and conceptual. Personal practical knowledge has emotional as well as moral elements and is heavily biographical in the sense that one's personal experience plays a large, if not defining, role in teaching. In this sense, teaching is a very personal practice. Finally, conceiving of teaching as an ongoing expression of one's narrative unities renders teaching meaningful and continuous with prior experience. But in trying to define the knowledge particular to teachers, Clandinin and Connelly choose to advance a distinctly stilted conception of teacher knowledge since inquiry into the social context in which teachers' understandings are nested is deemed unnecessary. Thus, it important to investigate what this partial view of teacher knowledge does not reveal. In the next section, ethnographies of schooling will be examined for their insight into teacher knowledge.

ETHNOGRAPHIES OF SCHOOLING AND TEACHER UNDER-
STANDINGS: AN OVERVIEW OF THE STUDIES

As noted at the beginning of this chapter, ethnographies of schooling have generally not been analyzed for their insight into teacher knowledge, although many of them
contain rich descriptions of teachers' understandings within the context of specific
school and community contexts. The five ethnographies examined for this analysis
are listed in Table 5.1 below, which provides information on the author, title, context
of the ethnography, and focus of the study.

All of these works are concerned with social stratification and examine the cultural knowledge or belief systems, as well as the structural mechanisms, related to
educational outcomes. For example, relying on the work of Erickson (1986) and
Spindler (1982), Page (1991) explains:

> Meaning is both patterned and idiosyncratic: Individuals express the world creatively,
> but their creativity is shaped by durable social precepts, such as those concerning social
> class or academic differences. Accordingly, rather than assuming that humans are either
> radically free or that they follow uniform, predictive, social scripts, interpretive studies
> acknowledge and seek to explicate a structured sociocultural world within which vari-
> ation, choice, and human agency are predominant features. (p. 12)

Table 5.1.

Author(s)/Title	Context of the Ethnography	Focus of the Study
Grant & Sleeter/*After the School Bell Rings* (1996)	Working-class, Midwestern junior high school	Attempts to describe the cultural knowledge of teachers, students, and administrators regarding diversity and determinants of that knowledge.
Wells & Crain/*Stepping Over the Color Line* (1997)	St. Louis, Missouri, and surrounding suburban schools	Examines how students, teachers, policymakers, and other participants in the St. Louis desegregation case view the court-imposed plan.
Page/*Lower-track Classrooms: A Curricular and Cultural Perspective* (1991)	Eight lower-track classrooms in two junior high schools in a mid-sized, Midwestern city	Focuses on curriculum differentiation and its meaning for teachers and students.
Mehan, Hertweck, & Meihls/*Handicapping the Handicapped* (1986)	A school district serving a small coastal community in California	Examines the process by which students are referred to special education.
Fine/*Framing Dropouts* (1991)	A comprehensive high school in the Bronx borough of New York City	Examines the structures, policies, and practices related to school retention.

From this theoretical perspective, curriculum activities are not simply enactments of personal knowledge, but of social and cultural meanings as well, many of which are so common sensical that they are taken for granted and, therefore, are unexamined. The meanings attached to categories such as "low track" student, dropout, or African-American student are not "created anew" (Page, 1991, p. 12) by individual teachers working in their classrooms, but taken from the broader culture and used by teachers in their local situations. In other words, teachers "bring conventional, historical, and institutionalized precepts of membership and differences from their families, their pasts, the larger school, and a wider community" (Page, 1991, pp. 12–13). Thus, these works study meanings as personally negotiated and socially impinged phenomena that are distinct from the social realities to which they refer. Each ethnography will be considered in turn, beginning with the work of Carl Grant and Christine Sleeter (1996).

In *After the School Bell Rings*, Grant and Sleeter (1996) reported a study of the cultural knowledge and behavior of teachers, administrators, and students with respect to human diversity in a working-class, Midwestern junior high school in a town they call Rivercrest. Five Bridges Junior High School provided a rich opportunity to study diversity, since it had been mainstreamed and desegregated in 1976, several years before the study began. While 67.5 percent of the population was White, 28 percent of the students were Hispanic. Blacks, Asian Americans, and Native Americans also attended the school.

Relying on conflict theory and drawing on anthropological methods, Grant and Sleeter (1996) sought to describe the cultural knowledge of the various groups at Five Bridges, as well as account for the determinants of that cultural knowledge. Relying on Spindler (1982), they state that cultural knowledge includes "the structure and content of meanings shared by individuals within a social group, and the sentiments attached to meanings" (p. 10). Grant and Sleeter point out that to merely attend to meanings is not sufficient to understand a culture. One also has to examine what individuals do and attempt to grasp the structural determinants that shape both understandings and behavior. Finally, Grant and Sleeter inquired into the consequences of the cultural knowledge held at Five Bridges for equal educational opportunity. In other words, despite whatever rhetorical interest was manifested by the teachers at Five Bridges with respect to equality of opportunity, what consequences did their behavior have for students attending the school?

Grant and Sleeter (1996) found that many teachers at the school "seemed to equate ability to think with proficiency in reading, and lamented students' reading levels because that made it more difficult to transmit academic knowledge to them" (p. 99). This difficulty was exacerbated because core subjects, such as math and English, were organized around textbooks. Furthermore, teachers did not tend to inquire into sources or explanations for students' deficiencies in reading: "The teachers assumed this problem stemmed from a lack of motivation, impoverished home experiences or general lack of ability" (p. 99). In short, many teachers, but not all, formulated expectations for their students based on reading ability and social class. These expectations translated into instructional activities that emphasized low-level skills and few opportunities for analytic or critical thinking. Grant and Sleeter observed that generally the teachers did not treat students' low performance as problems for inquiry:

> What could be done to help the students achieve success? If the teachers concluded that the students did have ability and several of them believed this—we wonder why they did not try various teaching approaches until they figured out what approach would be best. Instead, they continued to teach the students as they had always taught them—boringly, and achieved the same degree of success—minimum. (p. 192)

Stereotypic thinking about social class also played a role in teachers' estimation of student aspirations. According to Grant and Sleeter (1996), teachers generally believed that students had no aspirations beyond the completion of high school. For example, one teacher commented:

> They are not really interested in a career that will take a long time to prepare for. That seems to be quite an overriding thing. I think that many of them feel that once they get through twelve years of school they will have accomplished something. There are some of them who will even doubt that they will make it that far. (p. 99)

But, through their interviews with students, Grant and Sleeter learned that many had intentions of pursuing a college education and a middle-class career.

Grant and Sleeter (1996) described several instances of dissonance between what teachers said and what they actually did. Teachers at Five Bridges engaged in curricular practices that seemed contrary to their own assertions about needed curricular changes. For example, while the teachers recognized the importance of engaging students in a variety of instructional activities, the majority of teachers relied on recitation followed by seatwork (p. 116). Many teachers rhetorically acknowledged the importance of a multicultural education, yet few teachers actually attended to diversity in their instruction. Although many teachers acknowledged that students preferred activities that called for active participation, as opposed to lecturing and note-taking, the teachers' instructional activities were dominated by the latter. Student note-taking seemed to be a primary means of covering subject matter. Several teachers expressed a faith that student note-taking of lecture notes or from blackboards would enhance mastery of subject matter. In short, the majority of teachers at Five Bridges engaged in stereotypic thinking and relied on those stereotypes in making judgments about instruction, which Grant and Sleeter describe as generally lacking the opportunity for analytic or critical thought.

Finally, with respect to diversity, the teachers generally maintained a "color-blind" perspective, allowing few opportunities to discuss race and ethnicity in the formal curriculum. Few teachers expressed an interest in learning more about the students' lives outside of school or incorporating student interests into the curriculum.

In a follow-up study that traced 24 of the Five Bridges students as they went on to high school, Grant and Sleeter (1996) found that the students' aspirations had effectively been smothered. They conclude that the heavy remedial focus and passivity on the part of teachers with respect to diversity helped generate these low outcomes. In Grant and Sleeter's terms, these teachers were "representatives of the status quo" (p. 189).

Interestingly enough, Grant and Sleeter (1996) argued that teachers' accounts of the determinants of their practice were probably not the strongest ones. They write,

> The teachers did not include personal backgrounds as determinants of their actions in classrooms. Several talked about incidents with people and social experiences.... Yet we know several things about the teachers' backgrounds that we believe are very important. Most were white and had been raised in totally or predominantly white communities. A little over half were from middle class backgrounds; few were from economically poor family backgrounds. (pp. 189–190)

The majority of the teachers at Five Bridges, whose backgrounds were White and middle class, did not transcend their own experience. The understandings that they acquired from the dominant culture regarding race, social class, and gender generally persisted, even in this multicultural setting.

Reba Neukom Page's *Lower-Track Classrooms* (1991) focuses on curriculum differentiation in a small sample of lower-track classrooms in two comprehensive high schools. Designated by the school district as "Additional Needs" classes, these classes served students who had either failed or were considered unable to succeed in regular-track classes. Page's interpretive analysis focuses on the meanings that students and teachers attach to differentiation and how the particular manifestation of tracking at these two high schools is linked to "broader precepts of social and institutional differentiation and membership, such as academic ability, age, race, class or gender" (p. x).

Like many of the teachers in *After the School Bell Rings*, teachers of the Additional Needs classes in this study engaged in stereotypic thinking about their low-achieving students. Generally, the consensus at Maplehurst, one of the schools studied, was that lower-track students were deficient both behaviorally and academically. According to Page (1991), the students were viewed as "troublemakers" (p. 39). Appeals to this stereotype, in Page's view, carried a functional value in that it allowed "Maplehurst teachers to comprehend ambiguously specified social and educational phenomena. It is a professional and cultural resource, which teachers use and re-create as they define students in Additional Needs classes" (p. 39). In other words, the social construction of the lower-class student at Maplehurst is an image that teachers draw upon to help them negotiate complexity and ambiguity in their work.

According to Page, a key mechanism for maintaining these stereotypes are teacher stories:

Instead of formal diagnoses, stories form the stuff of teacher talk, and Maplehurst teachers rely on anecdotes to communicate notions about students' academic ability ... fleetingly articulated in 5 minutes between classes or over a hurried half-hour lunch in the lounge or the departmental offices ... stories are convincing because of their specificity and their drama. (1991, p. 40)

Page adds that the stories are compelling and "virtually irrefutable, given their form" (p. 40), and that further discussion or consideration of evidence that challenges the story's point are not invited nor could they "counter the symbolic impact of the teacher's story" (p. 41).

Page (1991) notes that while teachers as professionals might be expected to appeal to objective information in diagnosing students academically, instead portraits of students are "anecdotal, informal, and shot through with contradictions" (p. 40). The majority of the stories told by the Additional Needs teachers negatively characterize students. Page cites the following example regarding a usually talkative high school freshman whose interaction with an Additional Needs teacher attained the status of a story:

One day he "surprised" his teacher by accurately and vividly recounting a biography of Jim Thorpe he had read recently. His teacher interpreted the detailed account not as fluency but as possible evidence of "perseveration," a learning disability in which attention is fixated. Thereafter, the mention of the student's name almost always provoked a repetition by the teacher of the Thorpe incident, with a negative interpretation of it. Retold around the faculty lounge, the story spread the lower-track student's character as "learning disabled." (p. 41)

In Page's view, teacher stories are a vehicle for typing students in largely negative ways, these "types" persisting in the face of disconfirming evidence. Teachers engage in typing when they infer a students' character on the basis of a few actions (1991, p. 41). These stories "reduce the data to a convenient corpus that confirms a negative image of Additional Needs students as a group" (p. 43).

Page (1991) asserts that teachers' reliance on the negative image of the lower-track student results in teachers rendering different interpretations of similar events in lower-track versus regular-track classrooms. Thus, errors in recall of factual information in regular education classes are taken to be "momentary aberrations that instructors can correct, but in lower track classes, such lapses often are cited as stigma that inhere in persons and the group" (p. 43).

Finally, it is worth emphasizing the previous point that "typing" often persists in the face of discrepant information. One of the virtues of Page's (1991) study is that she chose to study lower-track classrooms attended by a heterogeneous student population. While some of the students were indeed working class, the majority were middle class and included the children of professionals. Yet, in spite of this heterogeneity, Additional Needs teachers characterized the families of their students as homogeneously deficient. Page notes:

In anecdotes similar to those they tell about students' academic disabilities, Maplehurst teachers simplify their characterizations of students' family backgrounds. For Additional Needs students as a group, families are "disadvantaged," "single parent," "not in the picture," or "do not care about education."(pp. 45–46)

While Page observes that there are indeed students for whom these descriptors would be accurate, they are by no means accurate of the entire group. She adds that "Maplehurst teachers readily remark the influence of social class on students' school success, even though they do not specify an explicit theory of class conflict or have regular contact with students' families" (p. 46). As in *After the School Bell Rings*, teachers seemed content to rely on the image or stereotype, rather than investigate the social conditions of their students' lives outside of school. Since teachers have little power to remediate students' home lives, the image of the deficient home serves a scapegoat function. Page observes "teachers suggest that the best they can do is maintain control of students who are academically deficient and socially disadvantaged" (pp. 47–48).

In short, like the teachers in *After the School Bell Rings*, these teachers had not transcended the ideas related to social class, race, and gender that they had absorbed from the dominant culture.

In *Stepping Over the Color Line* (1997), Wells and Crain examine the historical and social context of the efforts to desegregate public schools in St. Louis, Missouri. The desegregation plan called for the interdistrict transfer of Black inner-city students into suburban schools. Part of their study consisted of interviews with a sample of teachers from four suburban counties that accept transfer students. Wells and Crain classified some suburban teachers as "resistant" to the court-ordered desegregation plan, contrasting them with "visionary" teachers who saw the plan as an opportunity to re-evaluate the curriculum for *all* students.

Wells and Crain (1997) write that resistant teachers focus on student deficits, which in their view are both academic and behavioral. These teachers tended to "conflate the needs of transfer students ... with their low estimation of the students' 'intelligence' or 'ability' to comprehend difficult material and grasp complex concepts" (p. 273). According to Wells and Crane, resistant teachers placed a strong emphasis on students' deficits, providing a rationale for a rigid tracking system. Thus, schools were resegregated internally. Contrary to the stereotype of Black transfer students being unmotivated and difficult to manage, Wells and Crain observe:

It is interesting that many of the suburban teachers emphasize the problems of teaching the low-track or "deseg" classes in these schools and the joys of teaching the high-track classes, full of supposedly eager, motivated, polite and courteous white suburban students—the best of the best. In our classroom observations we did not see huge differences between the behavior of low- and high-track classes, try as we did. (p. 275)

Wells and Crane are quick to point out that the transfer students were by no means well-behaved by traditional standards, but they were not as disruptive as the teachers characterized them to be. Furthermore, White students' disruptions tended to be glossed over. For these teachers, the period prior to desegregation constitute the "the glory days," when "their students were all white and all above average" (p. 267).

On the other hand, the educators that Wells and Crane label "visionary" viewed the court-ordered desegregation plan as an opportunity for professional growth and development. These teachers, rather than designating the pre-desegregation era as "the glory days," concluded that the curriculum was failing to meet the needs of all students, including many of the resident White students. While some of these educators challenged the dominant ideology with respect to intelligence, all of the visionary teachers supported detracking the schools. These educators sought to teach in a more multicultural manner, seeing the diversity of the student body as a resource. Issues such as inequality were brought to the forefront of the curriculum and attention to meeting the individual needs of the students was emphasized.

In *Handicapping the Handicapped*, Mehan, Hertweck, and Meihls (1986) follow students' academic careers through the special education referral system in schools serving a small West Coast community. An outstanding feature of this study is the use of videotape to record the interaction of all the participants in the study (the teacher with the referred student; the psychologist with the referred student; and referral committee members with each other). Participants' accounts of these interactions could then be compared or scrutinized in light of the videotape record.

In order to examine the mechanisms which prompt a teacher to refer a student to special education, Mehan, Hertweck, and Meihls (1986) contacted 27 teachers who had referred a total of 55 students to special education. After selecting 17 cases for analysis, the researchers videotaped the referred student engaged in representative classroom events. The researchers then invited the classroom teacher who made the referral to review the videotape with them and to recount the reasons why he or she referred the student. One of the key findings of this analysis is related to Page's (1991) discussion of typing. Mehan, Hertweck and Meihls found that teachers, as they were reviewing these tapes, would cite a small number of exemplar behaviors that marked the student for referral, rather than enumerate a long list of referral behaviors. These exemplar behaviors served as symbols or representatives of a referral category, such as learning difficulties. According to the researchers, the exemplars and the referral category were used to explicate each other:

> One or two instances of behavior exemplify, stand for, and document the referral category, and the category is represented and elaborated by the exemplars of behavior. This hermeneutic spiral of a part-for-whole, whole-for-part relationship (Mehan and Wood, 1975) is signaled in the teachers' discourse by expressions such as "That is a frequent response of his" or "So watch what he does during the videotape, it's typical."(p. 76)

Interestingly enough, while reviewing the videotape, the researchers saw instances of nonreferral students engaging in virtually identical behavior as the referral students. As the lower-track teachers at Maplehurst interpreted failure to recall factual errors differentially in Page's (1991) study, Mehan, Hertweck, and Meihls found that referral behavior is given varying intepretations:

That is to say, we encountered instances in which the teacher identified a certain set of categories of behavior as reasons for referral and identified some of them in the behavior of the referral student on the tape during viewing lessons. On the other hand, instances of the same sort of behavior are apparent in the behavior of other students in the same event on the tape, but the teacher does not identify them as instances of referral behavior, nor is the child identified as a referral student. (1986, p. 76)

Mehan, Hertweck, and Meihls (1986) conclude that the teacher's referral judgement is highly contextual; that is, individual events, such as a student hitting another student, are considered in the context of the specific circumstances surrounding the action. They write, "It appears that the teacher's decision to refer students is only partially grounded in the student's behavior. It is grounded also in the categories that the teacher brings to the interaction, including expectations for academic performance and norms for appropriate classroom conduct" (pp. 86–87). In addition, according to the researchers, "Subjective interpretation is a mediating force in social and educational life. The educators in our study are not perceiving students' behavior directly. Their perceptions are mediated by categories that are provided by the culture and experience" (p. 155).

Finally, Michelle Fine's (1991) *Framing Dropouts* examines the attrition of high school students from a comprehensive high school in the Bronx borough of New York City, which at the time maintained a graduation rate of approximately 20 percent. In a context that Fine describes as totally disempowering to teachers, she asserts that teachers searched for belief systems that would render their experience intelligible in the face of the school's overwhelming failure. Interestingly enough, Fine notes that these belief systems assumed a defensive posture and that they "quickly calcified and disallowed the emergence of disconfirming evidence," (p. 155) a theme echoed in the work of Grant and Sleeter (1996), Page (1991), and Wells and Crain (1997).

Fine (1991) uncovered five belief systems, the most voiced of which were: "Things can't change" and "I do the best job I can in my classroom." As Fine explains, in the face of alienation and disempowerment, many teachers retreat to their classrooms. These belief systems functioned, in Fine's view, to "freeze, rationalize, and ultimately ensure institutional failure" (p. 157).

One of the most interesting insights in Fine's study is how the school inhibited both teachers and students from a process Fine calls "naming":

What became apparent was a structural fear of *naming*. Naming involves those practices that facilitate critical conversation about social and economic arrangements, particularly about inequitable distributions of power and resources.... The practices of administration, the relationships between school and community, and the forms of pedagogy and curriculum applied were all scarred by the fear of naming, provoking the move to silence. (1991, p. 34)

As an example, discussion of health and other social problems facing students and their families were marginalized into hygiene class or, as Fine described it, psychologized and treated as personal problems that required treatment by a school counselor. A biology teacher who attempted to address the issue of alcoholism in her class was reprimanded for including "extraneous" materials (p. 44). In this way, teachers and students both were "silenced" and discouraged from inquiry into their social conditions.

In conclusion, many teachers hold stereotypic images of students, a manifestation of unreflective thinking and that these stereotypic images are trenchant and immune to revision in the face of discrepant information. Page's (1991) analysis casts doubt on the idea that images provide the teachers' practice with coherence, yet they do serve a nominally functional value in interpreting and guiding practice in an ambiguous context. According to Page, teacher stories about students are a perpetuating mechanism of these stereotypes. Further, these stereotypes appear to have all the qualities that Clandinin (1985) attributed to classroom images, such as "classroom as home." These stereotypes are tinged with affect and emotion, have moral ramifications, and are embodied and enacted in the classroom. Because the stereotypes drawn from our dominant culture are so common sensical, they remain largely tacit as well. Thus, one conclusion that can be drawn about the majority of teachers described in the studies previously examined is they tend to have absorbed the prevailing or dominant view of social reality. For example, references or attributions to social class, as Page observed, are made in the absence of any evidence of a critical understanding of social class or class structure. Most of these teachers engage in unreflective thinking in the form of stereotyping with respect to race, class, and gender, although both Grant and Sleeter (1996) and Wells and Crain (1997) document some exceptions to this generalization. What is needed is a deeper examination of the factors that enabled these teachers to adopt a more critical stance toward social arrangements as they existed and to question prevailing institutional arrangements.

The second observation is that the teachers in these studies committed inferential errors based on these stereotypes, which carried negative consequences for their students. Thus, the image of "lower-track student as deficient," or "transfer student as academically and behaviorally deficient" as a form of prejudice resulted in policies that adversely affected educational outcomes. As already noted, Clandinin and Connelly's (1985) conception of personal practical knowledge cannot theoretically account for errors or mistakes in judgment. Furthermore, it has no way of discriminating between teachers who are guided by these images, as well as the very different images that guide the work of teachers that Wells and Crain (1997) call "visionary." For Clandinin and Connelly, it is all personal practical knowledge.

DISCUSSION

The topic of this chapter is the question: What do ethnographies of schooling tell us about teacher knowledge? The premise of this chapter is that ethnographies, which distinguish between meanings and the facts from which they arise, might inform conceptions of teachers' knowledge beyond Clandinin and Connelly's research, which focuses solely on finding biographical meaning in the classroom actions of individual teachers. As we have seen from an analysis of these ethnographies, most teachers, like most members of our culture, have adopted precepts about race, class, and gender from the dominant culture. Reflected in their practices are stereotypes and accounts of social reality that are hegemonic, since they are constituted of strands of dominant ideology and translated (see Page, 1991) into local contexts. As teachers tell stories, engage in low-level instruction, form low expectations for working-class or minority students, and so on, these apparently self-evident understandings are reified and are immune from modification, even in the face of disconfirming information. In short, the majority of teachers in these ethnographies generally do not have a coherent comprehension of the social world, and Clandinin and Connelly, in their efforts to bolster the teachers' authority and show that teachers are knowledgeable, have endorsed this mystification with the honorific term "knowledge" (see Fenstermacher, 1994).

By focusing on the question of how teachers know their classrooms, detached from any connections to the social and institutional context in which that classroom is nested, Clandinin and Connelly protect the teachers' practice from scrutiny and in doing so perform a legitimating function. Yet, as much as they would like to uncouple the teachers' acts from their social context, the teachers' actions are unintelligible without it. We literally do not know what the teachers' activities mean—or what their meanings mean—until we can connect them to broader social and institutional context and inquire into their consequences.

A concept borrowed from the work of historian John C. Miller (1977) is particularly apt. Miller, a biographer of Thomas Jefferson, noted that Jefferson was able to make assertions about the rights of man to freedom and the pursuit of happiness, while virtually not acknowledging the institution of slavery. In Miller's terms, Jefferson maintained a "convenient defect of vision" (p. 96), which allowed him to pronounce lofty principles while ignoring the reality facing Black people in the new republic. This defective vision, in Miller's view, served a protective function in obscuring present social conditions and "tended to diminish the need for the kind of incessant, dedicated, and uncompromising action that had distinguished Jefferson's career as a revolutionary" (p. 97).

Clandinin and Connelly assert a convenient defect of vision regarding teacher knowledge that serves a similar protective and cloaking function. This defect protects social arrangements as they exist for the sake of positing teachers as infallible. Their work provides no means of distinguishing the actions and understandings of teachers who engage in stereotyping and social control behavior from those who are reflective and serve democratic ends. For this reason, Clandinin and Connelly's non-judgmental stance toward teachers' practice is decidedly biased, favoring the social order as it exists. Like personalistic teacher education programs (see Feiman-Nemser, 1990) or child-centered progressive education, "personal practical knowledge" suffers from a relativism which is engendered by omitting, to borrow a phrase from Counts, "one-half of the landscape" (1932, p. 4), which is the social side.

This discussion concludes with two observations. First, while these ethnographies provide evidence that the majority of teachers did not have a reflective social ontology, it is important to point out that schools of education have generally not stressed the critical analysis of social structures, institutions, and social precepts. As Macedo (1993) points out, issues of race, ideology, and ethics are not studied rigorously in teacher education programs. In most, the study of the social foundations, whose task it is to promote a critical understanding of school and society, usually constitutes no more than 3 hours out of 120 hours or more of coursework. Some survey evidence reported by Shea, Sola, and Jones (1987) suggests that social foundations courses are increasingly taught by professors from fields outside the foundations (such as educational administration), or taught by adjuncts without a degree in the field. These staffing and programmatic decisions weaken the chances that teacher candidates will develop a critical and reflective view of social reality, rather than merely relying on common sensical understandings absorbed from the dominant culture.

Second, we need a theory of teacher knowledge that is less driven by the quest to legitimate whatever a teacher does and more intent on seeking out how we can conceptualize and recover the wisdom that teachers do develop through their experience. As a first step, teacher educators in their discussions of teacher knowledge need to stop referring to the findings of Clandinin and Connelly's work as evidence of teacher knowledge. To do so is to commit not only a dangerous equivocation, but also to endorse their "convenient defect of vision." It is difficult to understand how endorsing the faulty social understandings of teachers can be a means to empowerment and enhanced status. Ultimately, a true advance in understanding what teachers know will need to come about through a more realistic discourse than the one forwarded by Clandinin and Connelly.

REFERENCES

Carter, K. (1993). The place of story in the study of teaching and teacher education. *Educational Researcher, 22*(1), 5–12, 18.

Clandinin, D. J. (1985). Personal practical knowledge: A study of teachers' classroom images. *Curriculum Inquiry, 15*(4), 361–385.

Clandinin, D. J. (1989). Developing rhythm in teaching: The narrative study of a beginning teacher's personal practical knowledge of classrooms. *Curriculum Inquiry, 19*(2), 121–141.

Clandinin, D. J., & Connelly, F. M. (1987). Teacher's personal knowledge: What counts as "personal" in studies of the personal. *Journal of Curriculum Studies, 19*(6), 487–500.

Clandinin, D. J., & Connelly, F. M. (1988). Studying teachers' knowledge of classrooms: Collaborative research, ethics, and the negotiation of narrative. *The Journal of Educational Thought, 22*(2a), 269–282.

Clandinin, D. J., & Connelly, F. M. (1991). Narrative and story in practice and research. In D. A. Schon (Ed.), *The reflective turn* (pp. 258–281). New York: Teachers College Press.

Connelly, F. M., & Clandinin, D. J. (1985). Personal practical knowledge and the modes of knowing: Relevance for teaching and learning. In E. Eisner (Ed.), *Learning and teaching the ways of knowing* (pp. 174–198). Chicago: University of Chicago Press.

Connelly, F. M., & Clandinin, D. J. (1987). On narrative method, biography and narrative unities in the study of teaching. *Journal of Educational Thought, 21*(3), 130–139.

Elbaz-Luwisch, F. (1997). Narrative research: Political issues and implications. *Teaching and Teacher Education, 13*(1), 75–83.

Erickson, F. (1986). Qualitative methods in research on teaching. In M. Wittrock (Ed.), *Handbook of research on teaching* (3rd ed., pp. 119–161). New York: Macmillan.

Feiman-Nemser, S. (1990). Teacher preparation: Structural and conceptual alternatives. In W. R. Houston, M. Haberman, & J. Sikula (Eds.), *Handbook of research on teacher education* (pp. 212–233). New York: Macmillan.

Fenstermacher, G. (1994). The knower and the known: The nature of knowledge in research on teaching. *Review of Research in Education, 20*, 3–56.

Fine, M. (1991). *Framing dropouts*. New York: State University of New York Press.

Grant, C., & Sleeter, C. (1996). *After the school bell rings* (2nd ed.). Philadelphia: Falmer Press.

Lakoff, G., & Johnson, M. (1980). *Metaphors we live by*. Chicago: University of Chicago Press.

Lortie, D. C. (1975). *Schoolteacher: A sociological study*. Chicago: University of Chicago Press.

Macedo, D. P. (1993). Literacy for stupidification: The pedagogy of big lies. *Harvard Educational Review, 63*(2), 183–206.

McIntyre, A. (1981). *After virtue: A study in moral theory*. Notre Dame, IN: University of Notre Dame Press.

Mehan, H., Hertweck, A., & Meihls, J. L. (1986). *Handicapping the handicapped*. Stanford, CA: Stanford University Press.

Mehan, H., & Wood, H. (1975). *The reality of ethnomethodology*. New York: Wiley Interscience.

Miller, J. C. (1977). *The wolf by the ears*. New York: The Free Press.

Page, R. N. (1991). *Lower-track classrooms: A curricular and cultural perspective*. New York: Teachers College Press.

Polanyi, M. (1958). *Personal knowledge*. Chicago: University of Chicago Press.

Richardson, V. (1994). Conducting research on practice. *Educational Researcher, 23*(5), 5–10.

Shea, C. M., Sola, P. A., & Jones, A. H. (1987). Examining the crisis in the social foundations of education. *Educational Foundations, 2*, 47–57.

Spindler, G. (1982). General introduction. In G. D. Spindler (Ed.), *Doing the ethnography of schooling: Educational anthropology in action* (pp. 1–13). New York: Holt, Rinehart, & Winston.

Wells, A. S., & Crain, R. L. (1997). *Stepping over the color line*. New Haven, CT: Yale University Press.

Willinsky, J. (1989). Getting personal and practical with personal practical knowledge. *Curriculum Inquiry, 19*(3), 247–264.

6

Knowledge of Subject Matter*

James D. Raths
University of Delaware

INTRODUCTION

This chapter advances a conceptualization of two components of the knowledge base of teaching by building on the seminal work of Shulman (1986) and his colleagues (Grossman, 1990; Wilson, Shulman, & Richert, 1990), among others. Specifically, subject matter knowledge and pedagogical content knowledge are explored. As the essays in this monograph attest, there has been a significant change in the thinking of teacher educators about what constitutes these forms of knowledge and their implications for teacher education. For example, the idea that teachers transmit content knowledge to students is now commonly derided as "banking" education, borrowing a metaphor from Paolo Friere (1970, p. 59). In contrast with the growing interest in constructivism, teacher educators increasingly see knowledge as something that students themselves create. It is the key argument of this chapter that both groups, traditionalists and constructivists, must attend to helping students understand why some propositions or constructions are more warranted than others; that is, a major aspect of content knowledge for teaching is knowledge of justification itself. The first part of this essay rehearses a traditional definition of knowledge and illustrates its implications for subject matter knowledge. The second part extends the discussion to pedagogical content.

---

* I acknowledge the helpful criticism concerning earlier drafts of this chapter received from Professor Amy McAninch, University of Missouri, Kansas City; Professor Hugh G. Petrie, State University of New York at Buffalo; Professor Robert Ennis, University of Illinois; and many others.

SECTION ONE: SUBJECT MATTER KNOWLEDGE

One of the basic tenets about teaching is that teachers must know their subject matter. As Brown (1978) sees it, one of the principal responsibilities of teachers is *to give* students a better understanding of the content (emphasis added; p. 7).[1] Using the metaphor of "giving," we are reminded that teachers cannot give a student something they do not have. From a different perspective, Scheffler (1969) reminds us that teaching is a "triadic relation, describable by the form 'A teaches B to C,' where 'B' names some content, disposition, skill, or subject" (p. 260). Thus, Scheffler notes, "no one teaches anybody anything unless he teaches him something" (p. 260). This emphasis upon the importance of the "something" is reflected in almost all the recent reform proposals in teacher education, which generally forward at least two premises about subject matter knowledge. The first premise is that effective teachers know more about their subject matter than ineffective teachers; and the second asserts that a significant number of today's teachers do not know enough about their subject matter area—a factor contributing to placing our "nation at risk" (National Commission on Excellence in Education, 1983). These views are reflected in the following sample of prominent recommendations having to do with teachers' subject matter knowledge:

> Persons preparing to teach should be required to meet high educational standards, to demonstrate an aptitude for teaching and to demonstrate competence in an academic discipline. (National Commission, 1983, Recommendation D, Paragraph 1)

> All prospective teachers, as part of their liberal education, should be educated in at least one academic major. This is as true for the person who will teach first grade as it is for the person who will teach high school physics. (National Commission for Excellence in Teacher Education, 1985, p. 15, fn)

> The undergraduate years [in teacher education programs] should be devoted to a broad liberal education and a thorough grounding in the subjects to be taught. (Task Force on Teaching as a Profession, 1986, p. 73)

A similar position is also asserted by Wilson, Shulman, and Richert (1990):

> Because the goals of instruction include the transmission of knowledge and understanding to students, the question of what type of subject matter knowledge is needed for teaching is a compelling one. Intuitively, one would think that the effectiveness of any teaching is dependent, to some extent, on what the teacher knows about the subject matter to be taught. (p. 105)

While it has long been asserted that teachers need subject matter knowledge, it is unclear exactly what constitutes competence or thorough grounding in a teaching field. Subject matter knowledge is taken to be a vital part of teachers' knowledge, but the concept itself has been taken for granted and left poorly delineated. How would we discern a teacher with subject matter competence from one with inadequate subject matter knowledge?

For those engaged in the evaluation of teachers, this issue is of practical as well as theoretical importance. The criterion "subject matter knowledge" is frequently found on checklists and ratings used in both formative and summative teacher evaluation. All too often, we suspect, supervisors rate teachers "unsatisfactory" if, and only if, they have too frequently made some gross error pertaining to the content they are teaching. The standard for adequate content knowledge thus becomes the absence of factual gaffes, a minimal measure by any account.

At the outset, the idea that subject matter knowledge consists of facts or information alone is rejected. This conception of knowledge, which Dickens (1966) so effectively burlesqued in *Hard Times*, is a powerful legacy of the common school era. Just as Mr. Gradgrind saw his students as vessels to be filled with facts and not with understandings, teachers of the 19th century assumed the role of "drillmaster," leading students through tedious recitations of facts (see Finkelstein, 1986). Nevertheless, Whitehead noted in his discussion of the aims of education that "scraps of information have nothing to do with it" (1929, p. 90). Dewey (1910) commented in *How We Think* that "the aim often seems to be ... to make the pupil what has been called a 'cyclopedia of useless information'" (p. 221). If calls for more subject matter knowledge for teachers result in simply their acquisition of more facts pertaining to a particular field of study, then little qualitative improvement in teaching is likely to result.

A richer conception of subject matter knowledge might lead the way to improved practices in teacher education and teacher evaluation, but may also inform the disciplines which traditionally have carried the responsibility for the subject matter preparation of teachers. This paper will focus on what we think is a vital part of subject matter knowledge: knowledge of how knowledge is generated and claimed.

What is Knowledge?

First, in order to address the question about what teachers need to know concerning content, we need to ask, "What is knowledge?" Of course, philosophers have answered this question in many different ways and it would be difficult in this space to review all the different schools of epistemological thought. Instead, we chose to start our inquiry with Scheffler's (1965) work. We selected this perspective because it is rich in implications and because it poses significant issues to explore for those of us concerned with content knowledge. In the following paragraphs the main tenets of Scheffler's perspective are outlined, followed by a discussion of several of its implications for developing a fuller conception of content knowledge.

In a classic example of conceptual analysis, Scheffler (1965) describes a tripartite set of criteria that would be met if, and only if, we know something. The first criterion is: The knowledge claim is believed. Scheffler notes, "This condition stipulates that if X knows that Q, he believes that Q" (p. 75). According to this view, for us to claim that "Bill knows that the North won the Civil War," it is a necessary but not sufficient condition that Bill actually believes that the North won the Civil War. In other words, knowledge attributions require belief attributions as well.

Scheffler's (1965) second criterion is the evidence condition: If X knows that Q, he must have justification for Q. In other words, X must be able "to back up [his] belief [in Q] in a relevant manner, to bring evidence in its support, or to show that one is in a position to know what it affirms" (p. 9). This evidence condition separates knowing *in the strong sense* from knowing *in the weak sense*. Knowing in the strong sense requires the provision of reasons or other kinds of evidence to support the knowledge claim: it requires understanding why something is so. It therefore eliminates the case of attributing knowledge to someone who may indeed "know" something that is true, but for the wrong reasons or for no reason. In the weak sense, X may know that the North won the Civil War because he believes it and because it is true (a condition we will discuss below), but for X to know that the North won the Civil War in the strong sense would require more: it might require the ability to support this claim with knowledge of battles won and lost or the surrender at Appomattox, its source.

There are a number of very different sources which can serve to justify knowledge besides authority; several are described below, including analytic (a priori) and empirical (a posteriori) procedures. This second criterion for knowledge works to eliminate knowledge claims that may be right for the wrong reasons. Without learning about the score, I might simply "know" that the Yankees lost the game played earlier today. This assertion would not qualify as knowledge, even though it were true, because its source is not sufficient to justify it. The beliefs given as knowledge claims under the first criterion might be justified as follows:

- Most distinguished historians agree that the North won the Civil War.
- Since 22 can be factored into the form 2 times 11, it meets the definition of an "even number."

Do teachers present ideas or understandings to their students that they may believe are true, but which they cannot justify? The answer to this question is not rhetorical. The answer is not clear.

The third criterion in Scheffler's analysis is the belief advanced as a knowledge claim is true. This condition makes the concept of knowledge quite complex, because we do not have in our culture a litmus test for truth. The school's stakeholders cannot insist that teachers only share with their students understandings that are *true*. The truth of an assertion can be justified, but rarely established. As Brandon (1987) points out, we are aware that much of the knowledge that was taught to students in 1900, to pick an arbitrary year as an example, is not accepted as true today. And, he states, there is nothing "cognitively special about the present moment" (p. 4). It is likely that we will be teaching our students at least some understandings that are deemed as true today, but which will be discredited tomorrow. Indeed, it is probable that within a given time period, for instance during times of paradigm shifts in particular fields, two or more knowledge claims that are mutually contradictory could be justified as true. Do teachers engage their students only with ideas that are true? Again, the question is not rhetorical—almost certainly they do not.

It is important to note that Scheffler (1969) distinguished between knowing in a weak sense and knowing in the strong sense: We can know in the weak sense by satisfying the first and second criteria of knowledge, while knowing in the strong sense requires meeting all three of the criteria cited above.

It is interesting to note that some philosophers have found some dissatisfaction with the tripartite definition of knowledge and it too is subject to modification as scholars become more sophisticated about the concept.[2]

Implications for Teaching

The first implication stemming from this analysis of "knowledge" is that it is very difficult for any of us, as teachers, to claim that we are teaching the truth. One of the ground rules of educational discourse advanced by Edwards and Mercer (1987) is: "Try to make your contribution one that is true." Given that injunction, teachers can advance understandings as current explanations. That is, instead of saying that "diet influences health," a teacher could say that the current explanation concerning the relationship between diet and health is that certain eating habits contribute to well-being. This sort of tentativeness is not an effort to be evasive, but to contribute to the educational discourse in the classroom in a truthful manner.

The second implication is that the manner in which we present current understandings and explanations is dependent in significant ways upon the sources we have drawn upon to justify the beliefs we are sharing with our students. Assume for a moment that teachers intend to teach understandings to their students that they believe are true. What are the sources of their justifications? There are perhaps three prime sources of justification of knowledge that serve teachers well in the classroom: (1) authority; (2) personal experiences; and (3) standard procedures of inquiry.[3] The latter include both empirical (a posteriori) processes and analytic (a priori) processes. In the paragraphs below, each of the sources of knowledge is discussed in terms of its implications for demonstrating teachers' knowledge of subject matter in their teaching.

Authority as a Source of Justification

Much of the subject matter teachers teach to their students is derived in the main from what others have told them. The "others" might include their teachers, elders, parents, or the books they have read. In effect, teachers justify their beliefs in terms of the credibility of these sources. For example, no teacher knows for sure from first-hand experience that the Earth is round. Presumably, teachers have assumed that was the case from the first time they heard stories about Christopher Columbus. Do teachers know the names of Columbus's three ships? How is their knowledge justified? They probably justify their knowledge of the names of Columbus's ships on the basis of authority. And just as surely as authority is a source of truth, it is also a source of error. None of the sources available to teachers is a road to the Truth.

Assume for the moment that teachers would like their students to understand that the Constitution of the United States reflects a philosophy concerning the nature of man.[4] Where did they learn that was the case? They might have heard it from a charismatic lecturer in high school who asserted it as true. (Perhaps no one in the classroom was disposed at that time to ask about the justification of such an assertion.) What should teachers do if they intend to teach this "understanding" (or an analogous one) to their students?

1. It would be important to identify the source of the belief they are presenting to their students.
2. It would be important to identify the credentials of the source, as well as specify why it is reasonable to accept the authority as credible.
3. It would be important to identify other interpretations of the Constitution, if they are known, or to posit that other interpretations are possible.
4. It would be important to invite students to consider the views, to challenge them, and to seek out the arguments that might sustain or refute the position.

In sum, as teachers understand that they are teaching their students something about which they do not have direct knowledge, but which they are merely passing on, teachers take steps to make it clear to them exactly what they are doing.[5] In this example, the argument teachers elected to share with the class about the Constitution is not "theirs," but it belongs to an authority that has been cited. Disputes in class about this view are not between teachers and students, but between the authority the teachers have elected to share with them and their students.

Experience as a Source of Justification

Sometimes, teachers present our students with understandings that are rooted in their own personal experiences. Based on their successes with it, teachers teach their students the "best way" to solve rate-time and distance problems. They teach them a "proper" approach for writing essays. These precepts and others of this genre that teachers elect to teach may stem from authorities, and thus be justified by the credibility of their sources as outlined above. However, the ideas teachers teach in this regard and others may arise instead from their own intuitive interpretations of their personal experiences. According to Belenky, Clinchy, Goldberger, and Tarule (1986), "Truth for subjective knowers is an intuitive reaction—something experienced, not thought out, something felt rather than actively pursued or constructed" (p. 69). People using subjective processes prize their own observations, and their own experiences. In addition, they frequently reject authority and books and other traditional sources of knowledge based on authority. As with the blind acceptance of authority, this form of justification can be quite dangerous. It leads ultimately to a relativist view of truth: What is true for me may not be true for you, and each of our versions is equally valuable. If this view about knowledge and truth is taken to its extreme, there would be no intellectual or academic rationale for having schools. The understandings that students acquire in their neighborhoods as a process of growing up would be as valid as any taught in school. Furthermore, justification of action or belief could devolve into an "I did it because I felt like it" attitude. While some teachers may use intuition or feeling as a basis of knowledge, all teachers must be fully aware of the problems with this approach.

It is not unusual for teachers to share insights or intuitions with their students. Their insights are frequently products of their own personal experiences and observations. Very often, teachers resort to storytelling to convey to their students the understandings they are interested in sharing. For example, if a teacher is a veteran of the Korean War, he or she might want to explain to his or her students what it was really like in Korea during the early 1950s. The account would be a narrative of personal experiences and personal observations supported by claims such as "I was really there." What should teachers do if they intend to teach understandings to their students that are justified by appeals to firsthand experiences?

1. It would be important to remind their students that any one person's experiences are necessarily limited.
2. It would be important to give emphasis to the idea that interpretations of a subjective nature need to be squared with other accounts, other interpretations of persons who were present.
3. It would be important to qualify the claims embedded in the narrative with disclaimers such as "as I saw it...," "from my perspective...," or "I felt that..."
4. It would be important to invite students to read or search for other interpretations of the Korean War by those who have studied it from afar or who wrote of their own insights based on personal experiences in Korea at that time.
5. It would be important to emphasize that some interpretations are more accurate than others.

If teachers were to invoke these prescriptions in their teaching on the occasions they were sharing understandings that were justified by personal experiences, they would be demonstrating to an observer that they understood the difference between subjective justifications of knowledge and other sources of justification and the implications of those differences for teaching.

Procedure as a Source of Justification

Teachers might present to their students understandings that can be demonstrated in class through experiments or through logic. For example, teachers might feel confident teaching the process of the generation of oxygen in chemistry, since students can replicate the procedure themselves in the laboratory. Also, teachers might teach that the sum of the interior angles of a triangle in a plane is 180 degrees, since the proof is available to students. These examples suggest there are at least two classifications of standard procedures. The first category is the approach of the scientist, with knowledge claims resting upon the findings of experiments. The second has to do with the application of logic and reasoning to problems, independent of data.

Empirical (a posteriori) procedures. Here, persons justify knowledge claims by making use of procedures to measure, test, observe, and induce conclusions. The interpretations of their procedures are qualified by saying: "The results of my procedures support the claim that...." Proof is not available to persons using empirical procedures. They only generate support for or disproof of knowledge claims. Thus, science teachers can support the claim that an acid mixed with a base yields a salt plus water. Or mathematics teachers can demonstrate with a particular solid Euler's claim concerning the relationships between the faces, vertices, and edges of all polyhedra is represented by $V + F = E + 2$. The demonstration is not proof, but does provide support for the assertion. The procedures teachers invoke translate hypotheses into justified beliefs. What implications should teachers consider when they are teaching their students knowledge derived from empirical approaches?

1. It would be important for teachers to tell their students the nature of the procedure that is the source of the knowledge they are sharing. For example, students should learn to differentiate between experiments, quasi-experiments, and demonstrations.
2. As appropriate,[6] it would be important to allow students to replicate empirical procedures described in texts to gain understandings of how procedures can yield justifications for knowledge claims.
3. Teachers would need to differentiate between the proof of a claim provided by analytic procedures and support for a claim that is yielded by empirical approaches.
4. It would be important to share with students rival explanations for the findings that result from procedures. Since "data does not speak for itself," persons interpreting the results of procedures may differ in their accounts. Teachers must share with their students some of this ambiguity by asking them to expect and to use proper qualifiers in reporting results.
5. It would be important for teachers to share with their students what prior explanations were widely held to account for the findings that are under study in the classroom before the current explanations gained currency.
6. It would be important to encourage students to identify the assumptions that link findings with conclusions and to assess their reasonableness (Ennis, 1961).

If teachers were to invoke these prescriptions in their teaching, observers would have a sense that they understood their subject matter and knew its sources, as well as the explanations in the past that have been discredited by the application of empirical approaches.

Analytic (a priori) procedures. People making use of analytic procedures rarely collect data. Instead, they carry out thought experiments, apply logic to assumptions and axioms that are taken as true from the start, and deduce conclusions that are consistent and true within the logical system in which they ar generated. For example, the Einsteinian formulation $E = mc^2$ is the result of a series of deductions. The truth of the assertion has subsequently been supported by empirical evidence.

If teachers planned to teach the theorem that the sum of the internal angles of a triangle is 180 degrees in an Euclidian plane, then it makes sense to present proof of the claim to their students. What should teachers do in this case to demonstrate their knowledge of subject matter?

1. It would be important for students to know the difference between a valid argument and a true conclusion. That is, the argument that leads to the conclusion that "The sum of the interior angles of a triangle in a Euclidian plane is 180 degrees" may be valid, but the conclusion itself may be false.
2. It would be important for students to know that there are different ways to prove theorems—and that some proofs may be more compelling than others.
3. It would be important for students to know the roles played by definitions, assumptions, and undefined terms in the proofs they consider (Ennis, 1969).

If teachers were to invoke these prescriptions in their teaching, they would be demonstrating a profound knowledge of their subject matter. Observers of our teaching would recognize that they understood the sources of their knowledge, the extent to which they were able to discern the qualifications of authorities in their field, and the breadth of their knowledge, made clear by their familiarity with rival interpretations or understandings.

Back to the Questions

What does it mean to say that teachers have an adequate knowledge of our subject matter? Surely, it is important for teachers to have a "well-upholstered mind," furnished with concepts, facts, principles, and understandings associated with what they are teaching. But, as Wilson, Shulman, and Richert (1990) point out, knowledge at this level is not sufficient. Beyond that, teachers need to know the sources of the justification of the knowledge they are teaching and the particular implications each different source holds for educational discourse. Where did this understanding that teachers are planning to share with their students originate? How is it justified? What understandings were in place before this one came to the fore? So, to demonstrate a grasp of subject matter, teachers must know more than simply the facts, generalizations, or algorithms that are already widely taught.

If this is the case, do secondary teachers need to know more subject matter than their counterparts in elementary school? Do teachers of advanced tracks need to know more than teachers in curriculum tracks catering to slower students?

It is clear that different teachers need to know different things. That is, if physics teachers were presenting Newton's Third Law, then they would have to know it and all the other facets of it to demonstrate their knowledge of subject matter. On the other hand, first grade teachers may never teach Newton's Third Law to their students. It might be interesting if all teachers knew the Law, and invoked it at an appropriate time in the classroom when students experimented with balloons or when an inquiry is made about how jet planes fly. In the same vein, it would be wonderful if physics teachers understood the differences between art forms or musical genres if those topics arose during units on light or sound. However, the number of instances such as these are infinite, and it is unrealistic to expect teachers to know everything. It is reasonable for all teachers to understand the distinctions between sources of truth, and to expect that they have grasped the various approaches to knowledge specified in this essay. Furthermore, it is reasonable to expect that teachers can apply these understandings themselves when they are giving their students understandings of worthwhile ideas.

How do teachers manifest their knowledge of subject matter in a classroom? What would visitors to their classrooms see in their actions, comments, decisions, or judgments that would reveal the level of teachers' knowledge of subject matter? An elaborated answer to this question has been spelled out in the implications previously discussed. In sum, a visitor would observe that teachers are aware of the sources of the ideas being taught and are knowledgeable about the implications the particular sources hold for teaching by the ways the ideas are qualified, identified, and discussed.

Summary

These suggestions present a challenge to all teachers. Some administrators hold the position that "knowledge of subject matter" refers to the basics—knowing the elementary facts and presenting them to students in such a way as not to embarrass the school. For example, superintendents do not want to receive telephone calls from irate parents, charging that children were taught that Columbus's three ships were the Santa Maria, the Niña, and the Chiquita. The bane of schools' public relations is the teacher who miscites facts, who makes critical spelling mistakes or grammatical errors on tests, letters home, or on other official documents. Teachers who make errors such as these are seen as "not knowing their subject matter."

No one condones teachers making errors. If teachers had their way, they would all be perfect in these respects. But, given the nature of the process, almost certainly errors will be made. Surely steps can be taken to reduce their occurrence, such as providing teachers with spell checkers on their computers. However, it is the case that simply spelling words correctly and parsing sentences in an acceptable way falls far short of what is needed in our schools and misses the ideals of those who are calling for higher standards in subject matter competence of teachers.

If teachers are indeed going to invite their students to experience the complexity of subject matter, if they are going to trust their intellects and their abilities to cope with profound ideas, and if they are going to permit their students to comprehend and understand not only knowledge but the sources of knowledge as well, teachers need to manifest their own knowledge of subject matter in ways that are set down in this essay.

SECTION TWO: PEDAGOGICAL CONTENT KNOWLEDGE

What is pedagogical content knowledge? In his seminal Presidential Address to the American Educational Research Association, Shulman (1986) suggests that besides knowing subject matter and knowing how to teach, teachers also need to have a grasp of something he called "pedagogical content knowledge." It is a form of content knowledge that

> embodies the aspects of content most germane to its teachability. Within the category of pedagogical content knowledge, I include, for the most regularly taught topics in one's subject area, the most useful forms of representation of those ideas, the most powerful analogies, illustrations, examples, explanations, and demonstrations—in a word, the ways of representing and formulating the subject that make it comprehensible to others. (p. 9)

Perhaps the easiest example to illustrate the concept of pedagogical content knowledge, at least one element of it, is that associated with multiplying a negative real number by a negative real number. Almost all of us know that the product is a positive number. Surely all mathematics majors know this fact as a part of their "knowledge of subject matter." But, how would teachers explain this rule for multiplying signed numbers to a 13-year-old student in middle school. And if the student found the explanation incomprehensible, how many other explanations do teachers have in their repertoire to draw upon to help him out? The explanations teachers have at the ready to meet this challenge fall into the category of "pedagogical content knowledge."[7] One characteristic of this genre of knowledge is especially noteworthy. As a rule, there is little need for mathematics majors per se to know how to explain this algorithm to others. Indeed, they may have some explanations to offer to students, but they may also know the capital of Laos or the average rainfall in the Ukraine. The point is, as a rule, mathematics majors are not called upon to know how to explain mathematics to 13-year-olds. And furthermore, it is the case that most pedagogical content knowledge applicable to public school students is not treated in courses in the liberal arts.

This example, however, may trivialize Shulman's (1986) important distinction between content knowledge and pedagogical content knowledge. Before addressing the central purposes of this paper, let me share another example of pedagogical content knowledge.

In planning to teach a course or even a single topic, teachers often find it useful to represent the content they plan to teach by adopting some sort of framework or scheme. An interview with University of North Carolina history professor David Griffiths ("Ideas for teaching," 1989) is revealing. When Griffiths first started teaching, he relied more on his own enthusiasm for the materials than on organization or teaching methods to teach his students. He says that now he understands the necessity for structure and planning in a course, especially a course like History 30 ("1,000 years in one semester"), which he teaches every year. Professor Griffiths commented, "The first thing I do is say that the material is vast, I can't cover it all, but here are seven major themes that are going to come up again and again...." He then identifies the seven or eight themes that unify the materials and he carefully plans the entire semester of lectures and discussions to emphasize those themes.

Professor Griffiths's approach is of course only one way to represent the content. There are many others. Note how imprecise the narrative is about the seven themes. Is it seven or eight? It really doesn't matter. The point is that the content is themetized by the instructor to organize the course. Research and reflection may suggest that for subsequent courses, one of the themes could be dropped, others added, or some could be emended.

Two additional comments about pedagogical content knowledge are appropriate at this time. First, as Grossman (1990) points out, while the term Shulman used to describe this category of teacher knowledge is new, the idea of pedagogical content knowledge is not new. She attributes the idea to Dewey (1902):

It [subject matter] needs to be psychologized; turned over, translated into the immediate and individual experiencing within which it has its origin and significance. (p. 29)

Second, Shulman (1986) also suggests that pedagogical content knowledge includes aspects of an interaction of pupils with content.

Pedagogical content knowledge includes an understanding of what makes the learning of specific topics easy or difficult; the conceptions and preconceptions that students of different ages bring with them to the learning of those most frequently taught topics and lessons. (pp. 9–10)

Presumably, along with the knowledge of the most likely mis-perceptions that students are likely to acquire prior to a lesson, teachers need to know as well the strategies that would be useful in improving their understandings. However, as important as it is, this latter element of pedagogical content knowledge is not discussed in this paper. Grossman (1990) deals with it nicely in her seminal book concerned with teacher knowledge. On occasion, the narrative that follows alludes indirectly to teachers' knowledge of the interests and conceptions of students. On those pages, this fourth element of pedagogical content knowledge is implicitly acknowledged.

At this point, it would be important to give some illustrations of what *does not* count as pedagogical content knowledge. Such illustrations include knowing how to implement a cooperative learning lesson (pedagogy); knowing how children grow and develop (knowledge of human development); and knowing the causes of the American Civil War (knowledge of subject matter). All of these forms of knowledge as exemplified here are important for teaching. However, they do not fall under Shulman's rubric of pedagogical content knowledge.

In considering these other classifications of teacher knowledge, it is important to point out that the categories are never distinct. One may ask, where is the boundary between pedagogical knowledge and pedagogical content knowledge in the case where teachers elect to offer one explanation or another to our students. It is not clear. By and large, however, the principal defining element has to do with the subject matter knowledge that undergirds the decision or the action. Almost any teacher could use cooperative learning techniques or reciprocal teaching approaches, regardless of the class topic or subject area. But, only a history teacher with an intimate knowledge of history is likely to thematize a course. And only a mathematics teacher is apt to know several ways of presenting the epsilon-delta definition of a limit to a group of advanced placement students. All of this is not to say, however, that the classifications are pristine.

Finally, we should acknowledge that loosely defined constructs invite practitioners, researchers, and disseminators to develop their own definitions of what is meant by the term. We saw this occur concerning concepts such as "progressive education," "open education," and even "modern mathematics." The sharing of a variety of interpretations is not all bad, and the challenge invites each of us to reconsider our earlier interpretations of the concept. It is in that spirit that this essay is written.

Three Elements of Pedagogical Content Knowledge

The purpose of this section is to elaborate upon Shulman's (1986) ideas with some examples and to suggest ways that at least three elements of our pedagogical content knowledge might be observed in a classroom during one of our lessons. To address this purpose, I have conceptualized three aspects of pedagogical content knowledge: (1) representing the course content; (2) offering explanations; and (3) giving examples and nonexamples. As I have previously alluded, these three elements do not exhaust this important category of knowledge.

Representing the Course Content

To help make the content they are teaching more meaningful to students, teachers have learned how important it is to organize the material. The organization could pertain to a semester's scope of work, a unit, a week's series of topics, or to a particular lesson. There are at least five ways of representing course content, and that is through: (1) themes; (2) focus on the acquisition of intellectual skills and dispositions; (3) the use of analogies; (4) the exploration of perspectives; and (5) solving problems. Each of these is discussed below.

Representing the course content with themes. In this approach, a teacher elects a substantive theme that links together the topics that are covered or the genre that are read. Here are some examples:

- An English teacher elects "justice" as a theme for the course, and asks her pupils to read novels, poems, and essays reflecting on the issue of "justice." Each reading permits the teacher to ask how the concept of justice is illuminated by the literature.
- A geometry teacher organizes his course content based on the book *The Nature of Proof* (Fawcett, 1938). The study of triangles, parallel lines, and areas of polygons is related in each instance to synthetic proofs, indirect proofs, and analytic proofs. In each instance, questions are raised about particular proofs: Are they compelling? Are they elegant? Are they valid?
- A history teacher poses the hypothesis that economic interests drive historical events far more than idealistic views of freedom and liberty. As various events in United States history are studied, students are asked to test how reasonable this hypothesis is in explaining the events presented in the text.
- A sixth grade teacher chooses the theme of "families" to study stories about families in readers and to observe families in the animal kingdom—in zoos, in the class aquarium, and reflected in the patterns of other lands.

These examples serve to illustrate how teachers might present topics in our lessons, units, or courses to our students, so they might capture their significance and understand how they relate to other ideas or contexts.

Representing the course content though a focus upon the acquisition of intellectual skills and dispositions. Teachers who use this approach work to convince their students that they are acquiring intellectual skills and dispositions that will serve them well in many situations once the course is over. The content takes on a secondary role in these courses; what is important is the application of the skills that are being acquired. Here are some examples:

- A science teacher represents the course content as a study of the scientific method. Instead of discussing the scientific method during the first week of the class by covering the first chapter, and then proceeding to simply teach science through the discussion method, this teacher asks her students to resist accepting any information offered either by the text or by the teacher without experimenting to test its truth value. The class collects data, analyzes experiments, and critiques newspaper accounts of scientific claims offered by politicians, scientists, and even the school's superintendent, against the canons of science.
- An English teacher represents the course content as teaching an understanding of the "new criticism," circa 1950, advanced by Brooks, Purser, and Warren (1952). Poems, short stories, and dramas are studied, to which the procedures of the new

criticism are then applied. The teacher is convinced that these skills will enable his students to appreciate and enjoy all the poems, novels, and plays they will confront in their lives.

The point here is that the course content is represented not as a series of topics or lessons, but as semester-long themes. The themes, scientific method and new criticism, provide teachers with the opportunity of selecting a wide range of topics or specific readings that reflect their students' interests or abilities. The focus is on applying the understandings and skills associated with these themes in the future to new content. The particular plays under scrutiny in English class, the particular generalizations that are being tested scientifically in General Science, or the particular theorems that are the object of proofs in mathematics class make little difference to the teachers in these examples. The focus is on the application of new knowledge and skills.

Representing the course through the use of analogies. Wilson, Shulman, and Richert (1990) describe another approach to representing the content. A teacher was interested in teaching Shakespeare's *Julius Caesar* to ninth grade students as a play about moral conflict. To find an approach that would accommodate both his students' levels of interest and their levels of sophistication in these matters, he introduced Julius Caesar as the "Captain Kirk" of the Roman Empire. He began his teaching by advancing the following scenario:

> I said, "You are the first officer on the *Starship Enterprise*. Captain Kirk has been getting out of hand. He's a good captain; he's been made Commander of the Fleet. But, you, his closest friend, and your fellow officers have been noticing that he's been getting too risky, a little big-headed. You're afraid that he's going to endanger the Federation Fleet and might just seek glory in some farcical campaign." They really took off on that. (p. 112)

In this way, the teacher represented the content he was teaching by establishing an analogy between the popular television series *Star Trek* and the plot of *Julius Caesar*. His knowledge of the fit between the television series and the play is an element of pedagogical content knowledge that was applied in this instructional unit.

Representing the course content as addressing a problem. In this approach, a teacher works with his class to identify a problem that the class can study. The content of the course is reflected in efforts to solve the problem and the knowledge, skill, and understanding that are needed to get the job finished. Some examples of this approach to representing the content of a course include the following:

• Knowing that his first grade class members spent as long as 30 minutes each day on the school bus, the teacher posed the following problem to the group: "How can we improve the school bus to make riding on it a better experience?" The pursuit of this objective required making measurements, constructing plans, interviewing bus drivers and assistant superintendents, and preparing reports (Katz & Chard, 1989).

- A classic example of solving a problem was demonstrated in an old McGraw-Hill film (1955) on pedagogy. In this fictional account, a civics teacher turned his class loose on the project of improving the school cafeteria. The class took on the topics of budgeting, scheduling, interior design, and other fields as it tackled this problem.
- A secondary school aimed at giving all of its students the opportunity to provide service to the community elected to prepare a history of the town to display in the local historical society building. Students in the history classes had not used a textbook; by studying the history of their town and finding ways of relating that history to the concurrent events taking place in the nation and the world, they discovered ways of communicating historical ideas to the community, and also learned a lot of history on their own.

Representing the course content as a study of differing perspectives. This approach, proposed by Schwab (1971), is providing students with what is called "polyfocal conspectus." Several different perspectives are studied and applied to various cases. Students judge the extent to which each perspective contributes to understanding the elements of the case and even identify broader implications. For example:

- Several views of history could be studied in making sense of the United States Constitutional Convention.
- A number of theories of aesthetics could be taken on as perspectives and applied to outstanding pieces of art, music, or sculpture to better understand how the perspectives are used.

By representing a course or a lesson in this fashion, teachers assist their students to not only learn specifics about the topics under study, but also help them to better understand the various views or perspectives that are included in the course.

It is important to contrast teaching that attempts to represent the course content in some manner, and teaching where this does not occur. Indicators of the latter approach reflect the following well known methods:

- **Following the textbook.** The teacher takes no responsibility for representing the course content but instead defers to the textbook author. Some textbooks may indeed reflect some sort of representation of the content and not simply a linking-together of chronologies or discrete facts, but of course it would be important for the teacher to fully understand and appreciate the representation found there and to convey it to students.
- **Conceiving of the course content as a sequence of topics.** That is, someone might think of a literature course as dealing first with novels, then short stories, poetry, and finally, essays. Each genre would be taught by simply reading exemplars, only without a theme or an analogy to link the separate aspects of the course to help students make sense of them.

The matter of representing the content of a course is a very serious matter. It is not the case that any representation is as effective as any other. A teacher might elect to use the *Cosby Show* to represent Hamlet—and it probably would not work too well. Returning to the seven or eight themes Professor Griffiths ("Ideas for teaching," 1989) used to represent his history course, it might be the case that the themes a teacher or professor uses might be considered puerile or insipid by other scholars or by the students themselves. Besides being accurate and true to the content area, the themes or the analogies teachers select must "grab" students in significant ways.[8] Herrick (1962) suggests three factors that teachers might take into consideration when selecting a way to represent content.

First, the representation should be accessible to students. Herrick (1962) means that it should relate to what they know, with what they are familiar, and to readings and materials that they can use. For example, to organize a unit for fifth graders around the idea of "death" may be a good or bad idea, for many reasons, but there simply are not many instructional materials written about death that are available to fifth graders. To use the *Star Trek* theme as a way to organize a study of Shakespeare's *Julius Caesar* may have been a good idea when it was first introduced, but as time passes and fewer students have the opportunity to watch *Star Trek* on television, its efficacy as a representation of the content may fade.

Second, Herrick (1962) suggests that the representation be relevant to students. If the representation is to solve a problem, then the problem must be one in which students either are interested in or in which they could become interested. A teacher might be intrigued with the sources and solutions to the pollution found in a local pond, but the students might find the topic of little interest.

Third, Herrick (1962) proposes that a representation should offer students the opportunity to "succeed" at many different levels of accomplishment. That is, if the representation offers the students some flexibility in how they approach a problem, and how they in turn demonstrate their understandings of the ideas embedded in the content, the representation is likely to be successful.

Finally, a representation is useful if it provides latitude for students to explore a number of avenues—differentiated by time (the past and future) and geography (here and there). For example, the American Civil War is not an effective representation of content in its own right, in that it does not provide as much latitude for students as if the theme were instead "civil wars." The American Civil War is simply one instance of the general theme. The larger concept would allow students to explore civil wars in the past and present; and civil wars in the United States as well as those in Europe and Africa.

There are no doubt many other approaches teachers might use for representing the content of a course. The point is that teachers need to be involved in this process and their engagement with it calls on the application of pedagogical content knowledge.

Offering Explanations

According to Brown (1978), teachers are often called upon to respond to at least three different calls for explanation. His classification scheme included the following categories:

Interpretive explanations. What is a novel? What is regression? What is pedagogical content knowledge? Often, teachers make use of various types of definitions, such as denotative definitions, range definitions, and so forth to provide explanations of this sort (Ennis, 1969).

Descriptive explanations. How does Newton's Third Law work? How does a fax machine send messages? How are computers constructed? To respond to questions in this area, teachers often share physical models with students, provide them with manipulative experiences, or make use of metaphors and analogies to help improve their understandings.

Reason-giving explanations. Why are some people rich and other people poor? Why is Franklin Roosevelt considered to be a good president? In responding to students' wonderments about cause, teachers present chains of arguments to convince students of the credibility of claims found in textbooks and in other materials.

Brown (1978) acknowledges there may be demands on the part of students for other sorts of explanations, and also that these explanations may run into one another so that an interpretive explanation may well elicit from a curious set of students questions calling for descriptions or reason-giving. Clearly, some explanations work better than others in teaching. What are some criteria for assessing an explanation? Brown offers two:

- An explanation should be clear to students.
- An explanation should be interesting to students.

This criteria implies that the explanation offers ideas, facts, or relationships that are familiar to students.[9]

Two additional criteria seem appropriate:

- An explanation ought to be compelling as well as clear. Some explanations may be sufficiently clear, but serve not to explain.
- The explanation should not be false either in its source or in its implication. For example, a teacher striving to explain how the human circulatory system works might compare it to the hot water system in a house—establishing analogies between the hot water heater and the human heart. While the explanation by analogy might be clear, interesting, and even compelling, it might also lead to the drawing of inferences on the part of students that are false or misleading. A second example might be useful. A chemistry teacher helped her students recognize that whenever two chemicals are mixed together, sometimes there is a chemical reaction and sometimes a reaction does not take place. Why is that the case? The

teacher used a "boy-girl" metaphor to explain. Some male elements (metals) are simply not interested in the girl elements (nonmetals) and so the chemical reaction does not take place. This explanation may or may not be compelling and it may meet Brown's (1978) criterion of interest, but it certainly carries with it a lack of academic merit.

Teachers need to have at hand a number of explanations for the various claims, observations, or understandings they are trying to teach—and they need to gauge them against the four criteria just discussed.

Where do they come from? Teacher candidates may hear some good explanations from their college professors, although there is a chance that they may be too sophisticated or too complicated to be of interest to or compelling for students at the middle school level. Teachers may learn about some good explanations by reading professional journals or by attending workshops where various explanations are discussed and critiqued. Finally, some good explanations are simply made up on the spot, or in anticipation of a lesson that is to be taught. It is probably good practice to rehearse explanations with colleagues before they are presented to students to get help in de-bugging them, but of course that is not always possible.

A key matter in this process is that teachers and their students must recognize that the explanation that is being given is not Truth. It is important for all teachers to recognize an explanation offered in class for the role it is playing in the teaching-learning process. All participants in the lesson must fully understand that there are a number of explanations that might suffice to respond to puzzlements under study, and that some explanations are better than others. Indeed teachers need to strengthen the disposition of their students to ask the question: "Thank you for your explanation; what are some other explanations?"

Having explanations at hand to respond to the questions students have about the content that is being covered is another example of our need for pedagogical content knowledge.

Giving Examples

Joyce and Weil (1986), building on the solid research work of Bruner, Goodnow, and Austin (1956), describe in some detail the processes that are important when engaged in teaching concepts. In this formulation, a concept is the name of a set of similar elements. So, while all dogs are different, and no two dogs are precisely the same, it makes sense to classify this subset of animals into a conceptual category called "dogs." Teachers, at all levels, teach their students concepts. To do it effectively, according to the authorities cited above, a teacher should provide students with examples and nonexamples of the concept. That is, it is not sufficient, when teaching the concept of "dogs" to children, to have on hand only particular dogs as exemplars. It is important for children to recognize that "cats aren't dogs," that "birds aren't dogs," and, subsequently, that "wolves aren't dogs." Of course, it is the matter of borderline cases that makes concept-teaching difficult.

When engaged in teaching concepts, then, it is important for teachers to have on hand a large number of examples and nonexamples for their students to consider. The earliest examples proffered to the class should probably be clear-cut cases. But, in addition, teachers need to know the existence of borderline cases and what makes them either examples or nonexamples of the concept under study. Having this information on hand is another example of pedagogical content knowledge essential for teaching.

Teachers learn over time that some examples or nonexamples are more effective than others in getting the concept across. What are some criteria of good examples or nonexamples? Here are several to consider:

- *Examples need to be accessible to students.* They must grasp the example or have had experience with it. It makes little sense to tell students that "chows are dogs," if they don't have a clue what a "chow" is.
- Second, *an example should have an optimal level of reactivity.* That is, it would be important for the students to be interested in the example, especially if the example is something familiar to them. However, if the example elicits fear, anxiety, or other forms of disquiet, it may be less effective instructionally than one that is more benign. Using Nazism or death by cancer as an example of some concept might be less useful than some other choices.
- Finally, *examples that are quite frankly both examples and nonexamples at the same time would likely confuse the issue.* Care must be taken to reserve borderline cases for a propitious time in the lesson.

Here is yet another example of teachers' calling on pedagogical content knowledge in their teaching. To identify meaningful and effective examples and nonexamples for presentation in class calls on a full understanding of subject matter and teaching principles.

Summary

In a way, Shulman's (1986) concepts and our elaboration of some of them in this essay give the impression that teachers teach their students new ideas and better understandings as they react passively to the teachers' structuring and sage presentations. Several caveats need to be expressed to dissuade readers from arriving at this inference.

First, it is clear that whether teachers like it or not, their students will listen to their structures, explanations, and their examples and make sense of what they have told them. As the Holmes Group (1990) puts it,

What we are learning from cognitive scientists is, first, that people are inveterate constructors of meaning: They're going to make sense of it in some way. (p. 13)

Teaching is not a process of simply presenting or passing on information. Teaching is better considered as consisting of assisting performance in others (Tharp & Gallimore, 1988). The students play a critical role in the teaching-learning process.

Second, teachers assist their students by clarifying ideas, linking various experiences offered to students, and by sharing current explanations of various phenomenon. No one would seriously hold that students need to rediscover the world of knowledge all by themselves. Indeed, there is an important role for the teacher in setting the stage for learning. And teachers do this, in part, by exercising their pedagogical content knowledge. There are many arenas of ignorance in which teachers and their students might explore.

Third, just as teachers have skills they elect not to use, so they can have knowledge that they choose not to share. That is, just because teachers know five good explanations for the rule that a negative number multiplied by a negative number yields a positive product, there is nothing in what we have shared in this essay that demands that teachers share that knowledge with their students. For other reasons having to do with their knowledge of the particular children with whom they are working and with other goals of the lesson, teachers may elect to withhold this knowledge. The question is, given the freedom to share it or not, would teachers be better off knowing many explanations as opposed to not knowing?

Shulman's (1986) concept of pedagogical content knowledge has been elaborated here across three elements: representing the content, giving explanations, and offering examples. Students of teaching can observe a teacher's (or their own) application of pedagogical content knowledge matter in the classroom by responding to the following questions.

I. Representing the content
   a. How was the content of the lesson/unit/course represented to students?
      1) with themes
      2) as the acquisition of skills
      3) with an analogy
      4) as addressing a problem
      5) as dealing with different perspectives
      6) other
   b. How consistently was the representation reflected in the presentation, the assignments and the evaluation of the learning taking place?
   c. Did the representation of the content meet the following criteria?
      1) accessibility
      2) relevance
      3) multiple levels of successful accomplishment
      4) mobility
II. Offering explanations
   a. Were the explanations clear?
   b. Were the explanations of interest to the students?

    c. Were the explanations compelling?

    d. Were the explanations congruent with current scholarly understandings?

    e. Were students encouraged to seek other explanations?

III. Giving examples

    a. Were both examples and nonexamples shared with students?

    b. Were the examples familiar to the students?

    c. Were differentiations made between clear-cut examples and borderline examples?

    d. Were the examples optimally benign?

As teachers address these questions with their colleagues and with those who visit their classrooms, they will become engaged in a dialogue about the sources, the quality, and the effectiveness of elements of pedagogical content knowledge. The conversations prompted by these questions, and others, should help contribute to augmenting the store of pedagogical content knowledge of all who take part.

NOTES

[1] Brown's view of teaching reflects the "acquisition metaphor" (Sfard, 1998). There are other, competing metaphors.

[2] Poundstone (1988) demonstrates how the tripartite criteria for knowledge can lead to significant paradoxes, thus stimulating a search for a fourth criterion.

[3] Another source of knowledge often advanced as credible is revelation. This source of knowledge is not included in this analysis, since only rarely do products mined from the source of revelation find themselves in the curriculum of our schools.

[4] This was the principal theme of a lesson taught to students in a Washington, D. C., high school by then-Secretary of Education William Bennett. His lesson was discussed by a panel of scholars (Morine-Dershimer, 1986).

[5] The use of the word *merely* here should not be interpreted as being condescending of the teaching act. Clearly, in a professional manner, teachers must decide which ideas, interpretations, and authorities to share with students. This in itself is a profound act, calling for the invocation of judgment, values, and experience.

[6] Clearly, some procedures are too expensive, too dangerous, or too time-consuming to demonstrate in class. If teachers can convince their students that the inexpensive, safe, and relatively brief demonstrations that they do allow in class represent the more expensive, dangerous, and time-consuming ones, they will certainly be meeting the prescriptions in this section. Of course, any claim that the one set represents the other should be subject to scrutiny.

[7] It is interesting to speculate whether this example of pedagogical content knowledge meets Scheffler's tri-partite definition of knowledge advanced in Section One.

[8] Here is an area where we are approaching the fourth element of Shulman's (1986) concept, that of knowing what ideas students bring with them to the lesson.

[9] Here again, we meet an element of Shulman's (1986) definition that this essay ignores—having knowledge about the information that students bring to the lesson.

REFERENCES

Belenky, M. F., Clinchy, B. Mc., Goldberger, N. R., & Tarule, J. M. (1986). *Women's ways of knowing*. New York: Basic Books.

Brandon, E. P. (1987). *Do teachers care about truth?* London: Allen & Unwin.

Brooks, C., Purser, J., & Warren, R. P. (1952). *An approach to literature*. New York: Appleton-Century-Crofts.

Brown, G. (1978). *Lecturing and explaining*. London: Methuen.

Bruner, J. S., Goodnow, J. J., & Austin, G. A. (1956). *A study of thinking*. New York: Wiley.

Dewey, J. (1902). *The child and the curriculum*. Chicago: University of Chicago Press.

Dewey, J. (1910). *How we think*. Boston: Heath.

Dickens, C. (1966). *Hard times*. New York: Heritage Press.

Edwards, D., & Mercer, N. (1987). *Common knowledge: The development of understanding in the classroom*. London: Methuen.

Ennis, R. H. (1961). Assumption-finding. In B. O. Smith & R. H. Ennis (Eds.), *Language and concepts in education* (pp. 161–178). Chicago: Rand McNally.

Ennis, R. H. (1969). *Logic in teaching*. Englewood Cliffs, NJ: Prentice-Hall.

Fawcett, H. P. (1938). *The nature of proof*. Washington, DC: National Council of Teachers of Mathematics.

Finkelstein, B. (1986). *Governing the young: Teacher behavior in popular primary schools in the 19th century United States*. New York: Falmer.

Grossman, P. L. (1990). *The making of a teacher*. New York: Teachers College Press.

Herrick, V. E. (1962). Curriculum decisions and provision for individual differences. *Elementary School Journal, 62*(6), 313–320.

The Holmes Group. (1990). *Tomorrow's schools*. East Lansing, MI: The Holmes Group.

Ideas for teaching large lecture classes. (1989). *For Your Consideration, 2*(1), 1–4. (Available from the Center for Teaching and Learning, University of North Carolina, Chapel Hill)

Joyce, B., & Weil, M. (1986). *Models of teaching*. Englewood Cliffs, NJ: Prentice-Hall.

Katz, L. G., & Chard, S. C. (1989). *Engaging children's minds: The project approach*. Norwood, NJ: Ablex.

McGraw-Hill Educational Films. (1955). *Broader concept of method, part II* [Film]. New York: McGraw-Hill.

Morine-Dershimer, G. (1986). Introduction: Perspectives on a teaching episode. *Teaching & Teacher Education, 2*(4), 299–300.

National Commission on Excellence in Education. (1983). *A nation at risk*. Washington, DC: U.S. Department of Education. (ERIC Reproduction Service No. ED 226 006)

National Commission for Excellence in Teacher Education. (1985). *A call for change in teacher education*. Washington, DC: American Association for Colleges of Teacher Education.

Poundstone, W. (1988). *Labyrinths of reason*. New York: Anchor Press.

Scheffler, I. (1965). *Conditions of knowledge: An introduction to epistemology and education*. Chicago: Scott Foresman.

Scheffler, I. (1969). Justifying curriculum decisions. In B. Bandman & R. S. Guttchen (Eds.), *Philosophical essays on teaching* (pp 260–268). New York: J. B. Lippincott.

Sfard, A. (1998). On two metaphors for learning and the dangers of choosing just one. *Educational Researcher, 27*(2), 4–13.

Schwab, J. (1971). The practical: Acts of eclectic. *School Review, 79*, 493–542.

Shulman, L. S. (1986). Those who understand: Knowledge growth in teaching. *Educational Researcher, 15*(2), 4–14.

Task Force on Teaching as a Profession. (1986). *A nation prepared*. New York: Carnegie Forum on Education and the Economy.

Tharp, R. G., & Gallimore, R. (1988). *Rousing minds to life*. Cambridge, England: Cambridge University Press.

Whitehead, A. N. (1929). *The aims of education*. New York: Macmillan.

Wilson, S. M., Shulman, L. S., & Richert, A. E. (1990). "150 different ways" of knowing: Representations of knowledge in teaching. In J. Calderhead (Ed.), *Exploring teachers' thinking* (pp. 104–124). London: Oxford University Press.

Teacher Education, Knowledge Most Worth, and Ellwood P. Cubberley

Joe A. Stornello
University of Missouri, Kansas City

IDENTIFYING THE ISSUES

Just as one does not judge an individual by what he thinks about himself, so one cannot judge...a period of transformation by its consciousness, but, on the contrary, this consciousness must be explained from the contradictions of material life, from the conflict existing between the social forces of production and the relations of production. (Marx, 1970/1989, p. 21)

Over 150 years have passed in which to settle ontological questions about the historical conjunction between capitalism and the American system of public school education. Progress by educational historians toward congruent explanations of the relations between public school education and economic and political relations, however, is inconclusive. For example, in *American Education: A History*, Wayne Urban and Jennings Wagoner, Jr. (1996), write that

While Katz sees the public school as an institution imposed by the establishment on the lower classes, his critics tend to see the common school, and the public schools in the twentieth century, as imperfect institutions that nevertheless attempted to overcome, or mitigate, social divisions in American society and to help the members of the lower orders of that society to better themselves. (p. 112; see also Katz, 1968, 1971/1975, 1987)

As Urban and Wagoner (1996) present them, these opposing historical explanations of the role of public school education in American society are subjective *interpretations*. The issue between one and the other is rhetorical, such as, which is the more persuasive text. What must decide the issue between one interpretation and the other is now a question of internal textual *coherence*, coherence with other texts established within the discipline of educational history, and, perhaps, coherence with the teacher candidate's understanding. A historical social reality independent of the texts and interpretive arguments is absent, and what remains is a collection of more or less inscrutable texts of which the historian and/or teacher candidate endeavor to make sense. This is relativist and constructivist history. Teacher candidates are left to form their own opinion about the merits of one or the other argument in the discussion, because what cannot be done under these terms of discourse is to say this or that argument is true. Indeed, although Katz's excavation of the history of public schools in society is surely not the same as that of his critics, Urban and Wagoner reduce these very different ontological explanations of history to equivalents. In other words, what properly should be settled by an examination and explication of actual socioeconomic circumstances is instead reduced to what one thinks.

The effect of relativism is to make educational history a genre of fiction (Finkelstein, 1992). My contention is relativist history on the one hand and interpretive constructions of history on the other are deliberate political acts of ideological mystification dressed up as historical scholarship. And, as the textual product of deliberate authorship, these acts are meant to shape the beliefs of teachers about what constitutes the reality of public school education and economic and political relations through the manipulation of knowledge about the past.

Whenever a historian presents as explanation what is in fact an interpretation dependent for its coherence and persuasiveness upon the exclusion or diminution of knowledge about social reality and congruent evidence that would undermine his/her argument, then we have either ideological mystification, sloppy scholarship, or ignorance. Distinguishing one from the other is sometimes difficult, unless we have sufficient interdisciplinary knowledge of the object of study ourselves.

The determination of validity (or defensibility) for a historical explanation and knowledge claim depends in every case on established coherence *and* congruence.[1] Thus, ignorance as a cause of misrepresentations is most easily recognized, for the errors are many, often contradictory, and tend to be haphazard—explanations lack both coherence and congruence. Sloppy scholarship can usually be recognized through a close reading of the argument, which is largely a matter of assertions and coherent interpretation without much attempt at establishing a degree of congruence. Ideological mystification is the most difficult process to recognize and critique, for the author appears to have provided adequate documentation of his/her arguments and assertions may be many or few, but the undergirding assumptions and/or social agenda are hidden. Certainly the rhetorical strategy of presenting polemic as historical explanation is one of the conditions that makes ideological mystification difficult to recognize, but it is also one of its defining characteristics. Most often, the argument promotes a hegemonic perspective that obscures or misrepresents the historical particularities of actual economic and political relations within the context of specific socioeconomic circumstances, and presents as "knowledge" explanations or claims that contradict and/or mystify these conditions. One educational historian argues, for example, that capitalism benefited all citizens by engendering a society characterized by equal economic opportunities and shared political power; and, more subtly, he emphasizes only the benefits of capitalism—such as increased literacy or improved transportation— while the negative consequences—such as stratified economic and political relations, exploitation of the laboring class, and the concentration of wealth and power among a few—are given only passing mention, if mentioned at all (Kaestle, 1983). An ideological account posits as reality the assumption that increased literacy or improved transportation or the development of water treatment systems, for example, happen only because of a specific economic system; that, in fact, there are no viable alternatives that would have generated these benefits for individuals or to society generally. Moreover, Kaestle notes, an ideological account is one that insists—usually implicitly—that whatever the costs in social inequities and human misery, desperation, poverty, or loss, they were and are necessary to achieve industrial and capital progress and national supremacy.

My argument that the writing and publication of relativist or ideological historiographic texts are deliberate political acts will be developed and supported through my critique of Ellwood Cubberley's *Public Education in the United States* (1934a), which follows. I emphasize here, though, that the underlying purpose of the sort of political act I have described above is to obscure the connection between capitalist economic and political relations, which are inherently unequal and exploitative, and the state system of public school education. By obscuring this connection, the author contributes to the mechanisms of social hegemony. And, of greater importance, the mystification of the particulars of this relation distorts and/or obstructs the production of knowledge about the actual educational and social experiences of different ethnic groups of children.

In all the discourse about the public school education of children, for instance, it is easy to ignore or overlook the fact that the educational establishment is itself a multibillion-dollar business, which in turn is linked to local and national business interests. There are, in addition to the business of public school education, enormous economic and political forces that depend on a particular organization and ideology of public schooling. The stratification of society and the unequal distribution of resources and rights depend on the reproduction of certain kinds of unequal economic and political relations, and these relations depend for their legitimation upon the manipulation and control of what counts as knowledge about the constitution of society—and its history. Efficient hegemony depends especially on the ideological mystification of historical economic and political relations in society which would—were they and the social structures that generated them known—

reveal the processes and reasons undergirding the construction of particular types of state institutions, their development and change over time, and the positions and practices embodied within these institutions.

This program of social construction and engineering is one reason why teachers, as carefully screened and trained social agents, are, by necessity, inculcated in society's dominant and hegemonic ideology (Markowitz, 1993; Murphy, 1992). By fostering the internalization of this ideology as a system of beliefs, it is imagined (by Horace Mann and Ellwood Cubberley, among others) that teachers will uncritically (even enthusiastically) reproduce the ideology of individual achievement and self-determination (or the rationalization of social inequities as rooted in individual failings) through the inculcation of their students. This is a political process that perpetuates unequal social relations and protects those fundamental conditions of economic production that depend on the unequal distribution of resources and rights for their continuance.

Moreover, this political practice of ideological mystification to obscure the relation between public schools and capitalist society dates back to Horace Mann's invented mythic tradition of public education extending back in time to the Puritan settlements, and to his claims for social mobility through education.[2] As will soon become apparent, however, turning to Ellwood Cubberley, a less relativist historian than Urban and Wagoner, does not necessarily help our progress toward identification of real social structures, historical events and economic and political relations, or provide explanations that increase our knowledge of the past, or our understanding of the present.

ELLWOOD P. CUBBERLEY

The history of the state system of public school education, as it has been written in the 20th century, owes much to Ellwood Cubberley and his 1934 book, *Public Education in the United States*.[3] It is an indication of Cubberley's continued stature in the educational establishment, in the field of educational history, and in teacher training that he is still cited, quoted, and relied upon by numerous educators as the leading interpreter and/or authority on the development of the public school, its administrative organization, and its relation to American society (Button & Provenzo, 1989; Spring, 1994; Urban & Wagoner, 1996; Vinovskis, 1995).

In addition, no individual in the 20th century has had greater influence in shaping the state system of public school education, its physical and bureaucratic organization, its ideological and social aims, and what constitutes its reality and knowledge of it than Cubberley. He is the 20th-century educational establishment's first and most important master of ideological smoke and mirrors.

Between 1919, when first published, and 1934, when the revised second edition was issued, 80,000 copies of *Public Education in the United States* had been sold (Cremin, 1965). By 1960, Ellwood Cubberley's interpretive history of public school education in American society from Colonial times through the early 1930s had sold 100,000 copies (Bailyn, 1960/1972), and, in 1965, Lawrence Cremin confirmed its importance and influence by claiming that it continued to be used as a textbook in teacher education and had yet to be "superseded" (p. 2). The sales figures, however, reflect only new sales; they do not tell us how many of the 100,000 volumes were resold and sold again to successive classes and generations of teachers, American historians, or the curious. Bernard Bailyn's claim that *Public Education* was "exceedingly influential" (p. 12) is at best a conservative estimation. Cremin is not so reserved or circumspect about its importance:

> Indeed, its formulations have become so pervasive that we are largely unaware of them; yet they profoundly affect private practice, professional pronouncement, and public policy. In short, Cubberley's treatise remains contemporary, and almost a half-century after its appearance, it continues to define the nature and meaning of the American educational experience. (p. 2)

Cubberley would be pleased, for he wanted nothing less.

At the time *Public Education in the United States* (1934a) was published, Cubberley belonged to the educational establishment's select inner circle, which developed and directed public educational policy, and which dominated the training and placement of those men who were to become state and city school superintendents, as well as school principals—the men who would directly implement the policies and programs.[4] Other professional schoolpersons, educational entrepreneurs, and religious clerics before Cubberley had written accounts telling their story of public education's evolutionary progress. Cubberley gives passing notice to some (such as Small, Martin, and Graves), but in fact concentrates on Barnard as his most distinguished predecessor in educational scholarship and history (see Bailyn, 1960/1972, for an excellent survey of the field). With the possible exception of Barnard, none were positioned such as Cubberley in the upper echelon of a national organization economically and politically engaged in a complete reorganization of the public school system in American society and in defining how the reality of this relation was to be known, understood, and communicated. Cubberley tells us in his Preface to the revised second edition that his text "represented a method of treatment of the history of education that was new." And, "[t]hroughout, an effort was made...to set forth our educational history as an evolving series of events from which the recent advances in educational practice and procedure have had their origin..." (p. v).

Cubberley's position in the educational establishment as engaged propagandist for industrial efficiency and scientific management, as social engineer, as educational entrepreneur, as Dean of the School of Education at Stanford University, and as the designated historian among the leaders of the educational establishment make *Public Education in the United States* (1934a) a most peculiar text. It is stuffed with information about the legal, financial, and administrative development of the system of public school education and its integration into the State. *Public Education* is equally impressive in its near silence regarding historically specific socioeconomic circumstances that generated economic and political relations prior to the Civil War and after—unless one considers Cubberley's claims valid and fully explanatory that the War of Independence reduced the entire White population to poverty, or that World War I caused the Great Depression in the United States. But if his claim about the War of Independence, for instance, is valid, there is no explanation for grammar schools and academies for the wealthy, and charity or Lancasterian schools specifically for the working-class poor. If "the people" and the "nation" were so equally poor, where did the wealthy come from, and who organized and paid for these schools, and why the distinct class differentiations between them? It is not until Chapter XIV, where he shifts his discussion to the period between 1865 and 1930, that Cubberley has something substantial to say about society and what it had become by the year 1900, and what this signified for the state system of public school education. But even so, he sheds little illumination on how particular socioeconomic circumstances came to be as they are, nor does he explain why they must remain as they are or become progressively more so. Cubberley's discussion of society and problems generated by economic and political relations after the Civil War focuses almost exclusively on Eastern and Southern European immigrants, their biological inferiority and their corruption of American society, and upon the economic, political, cultural, and educational crises resulting from the emancipation of Black slaves. His discussion, however, depends on assertions, misrepresentations, and sweeping generalizations rather than on detailed inquiry, established congruences, and explanation.

It is because of Cubberley's peculiar rhetorical method of treating the whole of American history up to 1880 that his critics, and Bernard Bailyn in particular, have charged Cubberley and his cohort of presentism, for example, writing about and explaining the past through the categories, ideas, and values of the present. Objecting to presentism, however, may be a polite scholar's way of branding the text of another practitioner an ideological tract rather than a sincere explanatory effort to reconstruct the historical particulars of society in an earlier time. Or perhaps not. Labeling *Public Education* (1934a) as isolationist, presentist, and as consensus history, while in large measure true, is in fact to gloss over and obscure Cubberley's momentous, complex, labyrinthian rhetorical construction of American social history and the emergence of the state system of public school education.

To fully appreciate Cubberley's (1934a) concoction of historical details and interpretation, it is necessary to read *Public Education* twice, and from opposite directions. From front to back it is a 765-page rhetorical construct that Cubberley authoritatively claims is the new history of American education, of the public school system as it has evolved since the days of the first Puritan settlements to the present moment in 1919 (and extended to the 1930s in the second edition). From back to front, however, a radically different and less benevolent, less democratic history of the public school as social institution is revealed in Cubberley's text. In other words, the forward movement of *Public Education in the United States* is an interpretive reconstruction of American social and institutional history intended to legitimate and obscure under the mystifying rhetorical cover of *democratic progress* Cubberley and company's energized bureaucratic reorganization of the state system of public school education to secure the centralization and concentration of authority and policymaking for the purpose of more efficient social control and differentiation of labor. From back to front, however, it is obvious that Cubberley has had to peel away some of his ideological mystification of the 19th century.[5] To make 20th-century reorganization initiatives, which his "history" propagandizes and legitimates, appear to be evidence of both democratic progress and scientific efficiency, Cubberley reveals the 19th-century state system of public school education as a central mechanism of privilege and social control in the struggle between economic classes—to prevent class war, in the struggle of those in economic and political positions of governance against revolutionary democratic insurgents, in the struggle of elite and middle-class Protestant sects against working-class Protestant sects, and of Protestants collectively against Catholics and Jews, and in the struggle of Anglo-Americans with select allied groups from Western and Northern Europe against Black-Americans, Eastern and Southern European immigrants, and Asian immigrants.

Cubberley's (1934a) two opposing explanations of the public school's position in society can be visualized using Cubberley's own symbols: from front to back Cubberley tells the story of the American democratic ladder; but, from back to front, Cubberley explains the emergence of the American economic and political pyramid of hierarchically organized and differentiated classes and powers. In the first instance, the state system of public school education is a democratic vehicle carrying each American citizen socially upward as far as innate ability and economic means will permit.[6] In the second instance, the state system of public school education is an ideological and institutional hegemonic mechanism for securing and maintaining the stability of the American social pyramid in which economic acquisition and political power are concentrated at the top.

Something of Cubberley's (1934a) conceptual organization was revealed in his Preface, quoted above, and reappears as the first sentence of the last and shortest chapter of his history text:

> In the chapters preceding this one we have traced...the evolution of our American public schools from the days of their infancy...and have shown the connection between our more pressing present-day problems and our evolution during the past. (p. 750)

The past and the present are inextricably bound together. In Cubberley's history, present-day problems are rooted in a past that only makes sense in the context of the present. This is the present-perspective construction of history that Bailyn (1960/1972) protests with vigor, and rightly so, but it actually matters only if Cubberley is deliberately intent on writing *history*. But Cubberley is not writing history, he is writing propaganda to legitimate a particular social/educational ideology and a corresponding program of social determinism.

Cubberley's (1934a) rhetorical argument reconstructs the evolutionary development of a progressively "democratic"[7] system of public school instruction—one that overcomes the class-bias and rate-bills of early district schools,[8] that overcomes the incompetence of elected lay administrators of district schools, that overcomes sectarian opposition to secular public schooling,[9] and that by 1861 ultimately establishes on top of the elementary common schools a high school and, shortly after, a college education for all. This story is buttressed by a great many words and pages devoted to the needs and conditions required by children for healthy physical, mental, and social development.[10] This is Cubberley's construction of the democratic ladder. What he in fact identifies, establishes, and legitimates, however, is the progressive historical movement away from locally constituted district "public schools"—which tended to reflect objective conditions and antagonistic class relations, and which were more often than not only partially inclusive—to a system of State-imposed compulsory inclusion constituted by segregated and stratified schools organized along descending lines of race, ethnicity, and class,[11] as established by law and State policy, and under nondemocratic, hierarchical bureaucratic administration directed by nonelected experts (i.e., technocrats).[12] Undergirding all else (and a more coherent way to read his history in short) is Cubberley's account of a progressive institutional and social movement away from the inefficiency of democracy in an industrial capitalist society toward ever greater rule, order, and efficiency under the direction of the centralized State and administered by a strata of government bureaucrats and school superintendents—from the federal level, to the state, to the county, then to the city. This is his pyramid construct of the evolving system of public school education in its relation to society, and, too, this is the ideological conception around which his narrative is organized.[13]

Cubberley's (1934a) massing of historical details and his rhetorical strategy of describing the State's every advance over popular opposition as "democratic" progress act to obscure his ideology, just as his ideology is meant to mystify the processes and social reality of his program of radical public school reorganization. By abstracting his construction from its cloak of selective historical details and rhetoric, however, it is possible to see his undergirding ideology for what it actually is, and, too, to see how it informs the social construction of 20th century public school education.

Cubberley (1934a) is quite clever in the way he ideologically prepares for the "democratic" reorganization of the state system of public school education, which he explains in the latter third of *Public Education*. All along, Cubberley follows what appears to be a standard historical chronology. Occasionally, he steps out of strict historical narrative to tell readers that present circumstances, ideas, or practices owe their origin to this or that. To the New Englanders we owe the democratic ideal and the spread of public school education "open to all." We can thank James G. Carter and Horace Mann, for example, for establishing the precedent of the nonelective position of public school superintendence and the more efficient administration of the public school system. We can thank Mann in particular for helping the public school system break free from the stranglehold of the church and clerics. And for educational history and scholarship, we are deeply indebted to Henry Barnard. Also, Cubberley notes that William T. Harris, superintendent of St. Louis schools from 1867 to 1880, was our first great educational philosopher. To the uncritical eye, these asides do not distract from what otherwise appears to be a narrative of historical events and individual leaders important to the evolution of the state system of public school education. But, allowing Cubberley to say that something happened when he says it did,[14] his pretense of historical explanation is smoke and mirrors to cover up the simple fact that *Public Education in the United States* is an ideological polemic. And, as ideological polemic, his text has an internal logic of its own, even if it does not follow the disciplinary logic of historiography.

Cubberley's (1934a) construction of this embedded polemic follows the historical chronology of his sources, but, too, it is stratified. Thus, Fellenberg appears first in his narrative, followed by Johann Friedrich Herbart, and then Herbert Spencer. These three Europeans have their American counterparts in Horace Mann, Henry Barnard, and Frederick W. Taylor. The ideas and practices of the first group establish for Cubberley the defining stratification of public instruction along the lines of socioeconomic class, derived from Fellenberg; the proper relation of public instruction to the social and industrial needs of society, derived from Herbart; and the necessary and overarching reasons why the schools must be reorganized according to his explanations of society, derived from Spencer. The latter group exemplifies how the ideas and practices promoted by the first group were and are insinuated in and made over as the American system of public school education. In fact, Cubberley, to obscure what he is about, goes to extremes to keep the two groups separate in his narrative. For example, there is no explicit connection between the Prussian system of social inculcation through teacher education, public instruction and State-centralized administration, and Horace Mann. Barnard is an educational scholar and historian, not a capitalist seeking to generate a system of public school education dedicated to the secure production and reproduction of capitalist society. Taylor's systemic program of scientific management is poorly disguised as intelligent, scientific efficiency, and thus is not revealed as a social mechanism for establishing and reproducing unequal economic and political relations—without the danger of class consciousness.

Cubberley (1934a) has also identified the three Americans as role models for himself: As scholar and historian of the state system of public school education, he identifies Henry Barnard; as propagandist and social engineer for the reorganization of a secular (i.e., nonsectarian) public school education and its administration as a social institution dedicated to meeting the industrial and social needs of the State, he identifies Horace Mann; as strategic efficiency and management expert, Cubberley does not identify anyone, but in fact presents as his own program the hierarchical and systemic organization of management explicated by Frederick W. Taylor in *Principles of Scientific Management* (1967). The Americans are used, too, to obscure the ideological and social sources, and the historical socioeconomic circumstances that undergird the American system of public instruction.[15] Before Cubberley gets to

Taylor's scientific reconstitution of social relations, however, he first lays down a firm ideological foundation for the proper relation of the public school system, society, and the State—a relation that must be congruent with the undergirding social ontology for *Public Education in the United States*, which he does not make explicit until page 496 of the text.

Emanuel Fellenberg, Johann Friedrich Herbart, and Herbert Spencer are, according to Cubberley, European theorists whose educational and social ideas registered on American educational consciousness. In their historical roles, Fellenberg, Herbart, and Spencer are significant enough to warrant Cubberley's mention and his readers' attention. But more importantly, they have been given critical rhetorical and ideological roles to play in *Public Education* (1934a) that are central to Cubberley's larger project of explaining and legitimating the 20th-century reorganization of the state system of public school education. In the language of literary criticism, Cubberley uses these historical figures to foreshadow the historical future. In particular, Fellenberg is used to foreshadow the modern disciplinary institution, such as the reform school, but, too, his educational program, as explained by Cubberley, serves as the precursor for the stratification of schools and differentiated curriculum along lines of class and race, which Cubberley will eventually introduce as the new democratic public school system. Herbart is used to establish the argument for using the educational history textbook as instrumental to the proper inculcation of teacher candidates, and Spencer contributes to the development of the new curricula with his claims for the necessity of universal science education. Cubberley uses Herbart and Spencer as well to establish the ideological legitimation for the class and racial stratification of public school education, of which Fellenberg's program serves as the model. Cubberley's use of Fellenberg, Herbart, and Spencer to serve his argument and the needs of his project also poses problems; thus, his treatment of each is seldom straightforward. He is often at pains to focus on the content of their programs and/or ideas while simultaneously obscuring the substance and implications for society. Indeed, Cubberley's efforts to keep content and substance separate and to obscure actual social consequences of these ideas and programs when implemented, led him to make substantial omissions, especially in the case of his explication of Fellenberg.

EMANUEL FELLENBERG

Fellenberg's Manual-Labor system of education was introduced to the United States in 1829 through a series of published articles written by William Woodbridge. Cubberley (1934a) tells the reader that "Fellenberg's work was widely copied in Switzerland, Germany, England, and the United States, and contained the germ-idea of our modern agricultural, manual, and reformatory education" (p. 351). Several pages later, he is more emphatic about Fellenberg's influence on the development of the American public school:

The one European idea which we did adopt almost bodily...because we found it so well suited to early democratic conditions among a people of little wealth, was... worked out by Fellenberg and his followers at Hofwyl, in Switzerland, of combining manual labor with schooling.... The advantages, both pecuniary and educational, of combining schooling and farming made a strong appeal in the days when money was scarce and opportunities limited, and such schools...were founded first in Connecticut in 1819, Maine in 1821, Massachusetts in 1824, Kentucky in 1826, New York in 1827, Pennsylvania in 1829, New Jersey in 1830, Virginia in 1831, Georgia and Tennessee in 1832, and North Carolina in 1834. (p. 363)[16]

Cubberley (1934a) identifies six structural characteristics of Fellenberg's school that are meant to explain why American state public school promoters found it so well suited to socioeconomic circumstances:

1. A farm of about 600 acres.
2. Workshops for manufacturing clothing and tools.
3. A printing and lithographing establishment.
4. A literary institution for the education of the well-to-do.
5. A lower school that trained for handicrafts and middle-class occupations.
6. An agricultural school for the education of the poor as farm laborers, and as teachers for the rural schools.

Although he does not elaborate, Cubberley (1934a) at least points out that aspects of Fellenberg's conception served as the model for the American reform school. And elsewhere, he will explicitly identify the manual-industrial schools as reform schools. His fragmentary candor on these points, however, is counterbalanced by his studied omission of other social events and movements that might explain the attraction of the Fellenberg program of socialization and class-differentiated content and instruction better than his absurd claim that America was a poor country. In 1827, New York's law abolishing slavery in the state took effect. Andrew Jackson's election as President of the United States in 1828 was carried over venomous Whig opposition by the energized support of newly enfranchised, working-class, White males. In 1829, the New York Working Men's Association—under the guiding influence of Thomas Skidmore, the democratic revolutionary—issued its manifesto demanding structural reforms of the social order. Within weeks of their stunning declaration, they announced the formation of the Working Men's Party, which was specifically intended to lead in the organization of working men and their friends against the economic and political domination of the rich. This was also the year in which Thomas Skidmore and David Walker each published their revolutionary democratic treatises. About this same time, too, Robert Dale Owen and Franny Wright had been actively promoting a caretaker system of public education that would remove all children, rich and poor, and place them in secluded, State-run residential institutions where they would be housed, dressed, and educated alike (Wilentz, 1986).[17]

Cubberley's (1934a) silence on historical events and social movements has been noted by some of his critics, most often without the accompaniment of specifics, but no one to my knowledge has identified and established his engaged practice of ideological mystification or constructivism. His purpose in identifying Fellenberg is to leave a favorable impression of residential manual-labor education in his readers' minds, and to connect it in a positive way to the development of the agricultural state college system—where it will have lost all relation to the poor and to reform schools. Cubberley makes the Fellenberg program and its adoption in the United States appear innocent, a positive idea whose popularity crested too soon.

> It was at its height about 1830, but the movement soon collapsed. The rise of cities and wealth and social classes was against the idea, and the opening up of cheap and rich farms to the westward, with the change of the East from agriculture to manufacturing, turned the agricultural aspect of the movement aside for a generation. When it reappeared again in the Central West it came in the form of new demand for colleges to teach agriculture and mechanic arts, but with the manual-labor idea omitted. (p. 365)

Cubberley's (1934a) use of Fellenberg, though, is more than what it appears. He has told his readers that Fellenberg's ideas and program were introduced in the United States in 1829 through a series of articles, but within a year it was collapsing. There is no commonsense explanation to explain why a program of such tentative presence should be allotted the importance it receives in Cubberley's text, and he does not provide one. On the surface of his above statement, what he does establish by linking the Fellenberg idea to state colleges is it was not merely turned aside for a generation, but done away with entirely for the mass of working-class Whites who would not attend these state colleges in significant numbers until after World War II. Through this tidy bit of rhetoric, Cubberley has effectively directed attention away from reform schools, their parallel development with the system of public school education, and the increasing numbers of working-class children who came to occupy them.[18] He has in effect covered up Fellenberg's program as it was adapted for use in America.

Nearly 300 pages later, stripped of all Cubberley's (1934a) mystifying rhetoric, Fellenberg's program of a stratified education, divided along the lines of economic social positions, will reappear as democratic schools differentiated by students' capabilities: academic high schools for the capable and bright top 30% of students, and vocational and/or manual-industrial schools for the lower 70%. Cubberley is doing more than covering up Fellenberg's significant relation to American social education in this statement.

Cubberley's (1934a) explanation of the demise of the Manual-Labor school movement is an obscuring rhetorical maneuver. Cubberley claims Fellenberg's Manual-Labor idea was enormously popular for the education of machine workers in the cities. Logically, then, the westward movement of agriculture ought not to have had any negative effect on the continued popularity of the Manual-Labor schools in the cities. The only plausible explanation for their demise is suggested in his brief exclamation: "the rise of...social classes!" (p. 364). In other words, the working class for whom Manual-Labor education was intended rejected it, and Cubberley is doing his best to misdirect the reader's attention.

An important part of the consensus Cubberley (1934a) is drawing from and also promoting it is the story of the common bond between humanitarian public men as educational leaders and the supporting fellowship of enlightened working men— antagonistic class relations do not fit in this picture of social reality, nor does class conflict over equal general education. Yet Cubberley needs to acknowledge the early emergence of "social classes" to validate his claim of the "evolutionary development" of American society. By 1900, these social classes will have evolved in Cubberley's explanation into permanent social divisions. So here he rhetorically plants what appears to be a seed of the American society to come. The fact that he is obviously aware of class stratification and antagonistic class relations in the 19th century,[19] but does not explicate and elaborate these socioeconomic circumstances, indicates the high degree of authorial intentionality guiding what Cubberley chooses to explain, how he explains it, and where he places the explanation in his narrative. In short, Cubberley is constructing, rather than explaining, a particular historical reality.

To preserve the psychological impact of an invading immigrant and ex-slave Black laboring class, of emergent class and racial crises, which constitute his rhetorical emotional appeals substantiating the necessary reorganization of the state system of public school education at the turn of the century, Cubberley (1934a) does not reveal that class divisions were in fact already well developed, and the source of considerable antagonism and repeated eruptions of revolutionary democratic insurgency in the 19th century. His rhetorical tactic in constructing 19th-century history is to maintain silence or minimize the realities of class and antagonistic economic and political relations so that he can pose such conditions as unique to the decades following Reconstruction. At which point in his narrative Cubberley will stress the necessity of deliberately reorganizing the state system as the central "democratic" mechanism for responding to the social problems generated by class conflict—as if class conflict only emerged after the slaves were freed and certain immigrant groups settled in the United States.

It is no less interesting that the upstart and demise of the Fellenberg Manual-Labor school took place before Horace Mann was set to work energizing and reorganizing the Common School Reform Movement. Indeed, as Mann makes particularly explicit in his 1841 and 1848 *Reports*, the political expectation of the state system of public school education is it will specifically address the problem of class consciousness and antagonistic class relations in society that emerged in unison with the advance of industrial capitalism. But Cubberley (1934a) does not acknowledge Mann's or Barnard's positions, or the fact that Mann's efforts to secure a state system followed the general failure of charity schools, Lancasterian schools, and Fellenberg Manual-Labor schools to attract and inculcate the poor and the working class on the one hand, or, on the other hand, to answer the recognized need for an educational mechanism to distinguish and elevate the middle class from the lower classes. Therefore, according to Cubberley's construct of antebellum history, there is the indication of social class development, but typically antagonistic class relations go unexplored and unrecognized except for casual asides such as that evidenced above.

In addition to his silence on Mann's clear historical role in the context of 19th-century economic and political relations, Cubberley (1934a) is also silent about the obvious application of Fellenberg's Manual-Labor idea to the education of Black-Americans (Hampton/Tuskegee) and Amerindians (Carlisle). For example, if provision number 4 (literary education for the well-to-do) of Fellenberg's program is deleted, and provision number 5 is modified to delete instruction for the middle class, one has Samuel Armstrong's Hampton Institute for the education of Black-Americans (Anderson, 1986) and Pratt's Carlisle Institute, which followed for the education of Amerindians (Adams, 1995). In particular, provision number 6, which equates manual labor with teacher training, is precisely the Hampton Institute's program of training Black-American teachers for the task of inculcating Black-American children into a manual-labor work ethic (Anderson, 1986).

Cubberley's (1934a) silence is not oversight, but deliberate ideological mystification. First, he places the entire responsibility for the South's slow economic, political, and public educational development on the backs of Black-Americans, who were, according to Cubberley, slaves until the end of the Civil War, and who constituted two-fifths of the total population of illiterates in the United States as late as 1900. Second, Cubberley racially and ideologically mystifies the actual practices at Hampton and Tuskegee,[20] and the economic and political machinations of the Southern Educational Board, the General Education Board, and of Southern planters and capitalists generally to perpetuate illiteracy (or a delimited form of literacy) among Blacks and poor Whites. Their direct purpose through their public actions was to combat independent educational efforts and universal egalitarian democratic political aspirations by Black-Americans, and thus protect existing unequal social and economic relations, reestablish White political domination, and sustain and reproduce a large, Black, agricultural laboring class (Anderson, 1986; Holt, 1990). Cubberley won't mention Hampton and Tuskegee again for another 100 pages:

> The shop work, based on the "Russian system," included wood-turning, joinery, pattern-making, forging, foundry and machine work. Hampton Institute, after 1870, and Tuskegee Institute, after 1881, developed and applied the same type of technique for teaching trades to Negroes. (p. 464)

This passage specifically relates to Cubberley's elaborated discussion of the generative influence of the "Russian system" on certain American educators and industrialists intent on turning the public schools and colleges toward industrial skills and the applied sciences. He attributes the rise and character of industrial education to the "Russian system"—not to Fallenberg's school and curricular differentiation for a stratified class system. This passage demonstrates, in a small way, the multiple levels of mystification on which Cubberley's text operates. First, by linking industrial education to the "Russian system," and thus both to technical schools and colleges, he is redefining what vocational/industrial education is: training in skilled trades and applied sciences. Second, this looks forward to Cubberley's explication of vocational/industrial education for immigrant working-class children in the early 20th century, and will make the entire institutional socialization process appear to be benevolent and democratic—something it is not. But finally, the passage helps to expose the specific racist and ideological mystification that dominates these pages.

In his discussion of the retarded evolutionary development of the state system of public school education in the South after the Civil War, Cubberley (1934a) references W.E.B. DuBois's study of the Freeman's Bureau. But, significantly, he does not mention what DuBois had to say about Black-Americans' energized educational, economic, and political self-determination, and he does not cite DuBois in his index, nor include DuBois's work in his companion text of *Readings in Public Education in the United States* (1934b). Clearly, Cubberley (1934a) is aware of the actual socioeconomic circumstances in the South, and textual evidence strongly indicates he is also aware of the work of Black historians that refute racist mystifications of these circumstances.[21] There can be no doubt that Cubberley is thus deliberately covering up the fact that Hampton and Tuskegee were an insidious form of the Fellenberg Manual-Labor idea, where learning industriousness through long hours of arduous manual labor for scant wages, which must be turned over to the institution in payment for the privilege of learning to work, constituted enlightened educational practice (Anderson, 1986). Very little academic/intellectual education took place, and, for that matter, very little in the way of real craft skills were imparted to student-laborers (Anderson, 1986). When Cubberley's linkage between the "Russian system" and Hampton/Tuskegee is unpacked, the Manual-Labor/Industrial schools are revealed to be little more than "work-to-prepare-for-work" schools. This is a revelation, however, that is not anticipated in his text, nor is it addressed in any detail by any but a few educational historians who followed Cubberley (Anderson, 1986). As a matter of fact, by relying on Cubberley's explanation of the social and educational history of the South, teacher candidates would be no wiser about the actual relation between Fellenberg's program of education and the actual program at Hampton. Indeed, another 200 pages later, Cubberley returns us to Hampton Institute, which "the superintendent of public instruction of Virginia, Dr. Ruffner, declared it to be 'the most valuable of all schools opened on this continent for the colored people'" (p. 666).

Its founder, General Samuel Chapin Armstrong, had headed a colored regiment during the war, and in 1866 had been appointed superintendent of education for the colored people of Virginia under the Freedmen's Bureau. His training and experience had equipped him well to understand the needs of the Negro race, and during the twenty-five years he directed Hampton, until his death in 1893, he shaped the policy for the education of the Negroes and the Indians (included in 1878) of America, while the men and women he trained went out and became the leaders of their people throughout the South and West. The object of the institution was to train teachers and industrial leaders for the two races, particular emphasis being placed on character building, the missionary spirit, agricultural instruction, vocational course, and the home-making arts. (p. 667)

Cubberley's footnotes for Armstrong and Booker T. Washington, a graduate of Hampton, famous for founding the Tuskegee Institute and infamous as the Whites' Black spokesman for the Hampton idea, are also illuminating. Regarding Armstrong, Cubberley writes:

General Armstrong was born in the Hawaiian Islands, of missionary parents, and educated there and at Williams College. *For some years he was connected with the department of public instruction of Hawaii, where he obtained that knowledge of the education of backward peoples which proved of much use to him in his work for the Negroes of the South.* Realizing the need of the colored people for industrial training, he founded Hampton on the shores of Hampton Roads and began his great life-work. (emphasis added, p. 667, fn)

James D. Anderson is more forthcoming about the specifics of Armstrong's knowledge of "backward peoples" and his Hampton idea:

In his view, the "Colored people" could "afford to let politics severely alone." He maintained, for instance, that black participation in politics in South Carolina resulted in a "shameless legislature" that had "ruined the credit of a great state." Armstrong instructed black leaders to stay out of politics in South Carolina because they were "not capable of self-government," and he blamed the black voters for creating situations which "no white race on this earth ought to endure or will endure...." His idealized student was a hard worker with elementary education and industrial training. He did not believe that highly educated blacks would remain as "civilizers" among the rural masses. "There is such a thing as over-education," he warned. "A highly educated Negro is as little likely as a highly educated white man to do a work against which his tastes and sensibilities would every day rebel." The highly educated could not serve as models for the masses, who, according to Armstrong, were destined to plow, hoe, ditch, and grub. Therefore, manual labor rather than scholarship became Hampton's chief criterion for educational excellence. "One who shirks labor may be a fine mathematician," noted Armstrong, but "the blockhead at the black board may be a shining example in the cornfield." The idealized "blockhead" or "plodders," as they were called, became the standard by which all students were evaluated. "The plodding ones make good teachers." (1988, pp. 37, 48–49)

Armstrong's arguments found a sympathetic audience in Cubberley, who writes about Booker T. Washington:

Washington was born a slave...in 1858.... When fourteen years old, he walked five hundred miles to Hampton and asked for admission. His entrance examination was to clean out a dirty room. So well did he do the job that he not only was admitted, but paid all his expenses there for three years by janitor work. After some teaching experience, he studied further at Wayland Seminary at Washington, D.C., then became an instructor at Hampton, and, in 1881, he became principal of the new Institute chartered by the Alabama legislature at Tuskegee, where he remained the rest of his life.... He died in 1915. (1934a, p. 668)

What White, Anglo-American, Protestant male anywhere in the United States ever gained admission to college by passing an entrance examination consisting of cleaning out a dirty room? While pretending praise, Cubberley (1934a) is in fact declaring the backwardness of Black-Americans. Clearly, the reader is meant to understand that for Black-Americans the most appropriate test for school admission was (and, by implication, *is*) a set task at unskilled, tedious manual labor to determine the docility and obedience of the applicant. However, Cubberley's passage illuminates in the best possible way what actually constituted education at Hampton Institute. Such education and training as perpetuated there was not in the skilled industrial trades or applied sciences. And, too, the passage illuminates the manner in which Fellenberg's ideas were incorporated in the United States. But it is precisely this direct relationship between Fellenberg's program and the manner in which it has been adapted, promoted, and imposed in the United States for socially constructed class and racial division and subjugation that Cubberley covers up.

Central to Cubberley's (1934a) legitimation of State control of public school education, to centralized bureaucratic administration, and to a system of hierarchically stratified schools and differentiated curricula, is his argument that (1) Eastern and Southern European immigrants, and the great mass of Black-Americans, are backward, illiterate, and pose a dangerous obstacle to the State; (2) 70% of all young are incapable or unwilling to benefit from an academic education; and (3) Fellenberg's Manual-Labor idea provides the foundational model for the industrial/vocational school, which is the "democratic" answer to the social reality of the first two socioeconomic circumstances.

Cubberley (1934a) writes with at least two audiences in mind: First, college-educated men of the inner circle of superintendency, among whom Cubberley proudly includes himself, and school principals who, to efficiently fulfill the duties of their social positions and scientifically direct the manufacturing processes of the national school system and individual schools must understand the aim, content, methods of instruction, and the undergirding reasons of public instruction. And, given the high level of organized collaboration and coordination amongst these men in reorganizing and redefining the state system of public school education, it certainly appears that Cubberley expected this audience to make the connection between Fellenberg, as explained in his text and its manifestation as vocational and industrial education, and to properly interpret its meaning. Thus, for this audience, Cubberley can be said to be revealing. Cubberley's second audience are teacher candidates and practicing teachers, who, by virtue of their particularly delimited education and training, might not be expected to recognize the significant relation between Fellenberg and vocational/industrial public instruction.[22] As a matter of fact, by not making the relationship and its meaning explicit, Cubberley is mystifying the program of a socially engineered laboring force that is correspondingly subjugated politically and exploited economically. Were the reality of Hampton and its direct relation to Fellenberg's idea of stratified education explicitly illuminated in his text, training and practicing teachers might not be especially enthusiastic about their socially prescribed role as "blockheads" and "plodders," as agents for the reproduction of a socially constructed laboring force. Cubberley's explanation of the "democratic" vocational high school would be exposed for what it is. The exposure of Fellenberg/Hampton would reveal a social reality of antagonistic class and socially constructed race relations on the one hand, and on the other hand, reveal the antidemocratic ideology and processes undergirding the reorganization of the state system of public school education that his text is meant to advance. But, more importantly, were the truth known, Cubberley and company's program could easily have met the same fate as the Fellenberg Manual-Labor schools of the 1830s.

JOHANN FRIEDRICH HERBART

Cubberley (1934a) prepares the way for Herbart in much the same way he prepared for Fellenberg, by writing at length about Johann H. Pestalozzi.[23] Where Pestalozzi sought to transform the structures of society by giving poor children an academic education on one hand and teaching them skills for self-sufficiency on the other— and thus be prepared to take on the task of social transformation—Fellenberg is held up as more suitable, for he sought the transformation of the poor child without seeking the transformation of existing class relations. When he is ready for Herbart, Cubberley again uses Pestalozzi as his foil. Where Pestalozzi was a country farmer turned educator, "an impractical enthusiast" who defined teaching as spiritual, as an "act of love," Herbart was the son of "a well educated public official," "a well-trained scholarly thinker," and "professor of philosophy in a German University," who defined teaching as both an art and a "science" (p. 450). Cubberley clearly wants it understood that teaching as love for the child, teaching as dedicated to the healthy individual and social development of the child, is no good as the foundation for teacher training or as something upon which to erect an efficient system of public instruction. For this, science is required. But not just any science will do, a science of teacher training and a science of instruction that correspond to a science of society is needed. And, according to Cubberley, Herbart establishes this science.

Among the few things about which Cubberley is consistent is his attack against the "district schools." Scattered throughout his text, he gives various reasons against it, but his foremost reasons are local community orientation and governance, unsystematic criterion for teacher hiring, unsystematic selection of textbooks, and individualized instruction. Herbart provides Cubberley with both a theory and practice by which to promote an entirely different conception of the relationship between society, public school education, and teacher training.

> Herbart rejected alike the conventional-social education of Locke, the natural and unsocial education of Rousseau, and the "faculty-psychology" conception of education of Pestalozzi. Instead he conceived of the mind as a unity, rather than divided into "faculties," and the aim of education as broadly social rather than personal. The purpose of education, he said, was to prepare men to live properly in organized society, and hence the chief aim in education was not conventional fitness, natural development, mere knowledge, nor personal mental power, but personal character and social morality. This being the case, the educator should analyze the interests and occupations and social responsibilities of men as they are grouped in organized society, and, from such analyses, deduce the means and the method of instruction. (1934a, p. 451)

Certain social conditions and labor forces are necessary to fulfill the needs of capitalist society. Sustaining and reproducing these conditions and the necessary labor forces thus constitutes the legitimate aim of education. The educator's task is to inculcate the child into this society through a particular curricular content and method of instruction. The state system of public school education, therefore, exists not for the healthy development of the individual child, nor is it necessarily to reform, improve, or transform society; rather, its aim is directed toward meeting the social and industrial reproduction needs of capitalist society. Content and method of instruction are sufficiently and efficiently to prepare each and every child for their place, role, and function in meeting the social and industrial needs of the State.[24] Given the social aim of public instruction, the content and methods cannot be otherwise, for the individual's "social responsibilities and duties are determined by the nature of the social organization of which he forms a part" (Cubberley, 1934a, p. 451). In other words, the purpose of education is to reproduce the organization of economic and political relations as they actually and already exist.

But as the 20th-century state system of public school education is reorganized to meet the social and industrial needs of the State through its differentiated content and courses of study and its stratified levels of schools, it is essential that every subject of study at every level be commensurate with particular methods of instruction meant to establish and extend hegemony over all classes. Indeed, as Cubberley (1934a) warns, the real danger to society comes not from unequal economic and political relations, which constitute society as it actually is, but from the potential development of critical knowledge and class consciousness. Thus, in differentiated content and administrative organization, the school must be made consistent with actual economic and political relations of society, and this society must be made to appear normal and the best possible. The state system of public school education thus has two aims: first, to meet the social and industrial needs of the State, and, second, to prevent the emergence of class consciousness.[25]

To be met efficiently, both of these aims must be ideologically mystified. Cubberley (1934a) explains that the 70% of all children channeled into the vocational schools and into the Manual-Industrial schools are so directed because they are incapable or unwilling to learn from books. And if questioned by individual parents or students, administrators can point to Lewis Termin's (1919) scientific IQ studies, to his ethnically and racially differentiated statistical findings to show that Italian children, Polish children, or Black-American children, and so forth, typically score so low on the IQ scale of intelligence measurement that if such a child were placed in an academic school they would certainly fail. The teacher, parent, and child are meant to understand that placement in a vocational or industrial school is in fact a humanitarian act, a marvelous educational and training opportunity, and the children will now be able to contribute to the progress of society and of themselves (Cubberley, 1923a).[26] Providing for so many formerly excluded and academically incapable children is, Cubberley (1934a) claims, evidence of the progressive features of our democratic society. That these same children are identified, sorted, and sent into differentiated educational tracks before or shortly after beginning school, that their educational opportunities, that the content and methods of instruction they encounter, that the organization of social relations into which they are acculturated are all socially determined and constructed for them by a socially dominant class and race constitutes a reality that must be ideologically hidden if economic and political hegemony is to be successfully established—if a stratified, fragmented, and differentiated laboring force is to be produced to meet the social and industrial needs of the State—if critical intelligence and class consciousness are to be suppressed.

For such a program as this to take root and prosper, it is essential that teachers in particular be properly inculcated in the dominant ideology and that their training be carefully constructed and properly delimited. Having studied the Prussian system and having traveled there to observe it firsthand, Horace Mann clearly understood the necessary importance of State-regulated teacher training, and in short order after returning he set about implementing normal schools for this purpose. Child psychology (i.e., understanding how different groups of children learn most thoroughly and effectively), content (i.e., mastery of prescribed textbooks or building materials), and efficient methods of instruction (i.e., appropriate to age, capability, subject, and predetermined aims) soon came to dominate teacher training. But these areas of study and practice alone were and are insufficient to transform the teacher into a reliable and efficient agent of the State. Thus, it was necessary that teachers' training include a correct history of society and the relation of public education to it.

In the mid-1800s, it was, perhaps, enough for Horace Mann to dwell upon the Puritans and to tell of their dedication to schooling all children and of their commitment to bringing light into the darkness. By the early 20th century, the Puritan beginning provided a suitable point from which to start, but it was obviously insufficient. Hence, Cubberley's (1934a) teachers' education history for the proper explanation of what constitutes the reality of society, of economic and political relations, of different groups of children and races, and of the public school and its relation to this complex society.

Cubberley relies on Herbart to justify the sort of history he is writing and its aims:

> ...Herbart now added the two important studies of literature and history, and history with the emphasis on the social rather than the political side.... History in particular Herbart conceived to be a study of the first importance for revealing proper human relationships, and leading men to social and national "good-will." (1934a, p. 451)

Against the background of the Russian Revolution, of the recently concluded First World War, of Black-Americans struggling for integration and equality, revolution, or independent self-determination, of organized laborers' campaigns for democracy and their bloody confrontations with goons, Pinkertons, police, and military sent in to crush them, of populist farmers fighting bankers and politicians and the railroads, of increasingly popular socialists and Marxists, of decades of steady immigration from Eastern and Southern Europe, and of cycles of economic crisis, Cubberley's (1934a) choice of words and his purposeful vagueness appear richly connotative. The separation of "social" from "political" is most interesting; for how can one exist without the other? Without civic political behavior, without contested ideology, rule, and culture, one is confronted by the totalitarian State. To jettison the political dimensions of such a state is to posit the State's sanctity and supremacy as an unquestionable fact. And society within a totalitarian State must be rigidly organized and ideologically and culturally homogeneous if the State is to survive, or the State, representing the interest of those for whom it is energized, must rely on the uncertain and costly means of violent coercion to sustain and reproduce itself. In the context of the United States, therefore, to jettison the political is to jettison democracy (at least such notions as the *people* are supreme) and precepts of self-government. Thus, one of Cubberley's circle could read the above passage and understand him to mean an ideologically constructed history to indoctrinate, and to instill a narrowly conceived nativist nationalism to mean the inculcation of the teacher and student into the existing social order and for the production of conformism and social reproduction.

Cubberley, making his point explicit, writes:

> The chief purpose of education Herbart held to be to develop personal character and to prepare for social usefulness. These virtues, he held, proceeded from enough of the right kind of knowledge, properly interpreted to the pupil so that clear ideas as to relationships might be formed.[27] (1934a, p. 451)

Horace Mann also made this argument of the role of public school education in preventing class consciousness in a number of his *Reports*, but most pointedly in his *Twelfth Annual Report*.[28] But for Cubberley (1934a) to reveal this interesting correspondence between Mann's arguments and his interpretation of Herbart in this context and to his audience of teacher candidates would be to reveal too much. It would expose his manipulative use of Pestalozzi by making a clear connection between Mann, Herbart, and the Prussian system (one that is rather different from that which he has constructed)—a connection Cubberley has studiously ignored. And, too, that Mann and Herbart, whose active engagement in devising a form of public education, and its proper implementation to secure social control and order, might lead to the revelation that both men and their cohorts were responding to antagonistic class relations and social crises. And this in turn might raise questions about the historical socioeconomic circumstances that generated these particular relations, conflicts, and crises. In any case, it is too soon in his argument to make such a revelation, for he needs Herbart to be relevant to the present moment and transformed into an American presence.

Cubberley's (1934a) use of Herbart serves a number of his project's needs. Where Fellenberg has been used to delineate the class stratification of public school education, Herbart is used to define the essential pedagogy: aim, content, and method of instruction. Herbart is also Cubberley's compelling scientific authority legitimating the dismissal of child development as the aim of public education and shifting its aim to shaping social behavior, that is, "character," compatible with existing social relations and their organization in society. Cubberley also uses Herbart to validate the ideological centrality of the educational history textbook as the mechanism for the inculcation of both the training teacher and the school child into "the right kind of knowledge," which has been "properly interpreted...so that clear ideas as to relationships [in society] might be formed" (p. 451). If society is determining, then "proper human relations" are those that already exist. What must follow is making the child understand these relations and his/her place among them as correct, and that these relations could not be better otherwise. According to Cubberley, therefore,

> From full knowledge, and with proper instruction by the teacher, clear ideas or concepts might be formed, and clear ideas ought to lead to right action.... (p. 452)

Finally, Cubberley uses Herbart to speak directly to educators responsible for training teachers regarding what constitutes the appropriate learning environment, the proper relation between the teacher and the students, and the methods to be employed.

> Interest he held to be of first importance as a prerequisite to good instruction. If given spontaneously, well and good; but, if necessary, forced interest must be resorted to. Skill in instruction is in part to be determined by the ability of the teacher to secure interest without resorting to force on the one hand or sugar-coating of the subject on the other.... Herbart elaborated the process by which new knowledge is assimilated in terms of what one already knows, and from his elaboration of this principle the doctrine of apperception—that is, the apperceiving or comprehending of new knowledge in terms of the old—has been fixed as an important principle in educational psycholo-

gy. Good instruction, then, involves first putting the child into a proper frame of mind to apperceive the new knowledge, and hence this becomes a cornerstone of all good teaching method.[29] (1934a, p. 452)

The immediate aim, of course, is to follow a "methodical organization of the facts" directed by "some definite purpose...to secure certain predetermined ends in child development..." (p. 453). And, Cubberley might have said, to secure certain predetermined ends in teacher development. But he has said enough; he has established Herbart's theory of public instruction and its aims, he has validated the utility and centrality of an inculcating "history," and with these functional pieces in place it is time to bring Herbart to America.

Herbart died in 1841, and his works waited until 1865 to be resurrected and popularized by Tuiskon Ziller in Leipzig. American teacher educators studying in Jena, Germany, in the late 1800s became involved with the German Herbartian "scientific society" and returned to the States full of enthusiasm. Three of these American gentlemen proceeded to publish textbooks based on Herbart/Ziller: In 1889, Charles DeGarmo published *Essentials of Methods,* followed in 1892 by Charles A. McMurray's *General Method,* and in 1897 by Frank McMurray's *Method in Recitation.* Herbart's theory and practice of a socializing education is now both contemporary and American. Indeed, in 1892, the National Herbart Society was founded in the United States, which in turn became the National Society for the Study of Education in 1909, and was still active at the time Cubberley published his second edition.

Cubberley has now posited a model of his organization of stratified schools for differentiated groups of American children. He has set forth the socializing aims of these schools, and the ideological importance of the right historical knowledge to be interpreted for and to teacher candidates that they will become efficient agents of a prescribed socialization. What remains is a theory of society and State action that legitimates his program. For this he turns to his interpretation of Herbert Spencer's social Darwinism.

HERBERT SPENCER

Cubberley (1934a) constructs his theory of the relation between the state system of public school education and society on his understanding of Herbert Spencer:

In his essay he declared...that the only way to judge of an educational program was first to classify, in the order of their importance, the leading activities and needs of life, and then measure the instructional program by how fully it offers such a preparation. (p. 470)

This is a variation of Herbart's aim, content, and method of instruction. Cubberley tells us the worth of education is to be determined by "the leading activities and needs of life." And is this industrial manufacturing and commerce? Whomever owns the means of production, the bank, the insurance company, and/or the ships and rail-roads certainly has different "activities and needs of life" than the peddler, porter, or bricklayer, than the seamstress, laundress, or housekeeper. Cubberley implicitly acknowledges these divisions and differences, and suggestively posits the idea that a scientific and efficient public school education must be organized accordingly.[30] By way of an elaborated footnote, Cubberley reinforces his idea:

> Spencer's classification of life activities and needs, in the order of their importance, was:
>
> 1. Those ministering directly to self-preservation.
> 2. Those which secure for one the necessities of life.
> 3. Those which help in the rearing and disciplining of offspring.
> 4. Those involved in maintaining one's political and social relations.
> 5. Those which fill up the leisure part of life, and gratify taste and feelings. (p. 470)

This enumeration constitutes a rationalization of a class-based hierarchy and its status quo. The prescription of this program, as a matter of fact, calls for social domination through hegemony. But, embedded in this program is also the seed for antagonistic class relations.[31] In the competition for limited resources, (1) the economic and political elite want to preserve their position, and (2) their privileged necessities of life, which (3) depends on the proper rearing and disciplining of lower-class children, and (4) sustaining unequal social relations, which (5) thus enables leisure, luxury, and refined tastes. But from the position of the working class and the poor, securing one's self-preservation (item #1) depends on getting back some of what has been appropriated and acquired by the elite in order that their necessities (item #2) might be partially satisfied. The working class is thus pitted against the elite in a struggle for survival and basic necessities, which excludes them from overconcern about item #3—for they are working and such rearing and discipline is actually taken care of by the State (i.e., by schools, courts, and reform schools or prisons)—and they are confronted with the seeming perma-nence of item #4, and thus excluded from experiencing such things as leisure time and gratified tastes. But Cubberley does not want anyone to think the working class do not have leisure time. Quoting William Russell, Dean of Teachers College, educators and policymakers are asked "When does unemployment become a vaca-tion?"[32] And Cubberley, reinforcing this perverse idea, proceeds hereafter to sub-stitute the term "excess leisure time" for unemployment; thus, one is not so much unemployed as living life at one's leisure. However, late in the 19th century and well into the 20th century, society addressed leisure time and activity for the work-ing class through the mechanism of advertising, the ideology of abundance, and materialism fostered by time-payments and credit for commodity purchases (Lears, 1994), and through the provision of amusement parks, company picnics, team sports, and organized spectator sports (Nasaw, 1993; Violas, 1978), while keeping up a steady attack against taverns, speakeasies, and unions. Preserving the social order of political and social relations was and remains the item of greatest concern to the privileged in American capitalist society. Securing this order has depended largely on the State's policing powers and on the propagation of nativism and race ideology (Ross, 1935; Termin, 1919).

In short, through his explication of Spencer, Cubberley (1934a) promotes a capitalist social system organized around the unequal distribution of social positions, rights, and resources; it is clearly not a democratic program. It is a program that elevates acquisitive and appropriating behaviors to the status of natural law.

While the rich man's children ride their ponies or enjoy their European tours, the working man's children sweat in the mills and factories to generate wealth to satisfy the tastes and feelings of their "social betters"—or they stand in unemployment and/or food lines (see, for example, Covello, 1958; Gutman, 1987; Luther, 1962). And the preservation of elite privileges depends upon the consumption of the fruits of labor's life force and production. While the children of the wealthy enjoy small school classes of intimate to modest sizes, the children of other groups are sandwiched into classrooms of 25 to 50 students (or to 300 or more in the 19th-century monitorial schools)—if they attend school at all. And these social and educational inequities are precisely what item #4 of Spencer's evolutionary theory of social law legitimizes. In Cubberley's (1934a) program of centralization and consolidation of administrative authority and of social stratification and hegemony, sustaining and reproducing unequal economic and political relations are the undergirding motivations, and it is an essential social condition for the realization of the society he advocates. For such a reason, like Horace Mann before him, Cubberley rails against the small town and rural district system where far too many children enjoyed the benefit of small class sizes and individualized instruction. The district system was too localized and too independent to insure the program of systemic ideological and cultural indoctrination.

The problem for the state system of public school education is thus extraordinarily complex as Cubberley (1934a) will make explicit in Chapter XIV. To solve the problem, the state system of public education must be organized around these different and opposing social classes, activities, and life needs, and it must be done in ways that prevent the emergence of class consciousness and open antagonisms. A reorganized system of stratified schools and differentiated students, according to predetermined aims as set by the industrial and social needs of the State, can accomplish the first goal, but not the second. To achieve the second goal, and make it coherent with the first, requires properly trained teachers using a scientifically adjusted content interpreted by efficient methods of instruction that are fitted to each particular group of children. But here, Cubberley is laying down his ideological foundation, the undergirding theories and rationalization for the program of socially differentiated classes and educational reorganization. More importantly, he does not want these ideas or his program to appear as they actually are. So he is silent about social Darwinism, about survival of the fittest class, and about class conflict over the unequal distribution of life's necessities, and he endeavors to make Spencer over into a humanitarian:

> ...instead of a few being educated for a life of learning and leisure, he urged general instruction in science that all might receive training and help for the daily duties of life. (p. 471)

"Science" has become a code word for efficient regulation and reproduction of economic and political relations in society. On one side of the equation, a few are educated for a life of learning and leisure, but on the other side, the "all" are to be scientifically educated for their "daily duties of life." Some have leisure, and all the rest have duties. Leisure cannot exist without the performance of duties. The equation is based on a stratification of fixed classes.

Through his rhetorical exploitation of Fellenberg, Herbart, and Spencer, Cubberley (1934a) has effectively established the what, how, and why of the reorganization of the state system of public school education, which he will elaborate over the next 300 pages of his "history." Up to this point, however, he has been constructing the undergirding ideology and models that are essential to making sense of the present social reality, which he will soon make explicit, and an alternative society, which he will propose as one toward which his reorganized public instruction leads. Indeed, the first 479 pages of his interpretive reconstruction of educational history are a preparation for his explanation of the present, the specific nature of its social crisis, and his solution to this crisis.

Cubberley (1934a) addresses the present in two stages: the first is laid out in Chapter XIV, and the second in Chapter XX. The former identifies new immigrants from Eastern and Southern Europe as foremost among the threats to democratic life, institutions and government in America, and a dangerous obstacle to meeting the social and industrial needs of the State. The second identifies Black-Americans, freed at the conclusion of the Civil War, as the primary cause for the economic and educational backwardness of the southern states. Thus, a dangerous mass of poor, illiterate, and subnormal racial ethnics in the North and West, and a dangerous mass of illiterate, disease-spreading Black-Americans in the South[33] are jointly responsible for the economic and political problems plaguing American society in the first three decades of the 20th century. Cubberley informs his readers that as a consequence of these pressing circumstances, the state system of public school education has, for the first time, had to shoulder the burden of educating and socializing the children of these alien and dangerous classes for their place in modern society. This is made extraordinarily difficult by the popular but false and dangerous notions of democracy and equality[34] and the inefficiency of representative government. Cubberley writes,

> Compared with a highly organized and centralized nation, such as France, Germany, Italy, or Japan, we seem feeble in our ability to organize and push forward a construc-

tive program for national development. Many of the tools and methods they have used so effectively are entirely lacking with us. (p. 489)

Although we lack the fascist tools and methods to meet the alien and racial challenges to our national development, Cubberley (1934a) explains, the educational establishment has developed vocational education for White ethnics and segregated industrial education for Blacks in the South to provide for the particular capabilities and needs of these groups of children. Indeed, the entire system has been reorganized along scientific lines to meet the social and industrial needs of the State as it actually is.

According to Cubberley,

The modern city is essentially a center of trade and industry, and home life and home conditions must inevitably be determined and conditioned by this fact. The increasing specialization in all fields of labor has divided the people into dozens of more or less clearly defined classes, and the increasing centralization of trade and industry has concentrated business in the hands of a relatively small number of people. All standards of business efficiency indicate that this should be the case, but as a result of it the small merchant and employer are fast giving way to large mercantile and commercial concerns. No longer can a man save up a few thousand dollars and start in business for himself with much chance of success. The employee tends to remain an employee; the wage-earner tends to remain a wage-earner. New discoveries and improved machinery and methods have greatly increased the complexity of the industrial process in all lines of work, and the worker in every field of trade and industry tends more and more to become a cog in the machine, and to lose sight of his part in the industrial processes and his place in our industrial and civic and national life. (1934a, pp. 496–497)

However appropriate and rational this organization of society may be, there are inherent dangers:

With the ever-increasing subdivision and specialization of labor, the danger from class subdivision has been constantly increasing, and *more and more has been thrown upon the school the task of instilling into all a social and political consciousness* that will lead to unity amid our great diversity, and to united action for the preservation and improvement of our democratic institutions. (emphasis added, Cubberley, 1934a, p. 504)

Cubberley's concerns are not with class stratification, which he readily accepts as permanent, but with the *danger* that emergent antagonistic class consciousness poses to the social order.[35]

Those in positions of authority in the educational establishment are meant to recall Fellenberg, Herbart, and Spencer: A stratified system of public instruction that corresponds with differentiated social positions and classes; a socializing public instruction adapted to different capabilities and social classes/races; all of which is scientifically designed to insure the survival and reproduction of the capitalist social order as it is actually constituted, thus meeting the social and industrial needs of the

State. Of course, Cubberley (1934a) does not explicitly remind his audience of teachers of these three social theorists and/or educational practitioners, nor does he explicitly claim that fascism is a more efficient government by which to organize society. Cubberley merely asks his readers to compare a more efficient and ordered society with our own troubled one:

> Contrasted with a highly organized Nation, such as Germany was before the World War, we seem feeble in our ability to organize and push forward a constructive national program for development and progress. The State was highly organized; the people homogeneous; *the officials well educated, and selected by careful service tests; national policies were painstakingly thought out and promulgated; the schools were effectively organized into uniformly good institutions for the advancement of the national interests; the teachers were carefully trained in state institutions, and made into parts of a national army expected to follow the flag loyally;* the Church was nationalized, and in part supported by the Government; religion was taught in all schools, and the weight of religion and the backing of the priesthood were used to support the State; and *a great national army was maintained and used as an educative force for nationalizing all elements and training the people in obedience and respect for law and order.* (emphasis added, p. 760)

Through restrictive immigration laws, through an expanded police/military force, through the abolition of democratic elective processes for selecting school superintendents, and through the systemic adoption of scientific administration and scientifically reorganized public instruction, American society can effectively control racial heterogeneity on the one hand, and on the other, can effectively "nationalize all elements and training [of] the people in obedience and respect for law and order." The systemic adoption of the prescribed program for reorganizing the state system of public education will, according to Cubberley, simultaneously meet the social and industrial needs of the State and prevent the emergence of dangerous class consciousness, and thus the potential of socialist or Marxist revolution. This is the lesson of Cubberley's *Public Education in the United States* (1934a).[36]

Cubberley's *Public Education* (1934a) was last reprinted in 1947. Perhaps because of post-World War II, college-educated, working-class ethnic and Black-American veterans and women who chose teaching as a career, perhaps because of the demise of Joseph McCarthy and the 1954 *Brown* vs. *Topeka* Supreme Court decision, or perhaps due to a combination of many other factors, Cubberley's text as material artifact—as textbook—could no longer be persuasively reconciled with the changes occurring in American society by the educational establishment and its practitioners. Cubberley's blatant nativism and racism, his textual contradictions, the fallacy of much of his interpretive history, and its datedness, if not his thinly veiled enthusiasm for fascism, made the use of his textbook increasingly problematic. The challenge for establishment educational historians became how to preserve Cubberley's myth of humanitarian public men leading an enlightened intelligent working class in the progressive establishment and development of a democratic-ladder educational institu-

tion, and to preserve his ideological mystification of stratified schools and differentiated curricula—and the undergirding antidemocratic ideology and social structures of
the state system.

Much of the criticism of Cubberley's (1934a) educational history, therefore, has
been peculiar for its tendency to focus on particular historiographic interpretations
and some of his errors of historical fact, while leaving his undergirding ideology
untouched. In 1960, for example, Bernard Bailyn took aim at Cubberley, as well as
at educational historians generally, for constructing a presentist consensus history of
the American public school, and for treating it in isolation from other forms of cultural education and generally ignoring the contributions of American historians. The
blunt end of Bailyn's criticism is Cubberley was drawing on an interpretative consensus of the evolutionary development of the public school system already established by the end of the 19th century. Although Bailyn focuses his aim on
Cubberley's history in particular because it had been quickly taken up by the educational establishment after its publication in 1919 as the primary vehicle for disseminating this consensus tradition, he largely ignores Cubberley's social ideology. In
1965, Lawrence Cremin responded to Bailyn's assessment and agreed with him that
the history of the state system of public school education ought to be located within
the broader historical context of cultural production. The primary purpose of his
essay, however, is to identify and then downplay the importance of Cubberley's blatant historical errors, to contextualize his institutional history of public education
within the field of educators and historians, to protect the overall text (as it pertains
to the legal and administrative development of public school education) and interpretation (specifically the relation between the public school and social progress),
and to redeem Cubberley's reputation as preeminent among educational historians.
Indeed, despite Bailyn's specific criticism of Cubberley's treatment of the Colonial
period and his historiographic methods generally, Cremin asserts that even when the
flaws of Cubberley's history are acknowledged, *Public Education in the United
States* remains unsurpassed in educational historiography.

A decade later, in *The Revisionists Revised* (1978), Diane Ravitch recapitulates
the Bailyn/Cremin criticism of Cubberley, but puts her emphasis on his failure to
explicate the particulars of actual classrooms and the ways in which "education related to broad social and political currents, and how changes came about" (p. 28).
Ravitch's explicit criticism of Cubberley, however, is neither original or perceptive,
but her obvious silences are illuminating. She says nothing about Cremin's particular points of rebuttal to Bailyn's criticism or his zealous effort to redeem Cubberley's
reputation. By studiously ignoring Cremin's marshalled defense at the same time
rehashing those critical points he shares with Bailyn, Ravitch appears to distance
herself from Cubberley, his narrow perspective historicism, and his so-called promotionalism. But appearances aside, Ravitch's rhetorical ploy is not a critique of
Cubberley's history of the public school system or of his undergirding ideology.
Ravitch's desire to appear critical of Cubberley, and thus of a different camp or higher order of historians, is calculated, and is understandable. Cubberley's nativism,

racism, and fascist tendencies are everywhere explicit or exposed in *Public Education* (1934), and in 1975 one could not explicitly champion him without coming away befouled and stinking; but Ravitch in fact gets away with it through the rhetorical means of letting R. Freeman Butts (1974) implicitly legitimate Cubberley by attacking the "culture" premise of Cremin/Bailyn's criticism.

The sum total of these criticisms is: Cubberley's focus was artificially narrow; his writing was flawed by interpretive inaccuracies and overall by promotionalism; he subsumed actual instructional practice under legal, financial, administrative, organizational, and structural categories of study; and he failed to adequately explain the complex relation between the public school and society.[37] As a matter of fact, however, Bailyn, Cremin, and Ravitch go easy on Cubberley—he may have got the parts wrong, his historiographic methods may be wanting, but he got the whole correctly. They may chide him, they may prefer a different sort of historiography, they may have wanted more of this and less of that, but these are trivial matters compared to their fundamental agreement with Cubberley's ideological mystification of the actual relation between public school education, the expansion of the American State under capitalism, and achievement ideology[38] (see Bailyn, 1960/1972; Cremin, 1965; Ravitch, 1978). Thus, once the fight is over and the critics have returned to their desks, Cubberley, his history of the state system of public school education, and his ideology are seen to be very much intact and little the worse for the show of rough handling.

Subsequent assaults on *Public Education* (1934), however, have been less kind, but have generally limited their criticism to Cubberley's racist characterization of Black-Americans and the end of chattel slavery, and of all the immigrant groups from Eastern and Southern Europe and their participation in the American political system. A somewhat more serious inquiry into Cubberley's text was initiated by educational revisionist historians who were in fact the actual targets of Diane Ravitch's (1978) traditionalist doctrinaire essay. David Tyack in *The One Best System* (1974), and with Elisabeth Hansot in *Managers of Virtue* (1982), opened the door of explanatory critique wider by signaling that more than Cubberley's race prejudices deserved mention: Cubberley's candid dismissal of democracy in his 1909 *Changing Conceptions of Education* makes his ideological, institutional, and public policy efforts in constructing hierarchical bureaucracy, centralized authority, social and educational reorganization around differentiated races and socioeconomic classes, and his animated promotion of scientific efficiency look dangerously like fascism. David Nasaw, taking up this lead in *Schooled To Order* (1979), devotes few words to Cubberley, but links Cubberley's 1909 description of society and his prescriptive policy statement to similar ones by others to establish what he sees as the antidemocratic ideological foundation undergirding 20th-century bureaucratic and authoritarian public school reorganization.

Ellwood Cubberley, who was born in 1868 and had died in 1941, remains a potent ideological and directive force in educational historiography, public school administration, and in just about every other nook and cranny of the state system of public school education. Perhaps one reason is because what he and like-minded social engineers in the educational and industrial establishment brought to pass in the ideological and structured bureaucratic reorganization of public school education in the early 20th century is still with us today.

CONCLUDING REMARKS

Indeed, as Karl Marx, the great social scientist of capitalist society, Michael Katz, the educational historian, Michael Parenti, a political scientist, and Jay MacLeod, a sociologist, each demonstrate (Parenti, 1970), an adequate explanation of any historical period's social reality requires a complex excavation of its particular cultural, economic, and political relations *and* an identification and explanation of the social structures that determine the actual composition of these relations, as well as an accounting of what the participants think about their social experiences and actions. When the study of history—past and present—is pursued as a stratified and interdisciplinary activity, it is possible to identify people, their positions and practices within the context of social relations, their ideology, and, perhaps, their reasons as well. By seeking and identifying points of congruence, our explanations of people, events, and historical movements will be more complete, more complex, and more valid—and less susceptible to epistemic fallacy (for instance, mistaking ideology for what is actual).

Central to this essay and my critique of Cubberley's (1934a) educational historiographic text is my argument that public and educational policy, and people's actions, are generated from what folks believe. Controlling what people can know through the ideological construction of the history of American society and its institutions is therefore highly political. Hegemonic control of what constitutes reality is a political necessity because it conditions and privileges what counts ideologically as proper knowledge, for example, people are poor because they are lazy, are governed by their passions, or are biologically unequal (see Herrnstein & Murray, 1994); the working class is a dangerous revolutionary class unless indoctrinated through moral object education; capitalism and democracy are the same thing; "ending welfare as we know it" will make the poor moral, industrious, and productive; educating public school children for today's social relations and job market is the best possible education society can provide; and so on.

It seems significant to me, therefore, that all but the one most recent of Katz's (1968) relational class critiques of educational history are out of print, while Kaestle's (1983/1991) pro-capitalist tract remains in print. It is significant because the 12- or 16-week sessions into which teacher education courses are packaged forces teacher educators of historical foundations to rely on textbooks to cover 250 years of American social history. Engendering critical inquiry, reflective thinking, and knowledge about society through public school education and teacher education thus becomes a problematic exercise when some kinds of ideological history remain in print, become part of the dominant ideological canon in educational and American history, are widely promoted and cited, are treated as authentic explanations of "reality," while counterhegemonic explanatory critiques of historical phenomena, although published, are allowed to go out of print.

The fact that so much relativist epistemological interpretivism parades as historical explanation is not simply political, it is criminal. In the place of knowledge about society and its history, relativist interpretations mystify the actual social causes of human misery and construct lies, which legitimate and help reproduce those processes and mechanisms of oppression and exploitation that depend for their continuance on ideological hegemony. True historical knowledge, on the other hand, would guide teachers and their students toward emancipatory democratic projects. We must know something about a particular institution and its intended social aims (as well as unanticipated consequences), in other words, it is necessary to know about the society that created it, imposed it, and fortified it. Through such knowledge of society and its historical particularities it becomes possible to illuminate the political economy of social relations in which the state system of public school education is embedded. Of equal importance, knowledge about society and about its constituent economic and political relations, is necessary knowledge for teachers to fully comprehend their social position and agency in the classroom as well as their individual experiences. Perhaps it is for precisely this reason that Katz's *The Irony of Early School Reform* (1968) and Messerli's *Horace Mann: A Biography* (1971) are out of print, and Kaestle's *Pillars of the Republic* (1983/1991) and Cremin's edition of Mann's *Reports, The Republic and the School* (1957), are not.

NOTES

[1] *Congruence* is used in this essay to mean a correspondence between an explanation and the object of the explanation. For example, Cubberley's claims in *Public Education in the United States* (1934a) about Samuel Armstrong, the Hampton Institute, and the education of Black-Americans are not congruent with what was known at the time, or what has been established since.

[2] Lawrence Cremin writes: "Like any other crusader, Mann saw history on his side. The obligation to build common schools, he maintained, had been laid upon the people of the state by the founding fathers of the colony. 'We can never fully estimate the debt of gratitude we owe to our ancestors for establishing our system of Common Schools.... Can there be a man amongst us so recreant to duty, that he does not think it encumbent upon him to transmit that system, in an improved condition, to posterity, which his ancestors originated for him?' Building on the fact that the Puritan fathers, deeply committed to the preservation of learning, had at great sacrifice established schools in the wilderness, Mann conceived a historic tradition of education for freedom, a tradition which his own generation was duty-bound to perpetuate and strengthen" (1965, p. 18).

Mann did it; Cremin is doing it: constructing useful myths, folklore, rituals, customs, and duties; "building on the fact," "preservation of learning," and "schools in the wilderness," are phrases used to shape our historical understanding of the Puritans and their experiences in a land quite unlike the one they left behind. See also Welter (1975); Messerli (1971).

³ Lawrence Cremin, in his characterization of Cubberley's text, writes: "When *Public Education in the United States* finally appeared—it was apparently in the making for at least two decades—it was an immediate success. Charles Judd of the University of Chicago called it 'the first book which can in any proper sense be described as a history of American Schools,' while Frank Herbert Palmer pronounced it 'a treasure house of inspiration and information.' The book quickly captured the field...and it remains in use today as a textbook in educational history courses across the country" (1965, pp. 4–5).

⁴ Cubberley emphasizes the singular importance of: Thorndike, Judd, Strayer, Terman, Flexner, Bobbitt, Freeman, Russell, and Ayres. He quotes Harold Rugg's list, which adds Cubberley, Whipple, and Gray to the leadership of the new science movement. Among the nine educational histories published in the 20th century that he identifies, four are his own, two are by F.P. Graves, and one is by Paul Monroe, his mentor at Teacher's College.

Cubberley also makes use of others outside the establishment circle, such as John Dewey. He transforms Dewey into a staunch supporter of Industrial education and stratified schools with differentiated curricula for different groups of children. If, however, one turns to the companion text, *Readings In Public Education* (1934b, pp. 408–409), where Dewey is quoted at length, Dewey is not advocating industrial education, but the education of children of the industrial working class, the largest class in society "upon whom the whole world depends for the supply of necessities...." Dewey advocates an education "...that will as well give them enough control over their material environment to enable them to be economically independent." This is not one of Dewey's ideas that Cubberley entertains in his explanation of Dewey or public education.

Finally, there are few women educational leaders in Cubberley's history. He significantly ignores Ella Flagg Young, superintendent of Chicago's public school system at the turn of the century, the first woman superintendent of schools in the country, and who, together with Margaret Haley, led a strong opposition movement against Cubberley and company, as well as their industrial friends. Cubberley has erased from his history Young and the unionized Chicago female teachers, and with them he has erased their determined resistance to centralized bureaucratic administration and their legal battles against no-tax corporations. He limits his comments to two brief remarks about Chicago schools before the Civil War, and then writes as if Chicago vanished from the face of the Earth—except for a passage valorizing Judd at the University of Chicago.

⁵ See, for example, Cubberley, 1934a, p. 443: "a substantial middle class is necessary to the establishment of a public school system"; p. 483: "formation of public school education was a nativist and class reaction to illiterate and poor Irish, German radicals, etc."; p. 495: "upward social mobility is made possible by economic not educational means"; p. 498: "nineteenth century public school education was disciplinary for the purpose of inculcated docility"; p. 502: "public school education is determined by the nation's needs, not those of individuals"; p. 504: "nineteenth century public schools, especially the high schools, were for the well-to-do, and neglected the poor, immigrants, Blacks, and working class; and so on." Cubberley's argument at the end is new organization, new measures, and new curricular programs, all necessary because of the exclusive and undemocratic character of the 19th-century system of public school education.

⁶ "With the abolition of the rate-bill, which by 1860 had been done everywhere by the cities...this educational ladder [kindergarten through college] was finally open to all American children as their educational birthright. *The two requisites for the climb were money*

enough to obtain freedom from work in order to attend, and brains and perseverance enough to retain a place in the classes" (emphasis added, Cubberley, 1934a, p. 273).

[7] Cubberley has two standards regarding "democracy": When people are direct participants in self-government and self-determination, democracy is inefficient and chaotic and lends itself to corruption; on the other hand, under the modern system of centralized bureaucratic administration controlled by an appointed professional expert possessing appropriate authority, the inclusive school system, high school, or factory is efficiently democratic. Clearly, both of Cubberley's standards are a perversion, the first by interpretation and the second by misrepresentation.

Cubberley embraced Taylor's (1985–1986) "scientific" efficiency model of industrial management, social order, economic and political relations, and production. And, too, for Cubberley, like Taylor, workers had to be evaluated and differentiated in order to properly fit the required task, and workers had to willingly embrace their position and the task.

[8] "Rate-bills" were a form of tuition charged by district schools to parents of school children. This tuition was primarily for the material support of the school and the school teacher (Nasaw, 1979).

[9] One does not have to read too carefully, however, to see that contradicting his "secularization" section title and his claims is Cubberley's elaboration of an established nonsectarian Protestant system of public instruction.

[10] See, for example, Cubberley's commentaries on Pestalozzi, Froebel, the infant school, child labor laws, etc.

[11] "The vocational high school is the most effective agency so far devised for the training of that 70 per cent of all our children who cannot or will not continue in the regular courses of the high school, and who have, at the rate of a million a year, been entering industries for which they have been but ill-fitted and in which they could have little hope of advancement or success" (Cubberley, 1934a, pp. 647–648).

See, too, his commentaries on Black-Americans (chap. XII), and on Eastern and Southern European immigrants (chap. XIV).

[12] Cubberley writes: "The people seldom have an opportunity to vote for a really good man for the office, as the best men usually cannot be induced to become candidates...."

"In both county and state the demand today is for intelligent professional leadership...that the children in [the schools] may receive a better-directed education than they are now receiving. The important steps in the process of securing these results consist in...the reorganization and redirection of rural and village as well as city educational procedure; the abolition of the outgrown district system for a larger administrative unit; the elimination of politics and popular election in the selection of experts; and the concentration of larger authority in the hands of those whose business it is to guard the rights and advance the educational welfare of our children" (1934a, pp. 731, 733).

The tag-ending is an emotional appeal to distract from the nondemocratic program he has just outlined.

Throughout these passages, however, Cubberley is studiously silent about the strenuous opposition of citizens and public school teachers to centralized bureaucratic administrative authority (see, for example, Haley, 1982). And, too, he had nothing to say earlier in his commentary on the Colonial period regarding the 1760 struggle by aristocrats and Tory merchant elite to capture control of Boston town government and to exclude the artisans and journeymen from direct participation (see Nash, 1976). The idea of a supremely endowed, intelligent elite leadership is obviously not new to Cubberley.

For a persuasive challenge to Cubberley's interpretation of the district schools, see Barron (1997). Barron illuminates the protracted ideological and political battle of rural people against the machinations of the capitalist governing classes and the promoters and bureaucrats of the centralized, consolidated state educational system. According to Barron, rural Americans opposed—over a period of several generations—movements forced upon them from above and outside their communities to impose bureaucratic, centralized, impersonal, nonelective, and determining authoritarianism over their lives and their children. And, remarkably, rural opposition held its own, Barron reports, until after World War II, e.g., in Indiana until 1959. The locally administered district school remained a democratic fixture of the rural countryside well into the 20th century, and gave way to consolidation and centralization of authority only after the state and the federal government largely equalized the tax burden between farmer and town/city dweller, heavily subsidized the cost of transportation, and, significantly, only after capitalist economic and political relations had become thoroughly insinuated into the culture and customs of rural America (which paralleled the depopulation of the farming country).

13 Except for selectively quoting dominant members of the economic and political elite on the need for a state system of public school education, and, except for casting several of these gentlemen in roles of humanitarian civic and educational leadership, Cubberley has little to say about the positions or occupants located at the pinnacle of what he describes as the social pyramid.

14 Where it serves his purpose, or does not obviously undermine it, Cubberley does include information that can be useful, such as the dates on which different state legislatures enacted laws establishing a state system of publicly funded schools, or when a state office of school superintendence was established. He occasionally also provides interesting details about particular individuals, such as DeWitt Clinton's petition to Emma Willard that she relocate her female seminary to New York State, and a cursory treatment of the financial arrangements that made this possible. In a different but related context, Cubberley also reports that rather than establish an early system of normal schools, the New York legislature voted in 1827 to continue financial support of academies, of which Willard's was one, for the training of school teachers.

15 See, for example, Cubberley, 1934a, p. 75: "We note again the rise of a distinctly American educational consciousness and the development of distinctly American schools once more begins." Cubberley repeats his homespun, "all-American" claim frequently.

What he actually identifies and establishes, however, is that institutional organization, teacher training, pedagogy, grade differentiation, and social aims of public school education all have their origin in Europe, particularly in England, in the early decades of American nationhood, and, by the 1820s, Prussia. See p. 275n, for example, where Cubberley cites three city schools, each established on a different European model—Scottish, German, and English. The major influences on the development of American public education that he identifies are Lancaster, Cousin, Pestalozzi, Fellenberg, Froebel, Herbart, and Spencer. None of these men are American.

Nineteenth century American educational promoters—James G. Carter, Horace Mann, Henry Barnard, Calvin Stowe, John Pierce, Rev. Charles Brooks, Dr. Benjamin F. Smith, Henry E. Dwight, and William Russell—are distinguished within Cubberley's text for having popularized and adapted the Prussian (or German) system of social control and nationalism through public instruction to American circumstances. And, too, Cubberley consistently shows this system was (and is) the alternative preferred by humanitarian public men and educational leaders to the district school.

Cubberley is disingenuous about these things. On page 273, figure 68, he renders the American democratic educational ladder, and on page 352, figure 99, he renders the "German State School Systems Before 1914." Beneath the latter, he has written: "Compare with Fig. 68...and note the difference between a European two-class school system and the American democratic educational ladder." Cubberley's claims are consistent with his pictures, but not with his text. The "all-American" claims collapse under the weight of Cubberley's own text: First, American educational leaders are shown adapting the Prussian system and ideas to American circumstances; secondly, the claim of a democratic educational ladder is misleading because he deliberately ignores the elite private school system; and, thirdly, the two-class system of the German system, which he criticizes here, is hardly distinguishable from the reorganized American state system of public school education that he later promotes, rationalizes, and justifies. The only schools after the Colonial period that appear to have a claim to being homespun American institutions are the district schools, but these have been repudiated by every educational leader (including himself) identified by Cubberley in his text.

[16] This is one instance of Cubberley's sloppy scholarship. If Fellenberg's system was introduced in 1829, how does it come to serve as the basis for established schools before this date? If Cubberley knows, he does not tell.

[17] The notion of secluded or residential inculcation and socialization of children of the poor and working class apparently had considerable currency among both elite and middle-class reformers and conservatives alike. Such sentiments can be found in the 1809 pronouncements of DeWitt Clinton on the Lancasterian schools, and were again expressed nearly three decades later by Henry Barnard:

"No one at all familiar with the deficient household arrangements and deranged machinery of domestic life, of the extreme poor and ignorant, to say nothing of the intemperate—of the examples of rude manners, impure and profane language and all the vicious habits of low-bred idleness, which abound in certain sections of all populous districts—can doubt that it is better for children to be removed as early and as long as possible from such scenes and such examples and placed in an infant or primary school" (Nasaw, 1979, p. 35).

[18] Cubberley will return to methods and schools for disciplining behavior later in his narrative, where he explains the institutional means adopted to insure the ideological and cultural purity of White children from middle-class and professional families against the bad influence of other classes of children. But he does not connect these enlightened 20th-century institutional measures to Fellenberg or the 19th-century reform school movement.

[19] Cubberley posits a coexistence of manufacturing, different classes, poverty, and increasing promotion of public school education. But the context of economic and political relations remains obscured behind vague generalizations.

Interestingly, Cubberley takes from each of his sources here the argument that socioeconomic circumstances, social crisis, and human suffering are the product of ignorance arising from lack of education. *And*, the explicit charge that these conditions are largely the fault of the immigrants themselves. Clearly, then, public school education is the remedy. In addition, Cubberley advances the explanatory theory of breakdown: "The powerful restraining influences of the old home, with its strict moral code and religious atmosphere, seriously weakened."

The critical question that arises is: Does relocation lead to cultural transformation of the family and individual? The answer herein is yes. At the same time, however, the eroding influence is said to be the city itself. This latter conception is clearly inconsistent with the conception of individual improvement. For if influences are embedded in the structural organization of urban and industrial society, they are not manifestations of individual choice. The rationale of individual improvement is, however, that it will lead to the improvement of society. But this begs such questions as: Who determines the conditions and hours of labor and wages, and who is responsible for building the "ugly tenements"? Why did families abandon their farms and lives in the country, or homeland, in exchange for wage-labor in the factories? In other words, did immigrants in the cities and factory towns create their own misery, or did they encounter and confront miserable conditions?

20 Equating Tuskegee with Hampton is problematic: Although Washington promoted in public an enterprise at Tuskegee consistent with the subjugating program at Hampton, there are some indications that he may have been engaged in a radically different kind of education for Blacks. See, for example, DuBois (1903/1969); King (1971).

21 See Cubberley's acknowledgement on page 745, that without federal expenditures and intervention, such education as is available to Black-Americans benefits them little.

22 Cubberley's attitude toward and treatment of teachers in *Public Education* is inconsistent. He is certainly more generous with recognition and praise toward men (the Boston Masters an exception). When school teachers opposed the introduction of manual-labor subjects, Cubberley condemns them as narrow-minded conservatives. But when teachers opposed the academic curriculum of the Committee of Ten, they are good counsel ignored.

23 Cubberley has another use for Pestalozzi as well, which is to obscure the Prussian system of social control through public instruction behind Pestalozzi's dedication to children and his efforts to prepare them for the task of transforming society. In short, Cubberley uses what he describes as Pestalozzi's love and care for children to also describe the Prussian system.

24 Cubberley frequently equates "State" and "society," as in:

...as our social and industrial life has become more extended, and as production has come to be more specialized and the possibility of change from one vocation to another more limited, we have come to see that both the nature and the extent of the education offered young people in preparation for life must both change and increase.

...legislation has been enacted in the *interests of the State*, as well as in the interests of the child (emphasis added, 1934a, p. 574).

Cubberley uses similar constructions with regularity: "social and industrial life," "social and industrial whole," "social and industrial efficiency," "our social and industrial world," etc. His conflation and/or interchangable use of "State" and "society" is not an understanding of society shared by me. Indeed, the State is not an autonymous entity. The role of the State in capitalist society has a tendency to be dominated by capitalist class factions, thus when I talk about the role of the State, I'm simply highlighting the role of capitalist class through the mediation of the State. However, and importantly, I have synthesized the variations in form used by Cubberley to "the social and industrial needs of the State" as a means of clarifying and criticizing his argument and the socioeconomic and political aims of his policy proposals for the reorganization of public school education (see also Cubberley, 1909).

25 "Our city schools will soon be forced to give up the exceedingly democratic idea that all are equal, and that our society is devoid of classes...and to begin a specialization of education effort along many new lines in an attempt better to adapt the school to the needs of these many classes in the city life.

The evils and shortcomings of democracy are many and call loudly for remedies and improvement" (Cubberley, 1909, pp. 56–57, 64).

[26] When Termin's IQ studies of immigrant children and his "scientific" findings are compared with Cubberley's text here, it is clear that vocational education prepares these low IQ groups for productive and useful lives as unskilled and semi-skilled laborers. One of the worst faults of the public school system before the advent of science and efficient administration, according to Cubberley, was its tendency to inspire aspirations among certain groups of youths for positions of ownership, and of responsibility and/or decision making for which their IQs are clearly inadequate. Society could be spared much tumult, in other words, if Eastern or Southern European immigrant children or Black-American children were properly trained for occupations suited to their limited intelligence and thereby prevent frustration, resentment, and hostility.

[27] Cubberley is also looking ahead to his explication of Spencer. Compare "...the right kind of knowledge, properly interpreted to the pupil so that clear ideas as to relationships might be formed" (p. 451) to "help in the rearing and disciplining of offspring," and "maintaining one's political and social relations" (p. 470).

[28] "Now, surely, nothing but Universal Education can counter-work this tendency to the domination of capital and the servility of labor. If one class possesses all the wealth and the education, while the residue of society is ignorant and poor...the latter, in fact and in truth, will be the servile dependents and subjects of the former. But if education be equally diffused, it will draw property after it, by the strongest of all attractions; for such a thing never did happen, and never can happen, as that an intelligent and practical body of men should be permanently poor. *Property and labor, in different classes, are essentially antagonistic; but property and labor, in the same class, are essentially fraternal*" (emphasis added, Mann, 1957, pp. 84–87).

[29] See, too, Cubberley's use of John Dewey in this regard: "His work, both experimental and theoretical, has tended both to psychologize and socialize American education; to give to it a practical content, along scientific and industrial lines; and to interpret to the child the new social conditions of modern society connecting the activities of the school closely with those of real life...he has tried to change the work of the school so as to make it a miniature of society itself" (1934, p. 506).

Note the echo of Horace Mann (*12th Annual Report*) and of his own text in this characterization of Dewey's philosophy and educational pedagogy.

[30] For Cubberley's explicit argument, see the last chapters of *Public Education* (1934a), and especially see *School Organization and Administration* (1923b).

[31] See Cubberley, 1934a, p. 504: "the danger from class subdivision has been constantly increasing"; p. 575: "general legislation to protect youths from exploitation and the State from danger."

[32] Cubberley, 1934a, Fig. 136 (between pp. 548 and 549). Regarding industrial society in the late 1920s, Russell describes, under the heading of "Employment": "All of the workers idle some of the time. Some of the workers idle all of the time. Because of (a) Increasing technological unemployment, (b) Mergers, (c) Emphasis on the younger worker, (d) Closed frontier." And under the heading of "Tempo": "Quick Tempo/ Short Hours—High Productivity/ Periodic Shutdowns/ Much Idleness or Leisure/ When is a vacation unemployment?" And under "Control": "Increasing Government Control By/ Information/ Advice/ Direction."

And, perhaps because of socioeconomic circumstances generated by the Great Depression, Russell includes under "Possible Implications For The Schoolmaster" the caution to give "Much attention to problems of the use of leisure."

[33] "Brought in from Africa by former slaves, the disease [hookworms] had been passed on to the whites, who suffered more seriously from it, with the result that men of English, Scotch,

and Irish stock, who elsewhere in America had built up our civilization and been leaders in church, and school, and State, in the South had become the so-called 'poor white-trash' and were headed downward toward degeneracy and extinction" (Cubberley, 1934a, p. 677).

34 See the quotation from *Changing Conceptions of Education* (1909) cited above, and in *Public Education* (1934a), p. 745.

35 See, for example, Cubberley, 1934a, p. 574. And, in *Changing Conceptions of Education* (1909), we find the statement: "some way must be found to awaken a social consciousness as opposed to class consciousness...." (pp. 56–57).

36 Cubberley does not name fascism. He may well have been strongly attracted by what he perceived and understood as the efficiency, the scientism, and bureaucratic administration of society projected by the fascist countries he explicitly names without necessarily wanting to reproduce a fascist government. The problem, however, is one cannot energize fascist ideology and its mechanisms of social efficiency without also energizing those structures inherent to fascist economic and political relations. In other words, one cannot separate the cake from its ingredients. It is for this reason that I have not shied away from making explicit what Cubberley is in fact constructing and proposing in his text by repeatedly holding up first the Prussian social order and then the fascist social order as superior models of society that the United States might well emulate in its pursuit of greater social and industrial efficiency and order.

37 As I have attempted to establish and demonstrate in my critique of the ideological construction of his text, Cubberley did in fact address the complex relation of the state system of public school education to the "social and industrial needs of the State," or, to put it accurately, Cubberley's guiding premise in *Public Education* (1934a) is the efficient relation and integration of public school education in capitalist society. To declare that he did not, as does Ravitch, is to mystify this aspect of Cubberley's text and the purpose for which it was written.

38 Bailyn does not ever endorse Cubberley, but rather posits the ideology of education as the engine of progress. But, too, his pluralist liberal rejection of class structures in American society is intimately compatible with Cubberley's ideological mystification of the relation of public school education and capitalist society.

REFERENCES

Adams, D. W. (1995). *Education for extinction: American Indians and the boarding school experience, 1875–1928*. Lawrence, KS: University Press of Kansas.

Anderson, J. D. (1986). Secondary school history textbooks and the treatment of Black history. In D. C. Hine (Ed.), *The state of Afro-American history, past, present and future* (pp. 253–274). Baton Rouge, LA: Louisiana State University Press.

Anderson, J. D. (1988). *The education of Blacks in the South, 1860–1935*. Chapel Hill, NC: University of North Carolina Press.

Bailyn, B. (1972). *Education in the forming of American society*. New York: W. W. Norton. (Original work published 1960)

Barron, H. S. (1997). Teach no more his neighbor: Localism and rural opposition to educational reform. In *Mixed harvest: The second great transformation in the rural North 1870–1930* (pp. 43–70). Chapel Hill, NC: University of North Carolina Press.

Button, H. W., & Provenzo, Jr., E. F. (1989). *History of education & culture in America*. Englewood Cliffs, NJ: Prentice Hall.

Butts, R. F. (1974, Summer). Public education and political community. *History of Education Quarterly, 14*(2), 165–183.

Covello, L. (with D'Agostino, G.). (1958). *The heart is the teacher*. New York: McGraw-Hill.

Cremin, L. (1965). *The wonderful world of Ellwood Patterson Cubberley: An essay on the historiography of American education*. New York: Teachers College Press.

Cubberley, E. P. (1909). *Changing conceptions of education*. Boston: Houghton Mifflin.

Cubberley, E. P. (1923a). *The principal and his school*. Boston: Houghton Mifflin.

Cubberley, E. P. (1923b). *School organization and administration*. Yonkers-on-Hudson, NY: World Books.

Cubberley, E. P. (1934a). *Public education in the United States* (2nd ed.). Boston: Houghton Mifflin.

Cubberley, E. P. (1934b). *Readings in public education in the United States: A collection of sources and readings to illustrate the history of educational practice and progress in the United States*. Boston: Houghton Mifflin.

DuBois, W. E. B. (1969). The talented tenth. In *The negro problem* (pp. 31–75). New York: Arno Press. (Original work published 1903)

Finkelstein, B. (1992). Education historians as mythmakers. *Review of Research in Education, 18*, 255–297.

Gutman, H. G. (1987). *Power and culture: Essays on the American working class* (I. Berlin, Ed.). New York: The New Press.

Haley, M. (1982). *Battleground* (R. Reid, Ed.). Urbana, IL: University of Illinois Press.

Herrnstein, R. J., & Murray, C. (1994). *The bell curve: Intelligence and class structure in American life*. New York: Free Press.

Holt, T. (1990). "Knowledge is power": The Black struggle for literacy. In A. Lunsford, H. Moglen, & J. Slevin (Eds.), *The right to literacy* (pp. 91–102). New York: Modern Language Association.

Kaestle, C. F. (1983). *Pillars of the republic: Common schools and American society, 1780–1860*. New York: Hill and Wang.

Kaestle, C. F. (1991). *Pillars of the republic: Common schools and American society, 1780–1860*. New York: Hill and Wang. (Original work published 1983)

Katz, M. B. (1968). *The irony of early school reform*. Cambridge, MA: Harvard University Press.

Katz, M. B. (1975). *Class, bureaucracy, and schools: The illusion of educational change in America*. New York: Praeger. (Original work published 1971)

Katz, M. B. (1987). *Reconstructing American education*. Cambridge, MA: Harvard University Press.

King, K. J. (1971). *Pan-Africanism and education*. Oxford, England: Clarendon Press.

Lears, J. (1994). *Fables of abundance*. New York: Basic Books.

Luther, S. (1962). An address to the working-men of New-England (1832). In L. Stein & P. Taft (Eds.), *Religion, reform, and revolution: Labor panaceas in the nineteenth century* (n.p.). New York: Arno Press.

Mann, H. (1947). *Annual reports* (12 vols.). Washington, DC: NEA/Horace Mann League.

Mann, H. (1957). Twelfth annual report (1848). In L. A. Cremin (Ed.), *The republic and the school: Horace Mann on the education of free men* (pp. 79–112). New York: Teacher's College Press.

Markowitz, R. J. (1993). *My daughter, the teacher: Jewish teachers in the New York City schools*. New Brunswick, NJ: Rutgers University Press.

Marx, K. (1989). *A contribution to the critique of political economy* (S. W. Ryazanskaya, Trans. & M. Dobb, Ed.). New York: International Publishers. (Original work published 1970)

MacLeod, J. (1995). *Ain't no makin' it* (2nd ed.). Boulder, CO: Westview Press.

Messerli, J. (1971). *Horace Mann: A biography*. New York: Knopf.

Murphy, M. (1992). *Blackboard unions: The AFT & the NEA, 1900–1980*. Ithaca, NY: Cornell University Press.

Nasaw, D. (1979). *Schooled to order*. New York: Oxford University Press.

Nasaw, D. (1993). *Going out*. New York: Basic Books.

Nash, G. B. (1976). Social change and the growth of prerevolutionary urban radicalism. In A. F. Young (Ed.), *The American Revolution: Explorations in the history of American radicalism* (pp. 3–36). DeKalb, IL: Northern Illinois University Press.

Parenti, M. (1970, August). Power and pluralism: A view from the bottom. *Journal of Politics, 32*, 501–530.

Ravitch, D. (1978). *The revisionists revised: A critique of the radical attack on the schools*. New York: Basic Books.

Ross, E. A. (1935). *Civic sociology: A textbook in social and civic problems for young Americans* (Rev. ed.). Yonkers-on-Hudson, NY: World Books.

Spring, J. (1994). *The American school: 1642–1993* (3rd ed.). New York: McGraw-Hill.

Taylor, C. (1985–1986). *Philosophy and the human sciences: Philosophical papers* (Vols. 1–2). Cambridge, England: Cambridge University Press.

Taylor, F. W. (1967). *The principles of scientific management*. New York: W. W. Norton.

Termin, L. M. (1919). Editor's introduction. In E. P. Cubberley (Ed.), *The intelligence of school children* (pp. ix–x). Boston: Houghton Mifflin.

Tyack, D. (1974). *The one best system: A history of American urban education*. Cambridge, MA: Harvard University Press.

Tyack, D., & Hansot, E. (1982). *Manager of virtue: Public school leadership in America, 1820–1980*. New York: Basic Books.

Urban, W., & Wagoner, Jr., J. (1996). *American education: A history*. New York: McGraw-Hill.

Vinovskis, M. A. (1995). *Education, society, and economic opportunity*. New Haven, CT: Yale University Press.

Violas, P. (1978). *The training of the urban working class: A history of twentieth century American education*. Chicago: Rand McNally.

Welter, R. (1975). *The mind of America 1820–1860*. New York: Columbia University Press.

Wilentz, S. (1986). *Chants democratic: New York City & the rise of the American working class, 1788–1850*. New York: Oxford University Press.

Author Index

Subject Index